GIANT DESPAIR *meets* HOPEFUL

KRISTEVAN READINGS IN ADOLESCENT FICTION

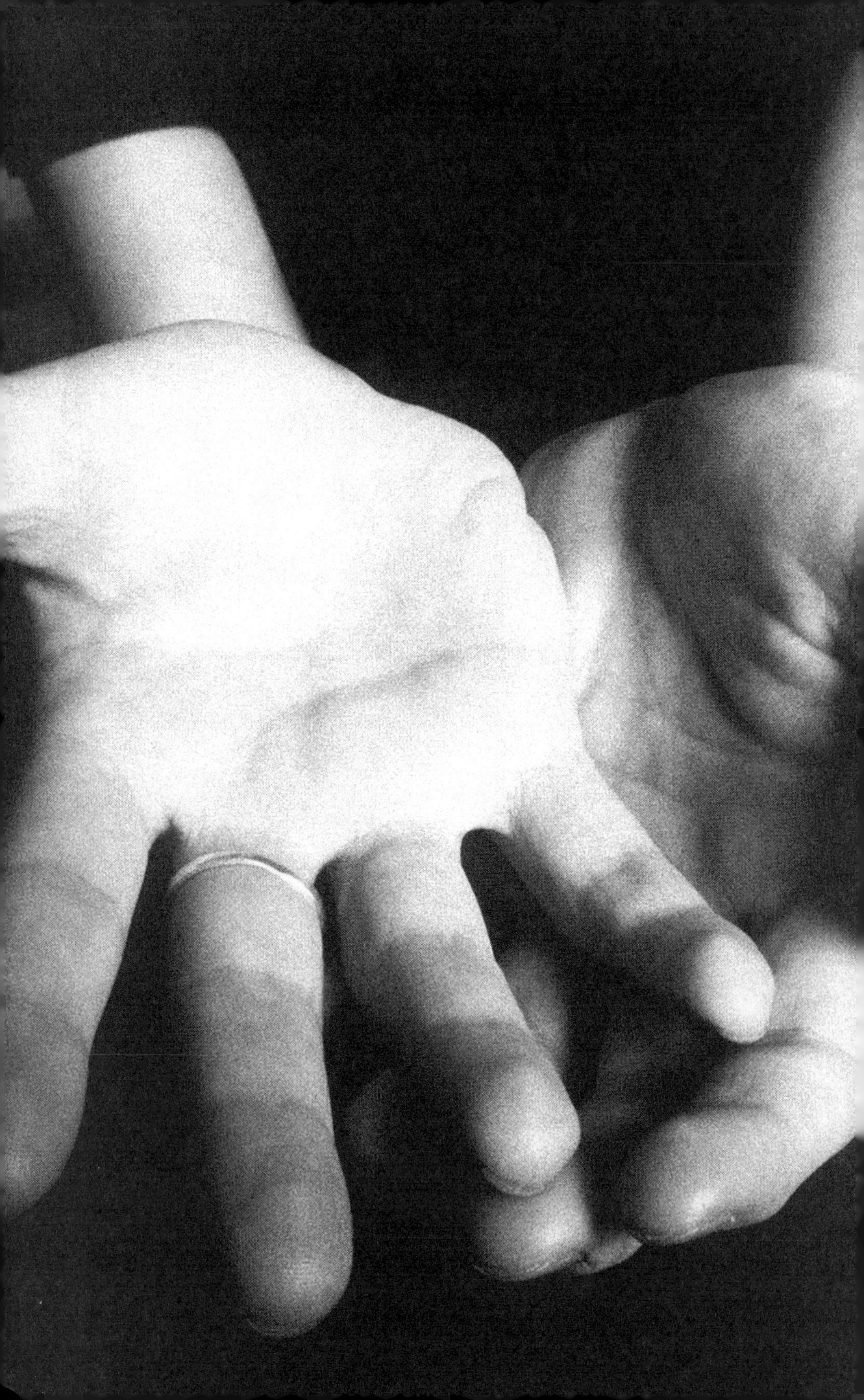

MARTHA WESTWATER

GIANT DESPAIR *meets* HOPEFUL

KRISTEVAN READINGS IN ADOLESCENT FICTION

The University of Alberta Press

Published by
The University of Alberta Press
Ring House 2
Edmonton, Alberta T6G 2E1

Printed in Canada 5 4 3 2 1

Canadian Cataloguing in Publication Data

Westwater, Martha, 1929-
Giant Despair meets Hopeful

Includes bibliographical references and index.
ISBN 0-88864-320-9

1. Young adult fiction—History and criticism. 2. Children's stories—History and criticism. I. Title.
PN1009.A1W47 2000 823'.914099283 C00-910105-5

Cover photography by Lara Minja. Interior photography by Tina Chang. All photos used with permission.

Printed and bound in Canada by Friesens, Altona, Manitoba.
∞ Printed on acid-free paper.

This book has been published with the help of a grant from the Humanities and Social Sciences Federation of Canada, using funds provided by the Social Sciences and Humanities Research Council of Canada.

The University of Alberta Press gratefully acknowledges the support received for its program from the Canada Council for the Arts. The Press also acknowledges the financial support of the Government of Canada through the Book Publishing Industry Development Program for its publishing activities.

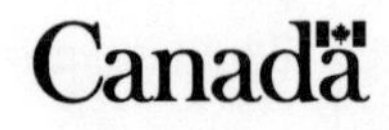

for Sisters Elizabeth Bellefontaine and Agatha Vienneau who died on October 9, 1998.

We were companions on the journey....

CONTENTS

ACKNOWLEDGEMENTS

For this work, as for others, I owe a deep debt of gratitude to the Social Sciences and Humanities Research Council of Canada which has generously supported all my research labours over the past twenty years. This programme provided me with several excellent, anonymous readers of *Giant Despair Meets Hopeful.* Their critique of the manuscript and their intelligent suggestions have increased the value of this book. Two of my colleagues, Peter Schwenger and Steven Bruhm, gave generously of their time, in the midst of very full teaching and research activities, to critique parts of the manuscript. I am deeply grateful for the encouragement and ever-reliable support of Mary Mahoney-Robson and Leslie Vermeer of the University of Alberta Press. I also wish to thank two perceptive student research assistants, Reina Greene and Nancy Richards. Finally, I wish to thank Sister Joan Verner and her staff, who rescued the manuscript during its final editing. Above all, my thanks to my students, whose buoyancy of spirit and whose insights have enriched my own reading pleasure and whose resiliency and joy have nourished my hope.

ABBREVIATIONS

Abbreviations Frequently Used for Kristeva's Works

ACW	*About Chinese Women*
"AN"	"The Adolescent Novel" in *Abjection, Melancholia and Love*
BS	*Black Sun: Depression and Melancholia*
DL	*Desire in Language*
IBWL	*In the Beginning Was Love*
KR	*The Kristeva Reader*
PH	*Powers of Horror: An Essay on Abjection*
PST	*Proust and the Sense of Time*
RPL	*Revolution in Poetic Language*
SO	*Strangers to Ourselves*
TL	*Tales of Love*

...ALL THE LAW IS NOT IN THE HAND OF GIANT DESPAIR...

—*The Pilgrim's Progress*

INTRODUCTION

In 1986, commenting on the status of children's literature in a university's literature curriculum, Zohar Shavit wrote, "Without exaggerating, children's literature is almost totally ignored."[1] Despite significant critical gains made over the past fifteen years—notably by such thinkers as Jacqueline Rose, Jack Zipes, Perry Nodelman, Rod MacGillis, and others—children's literature is still underrated.[2] It is underrated not only by some academics who consider it unworthy of serious literary criticism (Lesnik-Oberstein[3] for example) but also by publishers who go to the opposite extreme and extol every book ever directed at the lucrative market which youth provides. But when one examines young-adult fiction, particularly those novels which have avoided the deterioration of language, the violence, and the sexism of so much of present-day fiction, what emerges is a literature of great power that satisfies the human need for beauty of form and content, and at the same time challenges both the concept of the self and that self's expectation of stability and harmony.

The phenomenon of a burgeoning literature for teenage readers, one that challenges our notions of absolutes in a society increasingly cynical of values, is found in a number of writers from the United States, the United Kingdom, Canada, and Australia. Giving hope to the young by emphasizing that growth is possible, even in the most meaningless, chaotic situations, the writers selected for this study have exhibited independence, courage and unparalleled authenticity. And this at a time when Giant Despair seems to be vanquishing Hope.

It was the prevalence of so much disillusionment and despair that attracted me to a study of adolescent fiction in the first place. Novel after novel repeated the tale of contemporary youth suffering because of parental and peer pressure, violence, sexual abuse, divorce, and similar crises. What is to be made of this change in familial and social values? What is to be made of this despair as it is depicted in young-adult novels? Are parents and educators to believe that Giant Despair, ever more present now in a rapidly changing economy, will triumph? Must they learn to take more than a little comfort in the belief that perhaps we have arrived at such a point in evolutionary development in self-awareness that parental support may be relinquished earlier; that young people are weaned from the milk of illusionary parental beneficence at a much younger age? This book will grapple with these and many other questions. Reading several contemporary novelists in the light of Julia Kristeva's psychoanalytic theory might increase our awareness of the need for a more serious study of literature written for young people.

Many introductions include an apology which confesses a lack of some sort. At this point I should admit that I may disappoint those literary theorists who expect me to apply Kristevan theory to children's literature in the same way that Jacqueline Rose has applied Lacanian theory to James M. Barrie's *Peter Pan.* Rose's thesis in *The Case of Peter Pan or The Impossibility of Children's Fiction* splendidly argues that children's fiction is "impossible" because it hinges on "the impossible relation between adult and child." It "sets up a world in which the adult comes first (author, maker, giver) and the child comes after (reader, product, receiver) but where neither of them enters the space in between" (1-2). In her elucidation of this "no man's land" of children's literature, Rose has executed a literary *tour de force* by opening up the canon of children's literature and its semiotic opacity to serious literary scholarship. Praiseworthy as Rose's work is, however, I cannot follow her excellent lead because I fear she is somewhat dismissive of the importance of children's literature in Western culture. In discussing the purpose of Alan Garner's fiction, for example, she maintains that the British writer views literature as "the repository of a privileged experience and sensibility at risk in the outside world." Furthermore, she claims that the notion of cultural decay produces two assumptions: "First, that the child, if we get to him or her soon enough (or keep away long enough), is where this sensibility is to be found (childhood is therefore defined as something existing outside the culture in which it is produced). Secondly, that writing for children can contribute to prolonging or preserving—not only for the child but also for us—values which are constantly on the verge of collapse" (43-44). She objects to Garner's Rousseauistic romantic view of the child, and so do I. But I also believe, more deeply than Rose, I suspect, that we *are* in a state of cultural decay and that writing—whether for children or adults—may preserve for us values that are on the verge of decline.

If I read children's literature in the light of a new theory, I do not wish to discount the traditional values of Western culture. Nor do I wish to privilege theory over literature itself. In these "readings" I want primarily to demonstrate the literary value of several modern fiction writers who dared to unmask for the young the constructed nature of reality and to question the unitary nature of the self. (Perhaps a Kristevan reading may be a political, "salvational" act itself in the degree that it frees us from monoliths and allows us to embrace differences; but sometimes it is necessary to let go of certain cultural values, particularly if they suppress differences.) Secondly, I want to celebrate the psychoanalytic theory of Julia Kristeva, specifically her thinking on the illusionary nature of the self, as her theory appears, sometimes eerily, in the novels of these writers. My main intent is to deepen the reader's pleasure—be that reader adolescent, parent, teacher, or librarian. There is enormous joy in discovering meaning through affinity, particularly the private affinity between the reader's and the fictional character's imaginative experience. And meaning is also validly formed in the disjunction between reader and author—in dis-connections and dis-identifications. Meaning itself is a construct forged in a trinitarian symbiosis among author, reader, and text, and legitimized by the reader's own experience. In examining the novels presented in this book in the light of Kristevan theory, however, I do not wish to abandon the canonical elements of literary analysis. I am simply suggesting a praxis—putting theory into action. In literary studies, as in all areas of modern life, we are in a state of transition. Because "kiddy lit" is considered non-threatening, it might well be an ideal field for this integrating of theoretical and critical ideas. I have read contemporary adolescent fiction in the light of Kristevan theory simply because the theory illuminated for me the hope to be found in the fiction. Kristevan theory favours life and engenders hope. But whereas I am captivated by Kristeva's theory of the self as an ever-evolving construct, one that is capable of recreating itself, another reader might find enlightenment in a Bahktian, Foucauldian, or Lacanian approach. Indeed the novels studied in this book defy simple categorization as psychoanalytic, sociological, philosophical, just as readily as they resist the forms of modernism or postmodernism, realism or surrealism. In using Kristeva's psychoanalytic approach in reading adolescent fiction, I am making a very simple point: humanity cannot survive without hope, and hope cannot survive without the story, i.e., without narrative or the imaginary.

The six novelists whom I have selected for this study celebrate life and hope while at the same time offering profound, sometimes disturbing, insights into the consequence of cowardice which refuses to accept the ordinary burdens of humanity—the pains of birthing, of sharing life with others, of dying. Each writer, in a distinctly different way, relies on an invisible power beyond the self; that power may come from creation, from human imagination, from reason, or from a Divine Being. Finding meaning in life demands hope: not so much hope for a pristine, exemplary future, but hope in a present that is often infected with cruelty and neglect. In the ordinary realities of everyday life are found the seeds from which the fruits of hope spring and satisfy. Although I have concentrated mainly on works of realistic fiction, I could not ignore writers like Patricia Wrightson and Kevin Major who blend both realism and fancy in their writings. The mystic and the mundane often emerge in Wrightson's novels while the protagonist in at least one of Major's works literally enters into the imaginative fiction he is reading.

In choosing authors for this study, which concentrates on fiction whose antagonists are mostly adolescents, I had two criteria: the novelist, while being realistic, had to combat despair; and the writer had to be of acknowledged literary discernment, that acknowledgement validated by the writer's receipt of a major national award. I am aware that I have omitted other similarly gifted authors and I confess that my choice may be idiosyncratic, but the novels examined do expose the evils of disillusionment and despair, as well as their alarming reality. Each writer demands that the reader, young or old, confront Giant Despair with a hope-filled heart, for their protagonists refuse to accept hopeless cowardice. Patricia Wrightson, Kevin Major, Jan Mark, Aidan Chambers, Robert Cormier and Katherine Paterson—different as their philosophical or religious backgrounds may be—all share a fundamental belief in the human capacity to love. Whether it be transference love, so integral to the practice of psychoanalysis, or biblical love, as exemplified by the Judaeo-Christian God, the writers studied in this book all offer love as another name for hope and the only alternative to despair. They believe, as members of the human race, that whatever attraction love's enemy, despair, holds—whether it be fear, greed, jealousy, pride, anger, self-interest, or lust—we all have the capacity to reject it. We may fail, often and badly, because we have such an innate propensity for evil which will never change and which binds us in sympathy to past generations and to those yet unborn. Our glory, however, is that we sometimes succeed. So we continue to tell the stories of those who have the courage to take on the Giant and to overcome Despair. In a Kristevan sense, storytelling itself becomes an act of hopeful love because it engages the listener/reader in an osmotic bond of identification with the speaker/writer. The stories studied in this book take on Giant Despair in little as well as in great ways.

This book has an urgency and practicality about it which I cannot deny. I am concerned about the young students before me in the lecture hall who are already victimized by the violence of our society and discouraged in their own skirmishes with the Giant. They are the future parents and teachers who will one day face the next generation of suffering teens. I want to deepen in today's parents and educators an awareness of the power of fiction to sustain and preserve the ethical and social values of community life. I hope to demystify some of the terminology and jargon associated with present-day critical theory. Above all, I would simply like to share with adolescents and their guides the enjoyment I have found in a Kristevan reading of several fiction writers whose wisdom, wit, and grace flashed upon my own imagination and enriched my reading pleasure.

1

LOOKING UP THE DEVIL'S NOSE

In the autumn of 1989, I was riding British Rail from London to Westbury. In the same compartment was a group of teenaged American exchange students with their teachers, on their way to Stonehenge. The three thousand year mystery of that circle of stone had already exercised its magnetism on at least one of the students, for in a rare moment of quiet, a clear, raw American voice asked:

"Sir, do you believe in God?"

"No," was the quiet, laconic English master's answer. "Do you?"

"I don't know about God, but I sure as hell believe in the devil," was the student's firm reply.

The belief in a supernatural force which had inspired men to haul fifty-ton monoliths of stone twenty-four miles over the Marlborough Downs to Stonehenge still exerts its power. So does the glorious four-hundred-foot spire of nearby Salisbury Cathedral, uttering its sublime prayer in stone to the Christian God who has dominated European civilization for nearly two thousand years. But for this young student in the year 1989 A.D., the force of evil exerted more power. I think this book had its conception during that train ride.

Certainly the jagged edge of negativity which I heard in that young adolescent's comment has been echoed in the novels written for young adults over the past twenty years. And not mere negativity but oftentimes even an alarming despair pervades the lives of young protagonists who have become imaginary constructs exemplifying some sobering facts about contemporary society: that restless, bored youth, lacking stability, sometimes seek excitement in brutal and malignant ways; that parents and teachers seem to be losing their controlling influence over the young; and, perhaps most alarming, that suicides among the young have risen dramatically in the past twenty years (see Notes 6-7).

There is nothing new in the idea that the power of the good, or God, will be challenged by the power of evil, or Satan. Evil can be far more stimulating than the good. Even the unknown medieval author of that mystical classic *The Cloud of Unknowing* seems to have been fascinated by it. He writes of a discussion with a contemporary necromancer who told him that when the fiend appears on earth, "he will usually have only one great nostril, large and wide, and that he will readily toss his head back so that a man can see straight up to his brain, which appears like the fire of hell" (Johnston 119-20). The necromancer explained how the normal person's nose is divided into two parts, suggesting a spiritual discernment capable of deciding the good from the bad, or the bad from the worse, or the good from the better. The devil is well satisfied, the necromancer continued, if he can entice a human to look up that nostril, for the sight of it will either drive him out of his mind or drive him to despair. Indeed the Satanic cult that fascinated the medieval mind appears to be exerting a mesmerizing power over today's youth—not the belief of the "old religion" exemplified by the Stonehenge men of prehistory or the Kashubs of modern Ontario who seek to face the realities of evil, the terrors of death, and the challenges of life; but a Satanism that often leads to suicide.[1]

Parents and educators stepping into the twenty-first century seem to be looking up the devil's nose. We seem unable to discern between good and evil. We've lost our passion for absolutes and cannot find replacements. The ability to accept the distinction between good and evil, or at least the capability to discern between them, seems to demand more spiritual imagination than many adults possess. But what about our young people? Apparently, violence and ugliness have replaced idealism and beauty as youthful realities. Because beauty and idealism no longer seem to matter and are no longer capable of transforming experience, they have been denied the young. No wonder adolescent anger and pain lead to despair.

Not that adolescent rebellion and despair are new. Nearly four hundred years ago, in Shakespeare's *King Lear*, a masterful tragedy of doomed familial relationships, the young adult, Edmund, rages against an unjust universe and urges his goddess, Nature, to "stand up for bastards" (I.ii.15-22). The creature's subservience to a God has given way to a re-awakened consciousness of the creature's own powers, independent of God. And from the sixteenth to the nineteenth century, an immense transformation had been made. The theory of correspondences, where everything had a place in God's universe, was shaken. The family isolated on the lonely farm now became isolated in the crowded city. No longer was there a sacramental linkage among humans, their God, and nature, where all contributed to the meaning of the other. God became an absent Father, divorced both from Mother Nature and her children. The Great Chain of Being had snapped.[2]

The phenomenon of God's disappearance became particularly noticeable in the Victorian period. Paradoxically, in *The Idylls of the King*, the work in which Tennyson attempted to show the age-old conflict between good and evil, the pious Poet Laureate (no doubt unconsciously) had his evil daemon, Vivien, sing of the old God's repressive rule and of a new *jouissance:* [3] "The fire of Heaven is not the flame of Hell." The old sun worship, she promised, "will rise again,/ And beat the cross to earth" ("Balin and Balan," II.430-53). She celebrated the age's growing awareness of the sublime consciousness of self which the body's warming biological imperatives asserted. Tennyson himself clearly recognized that the old religious institution had begun to crumble and that two new surrogates would replace it: capitalistic consumerism and the dawning science of psychology. However, self-consciousness can create its own entrapment, perhaps even more confining than that imposed by any number of commandments in the Judean-Christian Western cultures.

Along with the institution of religion, that of the family has also lost influence and stability—a fact that is borne out not only by statistical data but also by fiction. If we examine the narrative voice and the imagery associated with that voice in teen fiction published between 1970 and 1990, we find recorded a distinct change in tone and attitude. In fiction written prior to 1970, the adolescent generally treated the parental figure with a modicum of respect if not always with love. There were not too many instances of parental failure. If there were angry voices, they were usually directed towards step-mothers or step-fathers. And the step-mother had to bear most of the opprobrium; the father was, at worst, the perpetrator of benign neglect.[4] But since the 1970s—in the aftermath of the tragic Viet Nam War, the rise of the drug culture, the new sexual freedom, the world-wide spread of AIDS—the adolescent seems to find in parents the very seeds of corruption. One of the earliest studies to focus on parent-child relationships in children's literature was Alma Homze's 1966 study of 780 books written between 1920 and 1960. She found that parents in these books were insignificant factors in the stories that centred on children's lives (*Elementary English* 43 (1966): 26-28). Seven years later, Selma R. Siege's study (1973) analyzed the voices of fourteen female heroines published in 1960 and found that the parents depicted in these novels were "confused, stubborn, self-centred, embittered and rejecting" of their offspring (*Elementary English* 50 (1973): 1039-43).

But during the last quarter of the twentieth century, there has been an increasing attack on the father figure in children's literature. Not only avowed feminists but also other writers for the young have rejected the Name of "the Father." That name has come to represent a repressive, male-dominated, authority-centred, power-driven principle that controls the individual's relationships both in the smaller unit of the private family and in the larger domain of politics and the law. In his 1974 study, Bernard Lukenbill concentrated on the father figure in adolescent fiction and rated half the fathers as "emotionally expressive," as opposed to "remote" in their dealings with their children (*Family Relations* 30 (1981): 219-229.). In Anita Kurth's 1982 study of books written in the late 1960s and early 1970s, the results were considerably different. Kurth sampled twenty-one books that featured twenty-five child-parent sets. There was an almost equal number of boys and girls as central characters, but male protagonists had much worse relationships with their parents. Fully twice as many parents were rated hostile and uninvolved as were sympathetic and involved. Kurth's study, corroborated by Lukenbill's, concluded that "fictional parents were apparently very much responsible for the mildly pathological global-psychological health of their families" (225). A cursory examination of teen-fiction characters substantiates these findings: John Gridley in John Donovan's *Wild in the World* (1971); Charles Norstadt in Isabelle Holland's *The Man Without a Face* (1972); Jerry Renault in Robert Cormier's *The Chocolate War* (1974); Dicey

Tillerman in Cynthia Voigt's *Homecoming* (1981); and finally Nick in Welwyn Wilton Katz's *Whalesinger* (1990). These are only a few of the many suffering, teenaged voices gone sometimes mildly, sometimes cruelly, cynical about the parent.

Along with despair, death, suicide, divorce, and negligent parents, some books deal with drugs, sex, and alcohol. When the anonymous *Go Ask Alice* was published in 1971, it shocked many adults and adolescents because they had no idea that "nice" girls from middle-class America would voice in print their problems with sex and drugs.[5] Within a few years, however (notably with Judy Blume's first books published in 1970), young readers were devouring books which treated of the dilemmas of the maturation process. The AIDS epidemic in particular brought sex education into the open (Donelson and Nilsen 93; see Note 5). In popular entertainment, nothing shocked anymore. Writers discovered a new, lucrative young-adult audience, and the market was glutted with despairing books of adolescent angst. These novels reveal a cosmic, increasingly isolating self-consciousness which has percolated down from the adult world to that of the pre-teen and teens.

Giant Despair manifests itself most conspicuously in ruptured familial relationships. Sociologists see the phenomenon of adolescent suicide as a reflection of the chaos resulting from the breakup of traditional family structure.[6] Granted that marriage has taken on a far wider set of meanings in the past several decades—for it includes long-term relationships not formerly sanctioned by church and state—statistically it has been proven that the family is in a state of flux. In 1980, for every 10.6 marriages, there were 5.2 divorces; in 1985, the rate was 5 divorces per 10.1 marriages. If there has been a slight decrease in the number of divorces (statistics reveal that in 1988 there were 4.7 divorces in 9.7 marriages), that knowledge is offset by the fact that the number of marriages decreased while the divorce rate increased (*Statistical Abstract of the U.S.* (1993) 113 ed. Table 140). The high incidence of divorce and the resulting single-parent family, with the concurrent changes in family lifestyles, add further strain to an already stressful period of life. Living in a non-supportive, hostile environment, one that lacks intimacy and affection, contributes to the development of despair and suicidal personalities (Hendin 327-8). Studies made on young people who have been hospitalized for attempted suicides have demonstrated that family disruptions and disintegration played a significant role in the maladaptation of these individuals. Close to one half (forty-three percent) of cases reviewed in one study showed that a family argument had preceded the suicide attempt (Litt, Cuskey, Rudd 106-108). Thus, unstable emotional and physical ties between adolescents and their parents are crucial indicators of despair's ascendancy. As Wallerstein and Blakeslee indicate in their study *Second Chances: Men, Women and Children a Decade after Divorce,* instead of getting over the turmoil of divorce, adults still feel angry, hurt, and rejected while children are being referred to school counsellors for aggressive behaviour, depression, and academic problems.[7] Divorce triggers stress, depression, and family and peer pressures that contribute to feelings of guilt and despair. More than from any other factor, this despair springs from a disastrous divorce—the divorce of parents and the subsequent separation of the child from at least one of his or her genitors. Besides spousal divorce, there is also institutional divorce—the separation of the child from those institutions which formerly functioned *in loco parentis*, church and school. These ruptures may lead the adolescent to that ultimate divorce: separation from life itself—suicide.

The epidemic of adolescent suicide provides the most compelling proof of adolescent hopelessness in a too-rapidly changing world.[8] Teen-age suicide is "anomic" (from anomie), a term which Durkeim uses to describe those suicides arising from a rapid change in the social order or social norms. A.R. Roberts further elaborates on the anomic suicide: "the individual becomes uncertain of the appropriate behaviour expected of him/her and experiences a state of anomic normlessness, an unbridgeable gap between aspirations and achievements where individual passions are out of control" (Roberts 27). Despair jeopardizes the adolescent brought up in a fast-changing world where ethical confusion abounds. Some thinkers stress the supremacy of the will of God and view suicide as an evil whereby a creature defies the will of the Creator. Other intellectuals emphasize the supremacy of the individual will and see suicide as the ultimate way of exercising free will (Atkinson 135-158). If academics are still debating issues surrounding suicide and cannot reach any rationally ethical consensus, is it any wonder the young are confused?

The confusion engendered by this staggering rate of change jeopardizes the stability of home, church, and school, which are losing their hold on the young. The entrance of what was once a dark secret into the public realm, namely, the betrayal of trust by churchmen who have sexually molested teen-agers; family breakups experienced either personally or observed in the homes of their contemporaries; a detrimental school environment, entered into at a very young age and often characterized by overcrowded classrooms where an impersonal atmosphere contributes to a sense of alienation—these are some of the causes reinforcing adolescent despair and potentially leading to suicide, which, following accidents and homicides, is the third leading cause of death in the fifteen to twenty-four-year-old age group (*Statistical Abstract of the U.S.* 1993). These statistics demand consideration.[9] But what makes these figures so frightening is that it may even be a conservative estimate because of the difficulty in getting unbiased reports. Parental pressure for confidentiality and/or the lack of investigative personnel sometimes cause probable suicides to be reported as accidents.[10] Reported deaths by suicide are the exception. Studies show that for every completed suicide there are between 50 and 150 attempts (See Note 10).

Despair-induced suicides are not peculiar to the United States alone but are prevalent in other English-speaking countries—Canada, Australia, and the United Kingdom.[11] Psychologists tell us that during adolescence the individuation process, the ability to cope with changing life situations, and growth in self-esteem are pursued. But the pressures that cause the adolescent to need both autonomy and affiliation often lead to a breakdown in self-esteem when the only remedy seems to be self-destruction (Jacobs and Teichor 139-49). Chronic inability to cope with the demands of maturation ranks as a major indicator in suicide attempts (see Walch 2892-93).

From *Hamlet* to *The Dead Poets Society*, serious writers of every age have attempted to understand the consequence of life's choices and to make the vision of those consequences comprehensible to others. But the contemporary vision is darker, at times outrageously so. Consider John Donovan's *Wild in the World* (1971), where young John Gridley's father takes his son to his mother's grave and shoots himself in front of the boy. With terrible episodes of violence, Gridley loses all his family—both parents, seven brothers and sisters; finally he himself dies, mourned only by the dog whom he called "Son." Darker still is the vision in Isabelle Holland's *The Man Without a Face* (1972). Charles Norstadt's mother has had a succession of husbands since Charles' father abandoned his family. When Charles does feel love for another human being, Justin McLeod, whose face had been cruelly deformed in an automobile crash, he is terrified by the emotions he holds for another male. *Perdita* (1983), another of Holland's novels (the name carries its own not-so-subtle significance), presents a young heroine who has been "lost"—sexually abused by her step-father who then attempts to kill her. Her mother remains uselessly incredulous throughout her daughter's ordeals. In Robert Cormier's *The Chocolate War* (1974), Jerry Renault views his parents as complete outsiders. His father, who nurses both grief and despair after the recent death of his wife, is indifferent towards his son. Such a loss would be a burden for any youth, but an even worse burden is Jerry's assumption of a parenting role to his father. The very fact that *The Chocolate War* invited such heated debate in assuming its place as an American tragedy marks it as a modern classic.[12] Even more significant, as will be demonstrated later in this study, Cormier's *The Chocolate War* refutes Jacqueline Rose's contention about the impossibility of writing children's fiction. Rose maintains that adult readers and writers want a fiction that returns us to "something innocent and precious which we have destroyed" and consequently impose their views on the fiction written for young people.[13] There is nothing "innocent and precious" about the ending of *The Chocolate War*, yet Cormier is not negative. Patricia Head makes a compelling argument for Cormier's "positive view of children's literature."[14]

A destabilizing vision of life appears regularly in adolescent fiction throughout English-speaking countries. Jennifer and Christopher Slade, for example, have rejected their alcoholic father in Kevin Major's Newfoundland novel *Far from Shore* (1980); and Michael Cameron rolls naked in the grass to show his contempt for his repressive father in Ivan Southall's Australian novel *Bread and Honey* (1970). One of the most creative of the serious writers for the young is Britain's Aidan Chambers, whose novels *Breaktime* (1978), *Dance on My Grave* (1982), and *Now I Know* (1987) are remarkable not only for their insights into the crumbling reality of a paternalistic society but also for their experimental form. Chambers chips away at the boundaries separating child and adult; his works reveal not only the child in the adult but also the adult within the child.

Even a cursory sampling of contemporary writers for the young demonstrates a growing appreciation of the profound changes which childhood is undergoing. Since the 1970s, social historians like J.H. Plumb have warned that the period of childhood is shrinking while that of young adulthood is expanding ("The Great Change in Children," *Horizon* (Winter 1971) 5-12).[15] Such expansion, which demands that the young remain in the educative process sometimes until their twenty-fourth year, has spawned a new millennialism for the novel. Subjects associated with the agonies of the young and formerly considered taboo are treated with surprising frankness and compassion. Divorce, sexuality, racial unrest, drunkenness, teen pregnancy, abortion—subjects which contribute to the growing despair of the young—are now found in the "Honor Sampling" of the best books for teens (Nilsen and Donelson 13-18).[16] Furthermore, most of the despair characteristic of modern adolescent fiction stems from a rebellion against the prolonged state of subservience, a subservience for which parents are usually castigated. Writers in the English-speaking world have creatively probed adolescent angst, and their very creativity demonstrates their profound appreciation of the great changes society is undergoing as it enters the twenty-first century.

Reading these modern adolescent novels can instill a feeling of melancholia and depression among adults. But great novelists have a knack not only of interpreting the age but also of generating a new understanding of it. They may claim to be uninterested in academic battles being waged in literary criticism over the relative merits of structuralism, deconstruction, reception theory, and so on; they may never even have heard of such modish, contemporary terms as "semiotic" "chora," and "abjection." It is not likely that many novelists have read the works of Julia Kristeva.[17] Yet these writers share with this literary-critic-turned-psychoanalyst a profound interest in the study of adolescence and an appreciation of its uncertainties. Life rarely presents us with unambiguous "either-or" choices between good and evil, hope and despair; and Aidan Chambers, Robert Cormier, Jan Mark, Kevin Major, Katherine Paterson, and Patricia Wrightson join with Julia Kristeva in celebrating difference. They face ambiguity and remain undaunted because both creative artists and psychoanalyst recognize the ongoing process of subject identity. In identifying Kristevan theories in the works of these six authors, Giant Despair meets Hopeful.

Julia Kristeva started her career as a semiotician. In 1979, however, she became a practicing psychoanalyst. Thus, formed by both disciplines of linguistics and psychoanalysis, Kristeva holds a unique position in post-structuralist criticism partly because she possesses an unusual respect for change. One of her earliest literary interests was in Russian formalism, but her subsequent study of Bakhtin made her see the necessity of going beyond formalism. As she admitted in her Introduction to the French translation of *Dostoevsky*, Bakhtin set Kristeva on a study for a "continent" which "the instruments of poetics [could] not attain." It entailed "a search for those rules by which the meaning and its speaker are brought into being" (Bann ix). Kristeva's search for rules governing the origin of meaning and its speaker set her on a quest for a theory of the subject, which led her to examine social and cultural evolution spanning more than two thousand years. More specifically, it led her to analyze language acquisition in very young children. Kristeva's early research demonstrated that children learn music before they learn syntax. The rhythm, intonation, and echoism of the mother's voice form the semiotic disposition that makes its way into language. For Kristeva, the semiotic is associative of the mother; however, it is important to note the distinction between *la semiotique*, the science of semiotics, and her particular "discovery," *le semiotique* (simply termed semiotic in this study). While building on Freud's and Lacan's studies of the unconscious, she concentrates on the importance of the semiotic in the formation of a speaking subject without denying the confluent power of the symbolic. She insists on a subject that is always individual and always in process.

Emphasizing that period before Lacan's mirror stage, the space before the child enters into the symbolic, the law of the father, Kristeva sees writing as a way of exploring the semiotic; writing itself, however, is a function of the symbolic, and Kristeva emphasizes the fluidity of both in facilitating the ultimate reorganization of the psyche. Kristeva's pre-symbolic, pre-oedipal space, the semiotic, is representative of the feminine, the privileged space of intimacy with the mother's body. Her study of the mother figure supplies a much-needed explanation of a lack found in both Freudian and Lacanian theory. Furthermore, as Bann noted, whereas Derrida applied himself to the deconstruction of the Western metaphysical tradition, "Kristeva pursued an alternative strategy" whereby her "major exegetic effort went into the reconstruction of Judaic law and Christian theology" (x). Her work has opened up a new conceptual area in language and literature without losing sight of their traditional roles in religion, politics, and society.

Kristeva asserts that the child/adolescent must eventually and irrevocably leave the mother and seek a new love object which is also susceptible to loss. In psychoanalytic thought, all love objects are replacements for that irreconcilable, unrecoverable abject, the mother. Thus a depressive, melancholic disposition is easily reactivated. In the refusal to accept loss and in the triumph of the Ego through the fetish of the text, Kristeva perceives writing to be an essential phallic complement, depending on an ideal paternity. In her *Tales of Love,* Kristeva postulates a paternity based on a loving father rather than Lacan's stern father, albeit a father of pre-history before gender division. In *Black Sun,* she imagines a father who is both stern *and* loving (Oliver 83). Although primarily oriented towards psychological analysis, Kristeva's theory stresses literature's therapeutic effect on both writer and reader in freeing the individual from a repression-induced melancholia. It comes as no surprise, then, that Julia Kristeva recognizes despair as a vital element in human existence, painful but necessary in that it provides a way of loosening the child/adolescent from parental domination and directing him/her to the Other. She believes that love alone can save us, but love is not something fixed: it is the only chance the individual has of passing through endemic narcissism toward the acceptance of the grace-filled moment of the symbolic. Her trust is in language, which gets us past narcissism but not necessarily into the castrating symbolic of Lacanian theory.

Kristeva's most pertinent insight, at least for the purposes of this study, is the contention that the novelistic genre itself is largely tributary to the "adolescent" economy of writing. Kristeva interprets the adolescent as mirroring the malaise of our society. In her essay "The Adolescent Novel," she describes the adolescent as a "mythic figure" whom we create in order to distance ourselves from our deficiencies by projecting them onto someone who has not yet grown up; she forces us to confront the perpetual adolescent in ourselves.

> It would be from this point of view, the work of a perpetual subject-adolescent which, as a permanent testimony of our adolescence, would enable us to retrieve this immature state, as depressive as it is jubilatory, to which we owe, perhaps, some part of that pleasure called aesthetic. ("The Adolescent Novel" 8, 11)[18]

In tracing the development of themes of betrayal, bisexuality, disguise, filiation, and seduction, Kristeva's essay explores the semiotic activity of written signs, the history of novelistic fiction, and the protective screening from phobic effects which writing ensures.

To illustrate her thesis, Kristeva analyzes de la Sale's *Little Jehan de Saintre* (1456), a work which is neither a courtly love lyric nor an epic. Up to this point, heroes and villains were "monovalent"—possessing a single strength—but with the adolescent Jehan and his little universe, a revolution of contrarieties is at work:

> Child and warrior, page boy and hero, deceived by the Lady, but conquering the soldiers, cared for and betrayed, loving the lady and loved by the king or by his brother-in-arms Boucicault, never fully masculine, child-lover of the Lady, but also comrade-friend to his tutors and to the brother with whom he shares his bed, Saintre is the perfect androgyne, the innocent and justified pervert. (13-14)

In her analysis of sexual ambiguities, Kristeva moves on to claim that ambivalence is the origin of psychology, and without the logic of pretense and betrayal, there is no psychology. Furthermore, ambivalence and psychology are synonymous with the novel as opposed to the epic and the courtly romance. In order to write of betrayal and loss, the fifteenth-century writer needed first to imagine this in-between space, this *topos* of incompleteness. Thus the writer, metaphorically speaking, "like the adolescent, is the one who will be able to betray his parents—to turn them against him and against themselves—in order to be free." (The writer's "parents" in this case being those institutions and social pressures which have formed him.) And Kristeva is alert to the consequences: "if this does not *mature* it, what an incredible loosening of the Superego, and what a recompense for the reader—this child, who, himself speechless, aspires only to be adolescent" (14).

Kristeva chronicles the development of inner psychic space in the novel and shows how the transition from the simpler man (e.g., "lacking both interior/inside and exterior/outside") to the more complex psychological man of the Romantics occurred in the eighteenth century. Remarkably, it is the adolescent character who serves as a standard measure in this involution of baroque man into nineteenth-century psychological man. Although the fact that Kristeva limits her discussion to the sexual identity of the Rousseauistic male raises some questions about female sexual identity, nonetheless her study underscores the ambiguities surrounding the whole area of adolescent sexual stirrings. Using Rousseau's tale *The Fairy Queen* (1752), Kristeva examines sexual ambiguity which "depends, at bottom, on the fantasies of the mother, and which must resolve itself providentially at the end of adolescence" (16). The adolescent becomes not only an emblem of a subjectivity in crisis, but also a means to display a psychic breakdown up to the point of psychosis. At the same time, the novel allows the adolescent to re-collect his subjectivity and to unify it within the unity of the narrative (18).

Kristeva continues her essay with a discussion of the father-son relationship in Dostoevsky's novel *The Adolescent* (1874-75). Noting particularly Dostoevsky's deliberate choice to write an adolescent novel "as a test of his thought" as a writer (19), she examines the adolescent hero's dilemma in having to choose between biological and spiritual paternity. Finally, in discussing the modern novels of Nabokov and Gombrowicz, she notes how the adolescent figure has become a metaphor "for what is not yet formed" (21). Thus, the adolescent is intimately connected to the beginnings and development of the novelistic genre. Its ambivalence, its more-than-oedipal pliancy, its dose of perversity, can be traced to the "open adolescent structure." In essence, adolescent writing is semiotic as well as symbolic:

> close to the primary processes awakened in adolescence, reproducing the dramaturgy of adolescent fantasies, absorbing stereotypes, but also capable of genuine inscriptions of unconscious contents that flower in the adolescent pre-conscious. This semiotic elaboration is the container—the form—and sometimes simply the mirror of adolescent transition. (22)

Kristeva has uncovered the basic component of the adolescent novel: its salutary incompleteness. At the same time, she may have tapped the secret charm of the novelists examined in this study: their comforting humility in accepting the enigma of incompleteness and in helping humanity bear its mysteries.

Kristeva uses language to link art, society, and consciousness in order to discuss the thought patterns underlying all human activity—patterns of which we are not totally in control and which constitute us as much as we do them. Essentially, Kristeva holds that consciousness, art, and society are all built "in the Name of the Father" and that, although western culture must free itself from this paternal, legislative domination, the wish to kill the father figure (civilization) can only lead to barbarism, further cruelty, and regression. But her writing does not minimize the very real threat of the mother figure; particularly in her study of the abject, she suggests that the return to the semiotic mother may also be destructive and potentially psychotic.

Julia Kristeva's writings are extremely dense. If her language is difficult, it is because she demands the total engagement of the mind, the reader's input as well as her (Kristeva's) output. Hers is the language of *materiality* as opposed to *transparency*. Her English editor claims that Kristeva's effort "is less to deal rationally with those objects or concepts words seem to encase than to work, consciously or not, with the sounds and rhythms of words in transrational fashion" (*Desire in Language* 5). Kristeva demands that we relearn the art of reading. In my own idiosyncratic readings, I will not attempt to "apply" but rather to "identify" or to "test" Kristevan theory. In this way I will be following the example of Kristeva herself, who, as Roudiez notes, never intended to follow any line *correctly*. When dealing with concepts borrowed from various disciplines, she "has fitted them to the object of her investigations." She does not "apply" a theory but allows practice to test theory (Roudiez 1).

The novels of Aidan Chambers, Robert Cormier, Kevin Major, Jan Mark, Katherine Paterson, and Patricia Wrightson acquire a new richness when read in the light of Kristevan theory because both novelist and psychiatrist give back hope. Change *is* possible. Because identity is not fixed, we are all subjects in process. The future can be good. In her essay "Women's Time,"

Kristeva writes about the "future perfect" in quotation marks. Here she develops a logic of anticipation based on a creative negativity through which she explores the possibility of transforming present time by exposing the potential of all that has been repressed in women. Alice Jardine sums up Kristeva's "future perfect" as a "modality that implies that we are neither helpless before some inevitable destiny nor that we can somehow, given enough time and thought, engineer an ultimately perfect future" ("Introduction," *Signs* 7:1 [Autumn 1981] 5).

Kristeva confronts negativity and despair in all her works; indeed, according to Lechte, negativity "comes to be the pivotal concept in [her] discussion of the relationship between the semiotic as embodied in poetic language, and the symbolic as embodied in the Law of the Father." Negativity, then, and not negation, leads the way to our understanding of the nature of repression as both constitutive and disruptive of the social order (*Julia Kristeva* 75). In *Powers of Horror,* Kristeva analyzes the logic of abjection and exposes religious taboos and institutional, cultural prohibitions that are necessary to the evolution of the speaking subject. The book represents a development of ideas found in *Desire in Language*, a collection of essays in which she explains how the literary text is the means by which a decisively innovative discourse is to be developed. The new literary work will move beyond the traditional subject/object dichotomy by dissolving those boundaries which traditionally separate the text as object from its reading and writing subjects. In *Tales of Love,* she explains how narrative can overcome narcissism's death and emptiness. Narrative is simultaneously that which is produced by the self and that which directly engages the desires of the other. It is always and never solipsistic. For Kristeva, the literary text does not merely reflect reality from an external position; it actually constitutes that reality. Thus, the reader does not extract the meaning implied in the text; rather, through interpretation, s/he participates in the creation of that meaning. In this way Kristeva alerts the reader to the deceptive nature of fiction itself. There can be no absolute view either of the world or of the individual.

As in the text so in the personality. Absolute meaning and identity are, as objects, unobtainable; they are always in process. Kristeva subverts a unitary view of the world and frees both the writer and the reader to explore the pain of a primal loss, the strangeness, the anomalies, the contrarieties that lie at the heart of human experience. At the same time, her work affirms that ordinary human consciousness can develop a sense of personal fulfillment which can put into a balanced perspective both the conflicting pleasures adult life has to offer and an understanding of those forces which are capable of diminishing these pleasures. Hers is an inestimable contribution to adolescent understanding because she emphasizes the relation between psychiatry and literature. She continually rejoices in the capacity of semiotic language to comfort the mind. Never losing sight of the often-chaotic origins of the creative act and its relation to social, cultural, and psychological conflicts, her works demonstrate that at least part of literature's value lies in the fact that the reader can lose self in chaos and then negotiate an ongoing identity. Kristeva scorns ideas of sameness and embraces those of difference, of multiplicity; she rejects unity as the gospel of male phallocentrism which has consistently repressed female expressiveness and heterogeneity. She reaches for a certain equilibrium in balancing social and psychic experience, but in doing so avoids imposing a single meaning on a subject's utterances, whether they be the words of the author or of the author's creation. For her, meaning and non-meaning reside in each subject—fictional or otherwise. In essence, Julia Kristeva brings us hope. She is optimistic about personality integration and individuality. As thoroughly learned as she is, of both the ancients like Plato and of the moderns like Freud and Lacan, she is equally independent, never intellectually dogmatic. Disagreeing with the structuralists, for example, she believes in the individuality of the speaking voice, an individual subjectivity which *can* intervene in history and actually change it. Kristeva considers herself a feminist; yet other feminists disagree with her theory of how language influences national character, a theory she advanced in *About Chinese Women.*

After reading Julia Kristeva, I found a new richness and originality in contemporary novels for the young. I could see Kristevan reflections in American novelists Katherine Paterson and Robert Cormier, British writers Aidan Chambers and Jan Mark, Canadian Kevin Major, and Australian Patricia Wrightson. In their literary creations, these writers acquaint readers with the stranger within; they confront the distress of "difference"; they help us understand the modern crises of ambiguity, of living with the possibility of never being able to understand the self or the other. These writers are a liberating influence because they always insist on a "subject in process": there is always hope for change—an ongoing change. They assure us that we continue developing in "monumental time" what we are now. These writers have enriched the inner lives of their readers by making them more aware of their place in time and by analyzing the significance of time in deepening one's interiority. The careful reader is also aware, however, of characters in the novels whose process is regression, who become lost to the psychotic rather than being liberated from it. These hope-filled novelists are unafraid to examine their subjects minutely in order to uncover the strange diseases of modern life. They have succeeded in coalescing a thorough knowledge of contemporary maladies with an appreciation of the power of the language of fiction. They have confronted the naked despair that grips modern youth and have explored new symbols that bind young and old in a spiritual poverty.

Representing a great tradition flourishing in the English-speaking countries of Canada, Australia, the United Kingdom, and the United States, each author seeks to unlock youth imprisoned in its extreme self-consciousness. These writers, however, do not attempt bibliotherapy. They write not so much for adolescents with problems as they do for all inhabitants of an ailing, though resilient, postmodern world. Their heroes simply happen to be adolescents. But the state of adolescence itself is indicative of a peculiarly contemporary frame of the global mind which, in seeking a societal unity that transcends geographical, political, even economic divisions, knows that it may never, nor perhaps should, find that unity. Aware of their power to represent realistically for their age the mystery of love's concurrence with pain, these authors are also interested in re-creating the world through the power of the word. The re-creation of the existential mysteries of life has occupied the imaginative mind since the beginning of literature, but few writers are more acutely aware of the mystery of the creative act itself than are the subjects of this study. These novelists who have taken on Giant Despair are among the most creative in the literature of their respective countries. Consciously or unconsciously, they are all experimenting with new forms of fiction, new ways of treating adolescence. All are unafraid to make challenging demands on the intelligence of their readers.

Cormier, for example, in *I Am the Cheese* (1977) brilliantly parallels a bike ride from Massachusetts to Vermont with a manipulated inner journey from a conscious to an unconscious reality that has become too oppressive to accept. The result is both chillingly and convincingly real because the novel is structured on the boy's account juxtaposed with a written report of a taped pseudo-psychiatric interview, and the reader is never certain which is "real." In *Breaktime* (1978), Aidan Chambers writes on three different levels. He narrates a simple journey to self-understanding by relating an adolescent's antagonistic relations with a father who has suffered a heart attack after a row with his son, "Ditto" (the name itself emphasizing the universality of the hero's plight). But *Breaktime* is also an intellectual challenge wherein the writer and reader engage in a game of metaphysical conceits. Furthermore, the book is a cleverly orchestrated exploration of the relations between art and life. For instance, Chambers has carefully structured a three-dimensional re-creation of the adolescent's first sexual experience by recounting the incident simultaneously in first-person narrative (regular print) with every half-page line interspersed with stream of consciousness reflection (italicized print). Counterpointed with this double presentation is the third dimension of patterns of love-making elucidated by Dr. Benjamin Spock's *A Young Person's Guide to Life and Love.* Kevin Major's distinctive ear for authentic dialogue, specifically in Newfoundland dialect, gives his novels a sense of place unique in Canadian literature. His realism, which demands that the narrative unfold from several points of view, resulted in his first book, *Hold Fast* (1978), receiving three major Canadian awards and his second novel, *Far From Shore* (1980), winning the Canadian Young Adult Book Award for 1983. Concerned with the theme of purification through suffering, in her *The Book of Wirrun* Australian writer Patricia Wrightson experiments with imagery based on the elemental trilogy of water, fire, and air. These elements reflect the psychological stresses concomitant with the pressures exerted on Aboriginal adolescents who are faced with the problems of being held in a subservient state in their own homeland. And the works of the American writer Katherine Paterson obliterate time and space distinctions by studying the abjection of the emergent self in settings as divergent as medieval Japan and modern America.

My "Kristevan" analysis of the six authors in this study has necessarily precluded countless other gifted writers for the young. During more than twenty years of lecturing on children's literature in the university, I have seen a burgeoning of creative talent in writers of children's and adolescent fiction. American writers like Sue Ellen Bridges, John Donovan, Isabelle Holland, Cynthia Voigt, and numerous others have had to be omitted; also reluctantly bypassed are Australia's Ruth Park, New Zealand's Margaret Mahey, and Britain's John Neufeld and Alan Garner. Neither do I give Canadian Budge Wilson and Australian Ivan Southall the critical attention they deserve. These are only a few of many talented authors who are none the less brilliant for not being included in this study. If, as I claimed in my introduction, the writers chosen are at all innovative, it is only fitting that I apply an innovative critical theory to their works. Because I wanted to test Julia Kristeva's theory, specifically on the fragmented but evolving nature of identity, the scope of the study by necessity had to be limited.

The authors who combat despair in this study do so from differing perspectives and in various ways, but their novels evoke responses from readers of all ages and illustrate Kristeva's thesis that adolescence is "less an age category" than an "open system" whereby, biologically speaking, living organisms live "only by maintaining a renewable identity through interaction with another" ("The Adolescent Novel" 8). The adolescent has a right to the imaginary, and it is the imaginary which helps to sweeten the adolescent's bitter initiation rite (11). Simply speaking (and really, Julia Kristeva is not simple), Kristeva gives fresh meaning to an old word: wisdom. So do the novelists studied in this book.

2

THE SEMIOTIC/ SYMBOLIC DYAD

Patricia Wrightson

> Paper bags and drink cartons scuttled furtively along pavements and lay still when Wirrun looked at them; then, as he passed, they rustled again, and were flung into spirit dances. Bits of paper that had been trees, thought Wirrun. Square-cut stones that had been rocks on a hillside. Bricks and concrete and bitumen out of the dark earth. All of them crumbling and wearing away; creeping secretly back into the earth, too slow for a man to see. Sometimes he was frightened and didn't know why.
>
> *The Dark Bright Water*

As he walks along a nameless Australian street Wirrun, the adolescent Aborigine hero of Patricia Wrightson's trilogy *The Book of Wirrun,* is frightened by the changing nature of the physical world: paper that had once been a tree, a stone that had once been part of a hill, he himself, an outsider, alone, an infinitesimal part of a predominantly white society. Loneliness and alienation are, however, only two of the problems confronting this destabilized subject. Wirrun has other sources of hopelessness besides his inability to find his place in life: aggressive impulses, the attempt to manipulate others, the inevitability of death—these are only some of the fears which Wirrun must confront in his attempts to find a niche in a society that he recognizes is crumbling like the "bits of papers that had been trees."

In Wrightson's novels we find ourselves in an ambiguous world—a stranger in a different landscape, a different culture. It's a limitless world where the boundaries between the mundane and the mystical blur, but in this new and strange world Wrightson voices her contempt for what she sees as the corruption of her own Western culture—its soul-destroying materialism. Thus, as her adolescent hero, Wirrun, saunters alone along a desolate city street, he epitomizes his creator's singular talent for combining the dynamics of the semiotic and the symbolic, the two components of the signifying process.

Wirrun, although fearful, must confront the changing nature of his own reality—his semiotic, drive-ridden instinct for survival in a white society and the symbolic nature of his Aboriginal Dreamtime which puts meaning into experience. For Wrightson, the Aborigine allegorizes a way of uniting with the maternal space of the Dreamtime, which heals the impending wounds of division. Wrightson questions the very foundations of meaning both in language and in civilization by bringing to the fore those primitive, unconscious drives buried in the human psyche—those pre-symbolic operations within language that precede signification. Her Aborigine serves as metaphor for the universal adolescent—the adolescent whom Kristeva defines as "one of those mythic figures that the imaginary gives us in order to distance us from certain of our faults" by "reifying" those faults—splits, denials, prejudices, and such—"in the form of someone who has not yet grown up"("AN" 8). As the Kristevan "writing subject" Wrightson sometimes seems to subvert the patriarchal and capitalistic structures of Western society by focussing on its marginal elements, and she converges particularly on the most marginalized of Australian society, the Aborigine.[1] In Aboriginal beliefs Wrightson discovers the re-birth of her own imagination. She creates life-like characters and immediate situations that help us "to arrive at truths that become absolute only because they first find their exact meaning in the evanescence of the imaginary construct" (*IBWL*, 18). Although words or signs are the key to the unconscious, they are not enough for Wrightson; they must be accompanied by productions of the imaginary, which fuse the semiotic and the symbolic elements, a fusing which Kristeva views as being constitutive of the subject. In reading Wrightson's fiction, especially in her construct of Wirrun as an adolescent Aborigine, we recognize a privileging of the semiotic over the symbolic. Wrightson appears to devaluate the symbolic as too representative of the European white man's over-reliance on reason and his over-estimation of the significance of his own culture. As an adolescent as well as an Aborigine, Wirrun embodies Kristeva's emphasis on the semiotic, an emphasis which Kristeva felt had been neglected in psychoanalysis, linguistics and art (Lechte, *JK*, 130).

All Wrightson's protagonists are fragmented and alone after leaving the maternal space. They need to learn, in Kristevan parlance, that they are always in a fluid state of becoming, "'destabilized' subject[s] constantly search[ing] for stabilization" (*IBWL* 19). Identification, always individual and always in process, requires a return to the security and safety of the maternal body.[2] The autoerotic, pre-oedipal body is what Kristeva calls the "semiotic" body. Semiotic activity begins in the mother's body; it is both biological and social, and it initiates those drives that Kristeva wants to bring back to Lacanian theory.[3] Wrightson found in her own reading of Aboriginal folk tales and myths an instinctive resolution of the semiotic-symbolic dialectic because Aborigines allow the world to be populated by spirit-drives, confluences which take up their bodily presence in humans, animals, and nature itself, but are never inexorably tied to these forms.[4] Her speaking subjects are split, "divided between unconscious and conscious motivation, that is, between physiological processes and social constraints" (*DL* 6). But in the Aboriginal network of relationships, each considers the "self" as the centre of a concentric circle enfolding "others," animate or inanimate; these "others" themselves form similar centres linking Aborigines in a kinship wherein boundaries are fluid and everything is interrelated: human and supra-human, semiotic and symbolic.[5]

Like Kristeva, Wrightson views adolescence less as an age category than as an open psychic structure. Because humans must maintain a renewable identity through interaction with others, the adolescent structure must open itself to the repressed at the same time that it initiates a psychic reorganization of the individual (Kristeva, "AN" 8). Wrightson's young protagonists usually make a breakthrough in the on-going process of identity formation by facing up to the self as revealed in the other; the discovery is facilitated by the wisdom and insight found in the story—the Aborigines' folk tales and myths. Perhaps even more importantly, Wrightson suggests that not only the individual but also postmodern Australia (indeed the West itself) is undergoing its own adolescence and must re-discover those common semiotic roots which would obliterate all divisions between male/female, proper/

improper, normal/abnormal, rich/poor and so on. Wrightson believes that, as surely as the paper cups return to the earth to nourish more trees and as inevitably as the rocks and bricks of our buildings crumble in order to prepare for their recycling, so does the adolescent, both individually and racially, share in nature's sublime power to renew itself. As a result, her heroes and heroines are always in a state of becoming. The wisdom of expectation operates as a subtle form of social criticism which opens up to the possibility of transforming the present by exposing potentialities that have been ostracized and repressed. Patricia Wrightson believes passionately that despair is "inherently wrong" and throughout her distinguished career she has repeatedly attacked the giant.[6]

Very early in her career, Wrightson established what would become the hallmark of all her fiction: the mystical unity of all living things.[7] Everything in nature—human nature above all—has the power to renew itself. Nothing need ever be destroyed or wasted. Wrightson sees Aboriginal culture as an antidote to the poison of modern materialism. Aboriginal culture also rectifies Western misrepresentation of Genesis, which understood that man had domination over the land and the animal kingdom (1:29). Domination, for her, is equated with responsibility and concern for the hunted—human and animal. From her first stories, *The Crooked Snake* (1955) and *The Bunyip Hole* (1957), Aboriginal folk characters co-exist with humans; both are situated in a distinctly Australian setting, and both must learn to share the land, the earth mother. A warm current is generated between Wrightson's voice and the land. Rocks, sand, water, and sky envelop reader and writer in a peculiarly profound relationship. Her feeling for place, particularly for the land, makes her stories essentially Australian; yet at the same time, this feeling for the land also marks the universality of her fiction, because it is through the land that humankind finds its essential unity with nature and with the protective power of the Dreamtime. For Wrightson, as for the natives of Australia and of North America, the land represents a promise of tomorrow. Money never mothered any culture as did the land.[8] Wrightson's Aborigines seek only to vanish into the land, become a part of it; never to stand out against it, never to conquer it. At death they return to its womb.

In Wrightson's view, Aboriginal culture regards itself as part of the totality of creation rather than in lordship of all it surveys. European culture valorizes the symbolic; it represents the paternal—masculine, competitive and exploitive—whereas the Aboriginal tradition is semiotic: maternal, conserving and caring. Thus Wrightson rejoices in the interconnectedness of all living things and celebrates:

> being a thread in the same fabric and knowing it; being aware of other lives driving in other directions yet interlocking; knowing that "your" land belongs also to a complex crowd who find you wholly negligible except as a resource, that "your" walls belong also to rats and ants, that "your" gutters belong also to frogs. And you can't live with it [interconnectedness] without somehow interpreting it. ("A Little Fear," *Reading Time* 92 [July 1984] 14).[9]

And she has imaginatively interpreted the interconnectedness of all life with wit, sanity and love because she has grasped the essential semiotic nature of the Aborigines' culture and made it central to her detestation of the white man's greed.

Because she felt her country had made little contribution to the field of fantasy, a field which she perceived being very difficult to break into, Wrightson, as "writing subject," believed Aboriginal folklore offered a rich, untapped vein of visionary ore that would be distinctly Australian.[10] Aware of the dangers and the difficulties that faced her, she wrote:

> This is a still-living folklore that we propose to handle creatively; it involves special ritual secrecy and the dividing lines merge and waver; it involves people at fifty different levels of acceptance and development, none of them readily agreeing with each other; it concerns two races forced to share a nation and between whom relations are strained; and it gives me nightmares.[11]

Out of Aboriginal folklore came some remarkable creatures tinted by her own colourful imagination—Bunyips, Nyols and, perhaps most compelling of all, the Nargun.[12] Hers is a particularly rich vision which relies on Aboriginal folk tales to dramatize the semiotic as a psychic component that is essentially maternal. Her special magic transforms perception, balances semiotic/symbolic needs, and stabilizes a destabilized subject.

After the somewhat quiet publication of *The Crooked Snake* (1955) and *The Bunyip Hole* (1957), Wrightson sharpened her imaginative focus in *The Rocks of Honey* (1960). Although the story is told through the eyes of the destabilized white child, Barney Willis, it is the young Aborigine, Eustace (Useless) Murray, who helps Barney to uncover the power of the Dreamtime past and to glimpse the invisible bridge that must be built between the emotional, drive-motivated, semiotic and the rational, logic-controlled symbolic. So too does Lindy Martin, the fifteen-year-old heroine of *The Feather Star* (1962), learn that when her imagined treasure the feather star is destroyed, new "stars" grow from the fragments. Every "death" brings another "birth." All returns to the Dreamtime; it's all in the way one sees.

Wrightson's tales of enlightenment with their imaginative enticements expanded with *Down to Earth* (1965), in which she explored how the ordinary may become extraordinary when our perception shifts: if, for example, a modern city like Sydney is seen through the eyes of a Martian who visits earth. In yet another story of mystification transformed, *I Own the Racecourse* (1968), she shows how the retarded hero Andy Hoddell creates his own "Dreamtime" reality by believing he owns a racecourse. Wrightson had won Australia's Children's Book of the Year Award in 1956, and with the "particularly striking" *I Own the Racecourse*, she won a place on the Hans Christian Andersen Honours List.

But it is with *An Older Kind of Magic* (1972) and *The Nargun and the Stars* (1973) that Wrightson's originality becomes most obvious. She has uncovered the psychological power of Aboriginal folklore to take us back to a semiotic Dreamtime where the imaginary not only accommodates but also nourishes the real. In *An Older Kind of Magic*, Wrightson explains that it was useless to try to plant the old Anglo-Saxon kind of magic in Australia. The signification of one culture is not readily absorbed by another. Australian vision must be shaped by the land itself:

> We need to look for another kind of magic, a kind that must have been shaped by the land itself at the edge of Australian vision. So I have tried, in a small way. I have pictured Pot-Koorok, Nyol and Net-Net, unsuspected in their own water or rock; creeping from tunnels and drains into our streets; never seen, but perhaps to spring out at us

> some day. I have put beside them for contrast a shabbier, pretended magic that has shrunk to an advertising gimmick and is real for only a moment in a thousand years. Perhaps this may be a beginning. (Epilogue)

It was more than a beginning; it was something entirely new. Wrightson had created characters who belonged equally to the real world of drives and instincts and to the symbolic world of signification. Stripped of their protective ferns and shut away forever from the sun, the rocks lie buried. But from these rocks the Nyols creep, the old creatures of the land. Wanting to feel the wind, they find their way up through tunnels and discover that the city is a dead place. Wrightson proved that the modern wizard of signification, the language of advertising with a "Save our Gardens" sign, was not nearly as effective as the older kind of magic epitomized by the Nyols of rock spirits.

More convincing in its uniqueness than even the Nyols is the Nargun who, in its fusion of semiotic and symbolic impulses, transcends the moral to show that a speaking subject is a social construct. The Nargun, in Wrightson's 1973 novel *The Nargun and the Stars,* is a rock beast and like the pre-adolescent speaking subject, Simon, is neither fully unified nor fully natural. It is as much a creature of destruction as it is an object of pity. The book, for which Wrightson won her second Australian Children's Book of the Year Award, challenges adult assumptions as much as it challenges children's. Is the Nargun real because the reader can comprehend it as a metaphor for Simon Brent's psychological state, bruised as it is after the death of his parents in a car crash? Or is the rock monster real because it can be explained as an equivalent for the scientific fact of erosion? In either case Wrightson has given her Nargun intense credibility, perhaps because she makes us feel the monster as well as understand him:

> The Nargun moves down the gorge to blink at the sun, to watch a river flow, to hunt savagely; but always it made the ponderous climb back, crushing ferns and grinding moss on its way, to drag itself behind the crystal columns. Sometimes it felt anger: for a fallen tree, a dried-up pool, an intruder, or for hunger. Then too it cried. It has a sort of love, a response to the deep, slow rhythms of the earth; and

> when it felt the earth's crust swell to the pull of the moon it sometimes called in ecstasy. It had no fear; but a wide sunny place, or any strange thing, made it uneasy. Then it crouched in stony stillness and little lizards ran over it. (10)

The reader feels that the Nargun is indifferent to humans and knows the rock monster threatens to crash down on the Waters' family home not through malice but simply because the house happens to be in its path. What makes the above passage more meaningful in a Kristevan sense is that it underscores the Nargun as a creature of drives, a semiotic creation; it also illustrates the importance of change, of movement. Nothing ever remains the same. The Nargun "moves down the gorge" and "blinks at the sun." It asserts those aggressive forces to "hunt savagely," "climb ponderously," "crush," "grind," and even cry. The Nargun is a signifier for the repressed, resentful Simon. Humans, with their logging of forests, have contributed to the Nargun's centuries-long movement until it finds itself in Australia's Hunter Valley at the same time when the orphan, Simon Brent, comes to live there. The Nargun's dislocation mirrors the dislocation of Simon whose name, associated with that of Simon Peter, suggests rock.

The Potkoorok, another spirit-creature of the valley (a trickster with a "golden eye"), is also a signifier. He watches Simon, waits and then curls "a coldness around his ankle slithering like an eel" (24). The Potkoorok shares in the symbolic, for it can speak, and Simon eventually becomes aware of "the gurgling voice and [hears] the words" (42). Other creatures of the forest like the Turongs are also signifiers for the dislocated Simon, who must move on in his life. The shadowy eeriness of the Turongs with their long, straggling beards, who spring from the highest branches, spreading their stick-like arms wide, frightens Simon. These displaced "ancient Turongs of the fallen forest" howl as they look for new homes when their ancient habitats are bulldozed.

With her power to create spirit voices in the wind's sighing or in a petal stirring, Wrightson encapsulates those wonders and fears that make everything in nature unique. Often troubled by his own uniqueness, the adolescent rejects difference. The orphaned Simon, through the semiotic signifiers of Nargun, Potkoorok and Turongs, discovers the connection between nature and culture, semiotic and symbolic; he learns to accept his uniqueness, his isolation. He discovers that the human psyche is more fragile than either the Nargun, the Potkoorok, or the Turongs; the human is more in need of assurance, of identity. Simon must not dwell on his own bitter loss; the "sullen boy who was a stranger" must leave off his narcissistic clinging to a dead mother and find the other. Despite the fact that Simon has seen the invisible spirits of the swamp, and learned of the power of the Nyols, he has yet to learn how to live interiorly. Simon, the speaking subject, is always "in process," always in a state of becoming.

There is a two-fold battle fought in *The Nargun and the Stars* as there is a two-fold quest. Humans have dispossessed the Turongs of their natural forest habitats in order to make new roads. No wonder the Turongs fight back by capturing the Bulldozer and confiscating it in a cave. But there is another battle going on between Simon and the Nargun, and Wrightson suggests the complexity of this skirmish. The Nargun is not a typical foe. After all, it had moved only "to escape from the throbbings and thunders [of the bulldozer] that killed the trees." It loves the mountain and "in its cold, still way the Nargun loved men; loved them even when it killed them" (77). Externally Simon fights the Nargun because it threatens his new home; internally he struggles because the Nargun signifies Simon himself. "Simon," the Nargun called silently. The boy "could see one dark cavity like an eye half turned to him, as though the darkness knew and watched" (80). Like the Nargun, Simon is cold and silent; he is battling his own deadness. And like the Nargun, Simon has to deal with his displacement. He is seeking a new home and a new identity. Simon's deadness is buried deep within the mountain's cave with the Nargun, and the faithful Nyols befriend the monster who "waits for the mountain to crumble … for time to wear away." Simon's name on the Nargun's back is "only a whisper in the dark" (160).

In *The Nargun and the Stars*, Wrightson makes a new Dreamtime possible for a young boy on the point of despair. What she does for the pre-adolescent with Simon, she tries to accomplish for the late adolescent in the character of Wirrun, hero of her trilogy *The Book of Wirrun*.[13] Here she extends her views on the "speaking subject" always "in process." Because Wrightson's characters survive only when they can maintain a renewable identity through their interaction with another, Wirrun must confront the fluidity of his own identity in discovering the semiotic/symbolic coalescence in his relationships with the other and with the "People," the Aborigines. For Wrightson, the wisdom of the past, specifically the recognition of racial intolerance, offers hope that the present can be changed by exposing potentialities that have been repressed (the semiotic). *The Book of Wirrun* is a studied response to oppression and repression: oppression of the whites over the blacks in Australia and the enforced repression of the blacks' Dreamtime-enabling culture. Furthermore, these novels underscore a new modern Dreamtime where a greater acceptance of cultural differences will obliterate the cruelty and intolerance of the past.

Wrightson's trilogy opens with *The Ice Is Coming* (1977), followed by *The Dark Bright Water* (1978), and *Behind the Wind* (1981). Her geography, although as specific as the southern tip of Australia which "lies like an open hand hollowed a little at the palm," is much more evidently the landscape of the inner psychic world—mysterious, dark and threatening. The greatest threat to this inner world seems to come from white Australians, whose institutionalized materialism Wrightson condemns in her satiric description of the "Happy Folk" who live only for happiness: "it is their business and their duty. They study it and teach it to their children, debate it, make laws to force it on each other, struggle for it, export it and import it. Most of them buy and sell it" (*TIIC* 11). In contrast to the Happy Folk of the city are the "Inlanders" and, more significantly, the "People." The "Inlanders" are of mixed race and claim to be of the same stock as the "Happy Folk," but the land has reclaimed them. The "People" are the Aborigines from whose ranks comes the hero, Wirrun, who is described as "a broad-shouldered, dark-eyed man with the heavy brow and wide smile of the People" (BTW 7). He is not a symbolically beautiful figure but rather a scruffy, eighteen-year-old gas-station attendant who, like many uneducated, deprived youth, speaks semiotically in poetic, if ungrammatical, English. His beginnings, like those of Jesus or Arthur or Teufelsdroch, are shrouded in mystery. He must learn to balance the deprivation and squalor of his actual position in a white, patriarchally structured society with the Dreamtime past of his Aboriginal roots. He has a choice between hunting with the pack—other Australians of colour who try to fit in with the Happy People—or going it alone. Both ways involve an inevitable sadness, but Wirrun chooses the destiny of his People and the trilogy examines the consequences of this choice.

Not so much actions as choices determine Wirrun's fate. All three novels present a simple quest which always involves the need for Wirrun to go back to his semiotic roots: he "had to find out from the earth things as he went" (*TIIC* 90). In *The Ice Is Coming*, Wirrun is commissioned by Ko-in, a wise man of The People, to rescue the Eldest Nargun, who holds the power of fire and who is imprisoned by the Ninya. Balance in nature is disrupted when the Ninya, who are ice people, threaten to freeze the whole continent. The second novel, *The Dark Bright Water*, finds the balance in nature disturbed by the erratic workings of the waterways which cause the stones to evaporate and the desert to blossom. Wirrun must restore harmony. In the third novel, *Behind the Wind*, Wirrun is asked by Ko-in to investigate the cause of nature's greatest agitation—death.

Although the plots are simple, the meanings are profound because through these tales Wrightson explores the disturbing, hidden powers of the semiotic/symbolic dyad in the teenager's psyche—the ways in which negation and identification operate—in alienation from society, in the struggles with aggressive impulses, in the manipulative drive to control others, in conflict with death and rebirth. Symbolic meaning is never completely achieved. Even at the end, Wirrun becomes a victim of the death he sought to destroy. Because *The Book of Wirrun* encapsulates the essence of Wrightson's despair-defying fiction, this study will concentrate on these three novels.

In *The Ice Is Coming*, Wirrun restores balance in nature by defeating the self-centered, white-blooded Nyols: "every man of the Nyols wants all and wants it for himself" (5); there is no "other." Wirrun is aided in his quest by the semiotic urges of his own needs and also by the symbolic power of the quartz stone wrapped up in possum fur and given to him by Ko-in, the wise old man of the People. With this stone he can "ride the wind," attain dominance over others, or—the stone's real power—recognize the spirituality of matter. The quartz stone is a powerful image of Wirrun's communication with the spirit world. Though his conversations with the shy Mimi, the rock spirit who shares Wirrun's quest to rescue the Nargun, it becomes evident that Wirrun has accepted his identity as a dark-skinned, low-browed, watchful-eyed Aborigine who belongs to the land: "it flows into them through their feet" (11). His unity with the land causes him to care for all creatures with whom he shares the earth: "There's a dung-beetle by that log. I care for that. There's a rotten toadstool with a worm in it: I care for both of 'em" (223). And in watching Wirrun, the spirit creatures, like the Mimi and the Nyol, recognize "the curious thing that men were made for: to care" (132).

But Wrightson remained unsatisfied after she completed *The Ice Is Coming.* She thought she had written a complete story and discovered it was only a beginning:

> It had employed an ancient, living and still adult folklore to do what a dead, long-handled folklore couldn't do: to place legend in the present time. It had taken its hero past the breakthrough point and put him in touch with timeless powers, initiated him into herohood and then dropped him. But the powers themselves, and the theme of the man appointed hero, were bigger than that. Legend is bigger. The folklore was bigger.[14]

The Dark Bright Water is itself a "bigger" book, bigger because Wrightson tackles dangerously complex subjects: the risk-taking involved in falling in love, the betrayal of friendship, the evils of guilt and abjection—all those enigmatic, semiotic elements which may transgress the encoded social constructs. She struggles fiercely to uncover those universal elements that make humans unique, vulnerable and alone.

Wirrun is pre-eminently a loner, living on the outskirts of society, treated contemptuously by whites, but nursed by hopes of the Dreamtime. The novel reflects back to the reader the need for a community of selves and the balancing of those separate selves. The time period is deliberately vague, and Wrightson suggests that the circumstances surrounding the most significant events in life are often casual, even trivial. Timeless fate and love entwine and tangle to complicate life; but Wirrun, more as an Aborigine, seems to grasp the enduring significance of his semiotic impulses. Nowhere is this more evident than in his complicated love for his friend Ularra and for his future wife Murra. Wrightson does not suggest that love's sensual pleasure is to be replaced by spiritual joy. The intensity of bodily pleasures is nowhere denied, but Wirrun's and Ularra's response to the allurements of jouissance is a study in contrasts. The reader may allegorize the boys' differences in a number of ways. Wirrun at one point represents the Kristevan symbolic while Ularra represents the semiotic. Each, however, needs the other, even though Ularra denies his semiotic drives and Wirrun refuses to accept the symbolic, first in the codes of his People and second in his call to be a hero—with all its responsibilities.

Ularra is the devoted friend, open-hearted and generous, paying for the jobless Wirrun's food and rent. He is more gregarious, more prone to beer-drinking than Wirrun, less subservient to social constraints but subject to Wirrun's manipulations. Generously rejoicing in his friend's status, he happily acknowledges Wirrun's power as a leader who possesses the great quartz crystal in its wrappings of possum-fur string.

But Wirrun is reluctant to accept the power of the quartz stone. He confesses that the power is for a man, and he "had never been made a man" (30). Even when Wirrun is counselled about the relationship between knowledge and experience, he refuses to listen: "You know only what you will not know, and what you will know is all greenness" (35-36). And again: "You cannot take back your name from the places where it is known. There are makings that cannot be denied, Hero, and names that must be accepted"(36). Wirrun, although recognizing his different selves, thrusts the power stone back into its hole and is enticed by the siren song of the water:

> Are you not coming?
> sings the bright water,
> are you not coming?

The "bright water" will become the "dark bright" of the title's oxymoron as Wirrun confronts the jealousy and violence masking love.

The semiotic/symbolic dichotomy is allegorized and given a specific cultural overtone when Wirrun and Ularra travel to Alice country in Australia's heartland. One night Wirrun awakes to see strange intruders hovering over Ularra. "They looked like wicked little men of the People, perhaps three or four feet tall, hairy all over and with long, dark beards. One of the pair was stick thin, the other stout and round-bellied" (64). The language and imagery suggest the excitement and enticement of pulsating semiotic drives from Aboriginal spirits like the Uthippa—shadowy women whom Wirrun observes dancing and singing in the moonlight. He sees "shields and spear-throwers lifted, and a flowing of limbs and breasts and hair" (72). Then, too, there are the Mungga, Mungga, "girl shapes who laugh and swing their hips in the moonlight" (79). Ularra is strongly attracted to the joyous abandon of breasts, limbs and hair while Wirrun, with his power stone throbbing, warns that they have fangs (79-80).

With Wirrun's "restless unhappiness" in repressing physical desire and in Ularra's dangerous dalliance with the moonlight spirits, Wrightson does not suggest moral evil, but rather an assertion of dissent from which an ethical standard surfaces. Hers is not the kind of ethics that consists of obedience and conformity to laws, but a necessary acceptance of the imbalance in nature from which the subject, always-in-process, emerges. The subject-on-trial reasserts its position in the transformation of the self and of the community. The aspect of Aboriginal communality is suggested in the language of the passage which evokes age-old land and border disputes, usurpation of territory, possessiveness—all of which are made analogous to the sexes' invasion of the others' territories. In rectifying the imbalance in nature, Wirrun and Ularra learn to control their own selfish acquisitiveness. But before Wirrun and Ularra enter into their climactic struggles as subjects-on-trial, discourse itself is transcended when the youths are "caught in a great stillness ... under a dome of glass." It is the point when Wirrun confesses to Ularra "how the mountain had caught him with a love-singing" (90-91).

The plot deepens and darkens in focus; violence and despair interact mutely in the novel's dramatic action wherein a double-heated intensity pulses underneath the central relationships—those of Wirrun with his friend and with his future wife. Perhaps the jealousy and violence throbbing throughout the friendship saga is even more intense than that echoing within the marriage. Ularra becomes enchanted with a broad-cheeked, dark-eyed Abuba "bright with mischief" (103); he spends the night with his Abuba and returns utterly transformed: "Baring its fangs and pleading with its eyes, the monstrous thing that was Ularra launched itself at Wirrun" (112). Renewal follows transgression, however, and it is at the boundaries of transformation that signification occurs. Wirrun learns how painful entering into the symbolic can be: he "must cook the sick and aching man gently in the earth with water and leaves" (120). The whole concept of the Aborigines' initiation ritual underlies this episode. Both Ularra's and Wirrun's youth will lie in the grave of pain—Ularra's of physical and Wirrun's of mental anguish. Wirrun conducts his first "turning" when he places his friend in a grave of hot coals covered with brush, and prays: "Take the evil out of this man." Keeping vigil through the night, in the morning he gropes "for hands and feet free of claws," gropes to wash his friend's sandy face and wet his "heat dried lips" (124-26). It would be days before his friend became totally changed, but through this trial the reader questions the sexual complexities of Ularra's and the Abuba's mutually inflicted violence. Wirrun hears his friend cry out to the Abuba, "Girl, girl... Why did you call me? ... What sort of thing are you? ... Did you want a beast to tear you?" (132). Ularra had tried to make the sexual experience something else, perhaps more than it was meant to be (134). The two black imps, one fat, the other thin, who first looked down on Ularra when he slept, seem to represent the immoderate, unbalanced expectations of human sexuality.

In relationship between the two friends, Wirrun and Ularra, the levels of interaction between the semiotic and symbolic can be represented. Ularra, a semiotic figure, is a creature of energy and drives, moved, however, by the influence of the symbolic figure of Wirrun, who reflects the social and cultural merits of the People. But the semiotic cannot be equated entirely with the physical nor the symbolic with the social. Wirrun himself will transgress the cultural norms of his people when he negates the urgings of Ularra, his friend. One incident, in particular, dramatizes the inter-relationship of semiotic/symbolic pressures.

Discovering an ancient cave (with its timeless, semiotic nuances of the first Dark, the womb), Wirrun hears the angry cries of tailed women, the furious cry of the dingo, the haunting sound of the water, and he becomes aware that the disturbances in nature, in his friendship with Ularra, and in himself are all inter-related. Against the advice of Ularra, Wirrun, as captivated by the tailed woman as Ularra was by his Abuba, goes into the cave. Darkness sustains the woman-womb imagery in two figures: guardian night in the "shape of a woman with a great sharp horn rising from each shoulder" (145) and the Bimpo, "a hag, cruel and cunning," who carries "a spear and a large net bag" [for human flesh] (146). The imagery connotes the murkiness of the semiotic/symbolic confluences along with those of the unconscious/

conscious, id/superego, feminine/masculine. In all instances a dialectic is constantly at work between nature and culture. Armed with his "uncovered" quartz stone and a fire stick (both sexual images here), Wirrun hears again the sound of the water and feels the presence of "ancient and formless things of the first dark"; spirits which had "no shape firm enough for speech of seeing." They only "rolled about him like smoke and thinned away from the light in his hand." More comforting is the sight of the Nyols, "the old bright eyes of the little grey people" who had helped him several times before and who now reveal that Ularra has followed him into the cave (151-52).

Wirrun's and Ularra's disturbing semiotic stirrings, as well as the uneasy coursing of the waters, enforce the semiotic/symbolic, nature/culture dichotomy: "his trouble and the land's were one; that to heal the land's trouble, he must meet and resolve his own ... that the singing and the howling, the hunger and the dread, were the same" (155). Wirrun, however, does not realize that the disturbances in his nature are more than sexual. He is jealous of his friend. Ularra has now entered into the symbolic; he too can hear and understand the language of the water spirit (161). Now it is Ularra who attempts to impose symbolic/cultural norms on Wirrun; he tries to keep his friend from the siren song. Infuriated, Wirrun berates Ularra for coming to him on the power of the quartz stone and excoriates his friend for dogging him like a beast. Ularra throws back the possum-fur cord linking the two friends. Meanwhile, on Wirrun's command, the tailed women are loosening rocks from a sealed pool. When an opening is made, out flows the captive Yunggamurra:

> She was silver like moonlight and lovely and dew-wet like a flower. Her dark hair flowed over slender shoulders to the rock where she sat and she combed it back with delicate fingers. (164)

Wirrun is smitten by her loveliness but Ularra, trying to save his friend from the love-torment he himself had suffered, flings himself into the pool to prevent Wirrun from going to the seductive water spirit and drowns. Even as Wirrun rolls him over on the bank of the pool, "the ancient air of the cavern stirred and sweetened." Something "warm and strong and gentle" passes him (169). It is Ularra's spirit.

For all the similarities among the semiotic/symbolic analogies, the operational sphere is always language; language allows for different modes of articulation for both. There are non-verbal signifying systems that are constructed exclusively on the basis of the semiotic, like the sound of water rushing or the cries of the dingo or the ancient air, warm, strong and gentle. As Kristeva reminds us:

> Because the subject is always both semiotic and symbolic, no signifying system he produces can be either 'exclusively' symbolic, and is instead necessarily marked by an indebtedness to both." (*RPL* 24)

But in the symbolic/semiotic, Wirrun/Ularra relationship, the symbolic includes the separation of the subject from its object. Thus Wirrun leaves Ularra. He gives his friend a hero's grave deep in the silent underground, and the hands of culture, through his Aborigine ancestors, reach in pity from the past. These spirits "knew he had faced his haunting and found no power of himself" (173). It is Ularra's spirit that brings him comfort both in his remorse and in his ambiguous attraction and repulsion for the Yunggamurra. Ularra's voice is heard in the sound of the wind in the grass; he whispers, "A man can't drown so quickly ... unless he wants to ... a beast's too much for a man" (178).

Culture demands that Wirrun bring Yunggamurra, the water spirit, to his home. Another semiotic/symbolic coagulation occurs in the water/fire dyad because, as subject, Wirrun must posit himself as something different from his object (the Yunggamurra water spirit), whom he takes into the human world through the civilizing influence of fire.

> He held her over the small licking flames and saw strips of dried slime fall away and burn. He watched with hard disgust something more horrible: a million tiny leeches crawl from the pores of her skin to fall into the flames ... When there were only dead fires and lazy smoke, he lifted her and kissed her, and her lips were smoke-dried but soft and cool and clean.... (204-05)

Wirrun names his "golden girl" Murra. Instinctual rather than intellectual, Murra is another semiotic figure acting on drives and impulse. A prisoner of male domination, subjected to the jealousy of the wives of Kooleen, she refuses to become the potential victim of Wirrun's manipulations. When she is asked to put on clothes, she resists Wirrun's social injunction, claiming that the body is beautiful and should not be hidden. Murra is not a passive recipient of male domination. When Wirrun tries to tell her about money, the world of the Happy People, jobs, cities, settlements, and so on, Murra scorns them all. As long as she is Wirrun's wife, she will stay in his world, but he must learn to accommodate himself to her spirit ways as much as she conforms to his human ways. Thus the semiotic/symbolic dichotomy continues to be in process even in the final part of the trilogy, *Behind the Wind.*

In the third novel, the semiotic/symbolic is played out in the country/city bivalence. Wirrun has given up the shoddy cheapness of the city in order to live freely with his wife in the old Aboriginal ways. And just as Ularra as spirit became a teacher for Wirrun, as he never was in his human state, so does the anti-materialistic Murra teach Wirrun how to transform life. She is the source of joy and playfulness in the novel. The Happy Folk, in their search for money and possessions, have lost their capacity for joy. Murra questions Wirrun's own values when she asks, "Why do you need this crazy money?" She possesses the fundamental spirit of true detachment from material things and a profound love of the elements—first of water, now land. At one point Wirrun wants to work for the Happy Folk in order to earn money to buy her a dress so that she will not look like something the cat dragged in. Murra's response is, "to be Yunggamurra is to be beautiful when the cat drags you" (13).

Wirrun as subject must once again separate from his object. Murra unwillingly returns to the Yunggamurra when "the whiteness of rain came roaring over the water" (37).[15] But the greatest separation is yet to be faced: Wirrun is charged to answer "the call of earth things and spirits" (44). Wirrun must confront death, made tangible, easily comprehensible, in a figure like Wulgaru, the name given to Death by North-country Aborigines. Wirrun acts out his final semiotic/symbolic testing in death's spiritual/physical confluence. The Aborigines believe that death is man-made, caused most commonly by "pointing the bone." Emphasis is laid on the fact that man, as part of the land, cannot be annihilated because the land is a spirit. Sorcery may very well "inflict death, injury or other misfortune by carrying out physical and hence empirically observable operations possessed of mystical efficacy"; furthermore, death may be caused "by the sorcerer using his art to separate irrevocably the bodily and spiritual parts of his victim's person" (Maddock 161-62). But death can never extinguish the spirit. So Wirrun, overcome with loss of his others, Ularra and Murra, "risked his naked spirit again and hunted the mash-face Wulgaru in sleep" (106).

Kristeva's dissolution of the myth of permanence makes comprehensible Wirrun's confrontation with death. In this final confrontation Wirrun recognizes that every loss or disintegration is replaced by another force, and the force of life prevails over that of death as is evident when, one night in sleep, he sees his lovely Murra, "Shining by moonlight" in the land that was old by day and young by night. She is transformed:

> ...he glimpsed her high in a tree and shining gold as the moon with the breeze wrapping her long dark hair about her. The song broke—she slid down from the tree and vanished and Wirrun fled too. They had found their ways out of the net and must not be caught again. (106)

Wirrun begins to understand that only in the spirit world of sleep and death (both are parts of nature) can he find union with Murra, who is herself freed from control of her Yunggamurra sisters and has tasted human individuality. In his critical meeting with Wulgaru, Wirrun concretizes the meaning of death as a natural part of rebirth and transformation. Wulgaru, in the shape of a faint green glow under the grave tree, demands of Wirrun, "Say what you are." Wirrun answers resoundingly, "I am" (121). Wulgaru sneers at man "who came from shadows and nothings, things that creep like beetles out of the land and are bound by law." But it is precisely because the land is more powerful than man himself that Wirrun gains his trust. Wulgaru speaks of the land as "a law of beaten sand and crumbled rock and dust carried on the wind, a law of lost water and dead seas." Wulgaru takes his law from "the living and knowing, from Man" (121). In creating Wulgaru, man has lied in denying the spirit in the land of which Wirrun is a part. Defying the cheater Wulgaru, Wirrun cries, "I just spit on you because I am" (122). Wulgaru triumphs in his fight with Wirrun boasting, "though I am man-made, a bit of tree, I am death. You cannot meet me unchanged." And Wirrun is changed, transformed:

> "I am ... I am ... The bit of me here; it's spirit." ...he knew he had been changed as ancestors and heroes and lesser men before him had been changed. The land was silently peopled with them; among its ancient rocks their stone bodies lay in waiting or in promise while they themselves lived on; behind the wind as the old men said. Now he too lived behind the wind. He had grown out of now into forever. (152-53)

In the course of the trilogy Wirrun undergoes the repressive-jubilatory states of youth, adulthood and old age while still remaining an adolescent. In all three books Wirrun has been questioning subjectivity by revisiting the semiotic/symbolic roots of his Aboriginal culture. First he is Ice-Fighter, then Peace-Bringer, and finally, the powerful Spirit "I am" with its shades of the Judeo-Christian God's "I Am who I Am" (Exodus 3:14). Only by entering the silent abode of death, returning to the womb of earth, does he learn to understand that death always has a place in life. Death is a creator as well as a destroyer. In releasing those barriers imposed on spirit, Death reveals the ultimate potential of human life.

What a condemnation of racism, of the notion of the supremacy of European civilization, and what an incredible loosening of the Superego Wrightson has unleashed in her trilogy! In her emphasis on the semiotic both in the Aborigine and in the adolescent Wirrun, Patricia Wrightson has exposed not only the wisdom of recognizing the significance of the semiotic, but also the greed of the white man's culture—paternalistic and dominant—which has made the colonizer both victimizer and victim. With wit, sanity and love she has imaginatively interpreted the interconnectedness of all life because she has grasped the essential spirituality of the Aborigines' culture and made it central to her detestation of the white man's greed.

Since 1788, European settlers have almost decimated a culture and a race which, when they first came to Australia, numbered approximately 300,000 natives but which is now in a rapid state of decline. Passionately indignant at the destructive effect of Western domination on the Aborigines, Wrightson recognizes history's irony in that, while the past twenty years have witnessed the Australian government's attempts to redress the injustice done to its native people by allowing them greater access to economic and political power, the Aborigines themselves are trapped in a situation in which they view their traditional spiritual power as no longer effective in a power-driven world.

The "writing subject" includes not only consciousness but also its unconsciousness. Even though Wrightson has never studied Kristevan theory, her appreciation of the earth as mother provides a more compelling illustration of Julia Kristeva's semiotic principle than do the psychiatrist's treatises. In any case Wrightson as novelist has made us more intensely aware of our essential linkage to the earth mother. Patricia Wrightson's trilogy, *The Book of Wirrun*, reveals to Australians and non-Australians alike the singular beauty of the Australian bush, the rich mysteries of the Aborigines' ties with the land, and the destructive effects of genocide—not only on the victims but also on its perpetrators. As Jeanette Manyweathers writes of Wrightson:

> She has written ironically, sharply, critically and yet lovingly of Australian Society; she has, with great sensitivity, unlocked for non-Aboriginals the rich and perceptive Aboriginal view of a people bound with close physical and psychological ties to the land; and she has let us look through the calm and joyful eyes of the wise fool at the world's fragile, accidental beauty. (78)

But Patricia Wrightson has realized even more. Intuitively grasping two central concepts of one of the foremost contemporary intellectuals, she has illuminated Julia Kristeva's concepts both of the semiotic/symbolic confluence and of the non-chronological understanding of adolescence as an open system, a *topos* of incompleteness, applying equally to the race as to the individual. There is probably no other Australian writer of children's and adolescents' literature who demonstrates so much literary grace and human wisdom.

3

KEVIN MAJOR AND THE CHORA EXPERIENCE

AS A CANADIAN, but more so as a Newfoundlander proud of his isolated island,[1] Kevin Major's imagination reveres the stranger within, that "foreigner" whom Julia Kristeva in *Strangers to Ourselves* terms "the hidden face of our identity, the space that wrecks our abode, the time in which understanding and affinity founder" (1). It is the hidden face of our identity that absorbs Kristeva's thinking, and that face is found not in the ego or the personality, but in the unconscious. Kristeva works to decentre the ego and dethrone consciousness. This decentring takes place not only in psychoanalysis but in art, in literature, and, to some extent, even in theology. According to Lechte, Kristeva's work can be seen "as a prolonged meditation on the effect of the unconscious in human life, an effect psychoanalytic discourse is charged with rendering thinkable, symbolizable, and perhaps explicable" (*JK* 33). The structure of the unconscious, like the structure of language, is not completely representable. If rules of grammar and syntax, the lack of intonation, timbre of voice, insufficient vocabulary, and similar factors limit the reliability of the written or spoken word, rendering it difficult to present the real, how much more difficult it is to present the reality of the unconscious. Moreover, the written and spoken word belong to the symbolic; what engages Kristeva's thought is the break between the two. Her work centres on the pre-symbolic function, the semiotic. Breaks and splits in individual, familial, and social relationships are imaginative engagements for Kevin Major as well, and these fractures provide a fertile field for a Kristevan meditation on the unconscious of the speaking subject caught up in these lesions.

In discussing the semiotic/symbolic function in Patricia Wrightson's work we have seen that there is no clear separation between art, society, and language on the one hand, and the individual subject as the outcome of interaction between the semiotic and the symbolic on the other. The interaction between the semiotic and the symbolic was made representable in the figure of Wirrun in Wrightson's trilogy. Separated from the earth mother at the beginning of the novels when he accepts a position in the white world as a gas-station attendant, Wirrun returns to his mother at the end. Wrightson's works present a study of the semiotic function of the unconscious in a social dimension. In Major's fiction, we reflect on that separation on an individual, familial, and historical level. We will study that prolonged separation process in particular by examining the chora as it manifests itself: on the individual level in *Hold Fast* and *Far from Shore*; on the familial level in *Eating Between the Lines;* and on the historical level in *Blood Red Ochre.* But even a cursory reading of Kevin Major's work demonstrates the writer's preoccupation with those morbid breaks in individual, familial, and societal order caused by death, divorce, or the natural processes of change.

Hold Fast (1978) begins with a powerful graveyard scene in which Michael grapples with the wrenching lesions caused by death. In *Far from Shore* (1980), family cohesiveness breaks down because of economics: unemployment and the father's subsequent alcoholism. In *Thirty-Six Exposures* (1984), the break is with the past. In *Dear Bruce Springsteen* (1987), familial security is ruptured by divorce, while in *Eating Between the Lines* (1991), although the rupture appears within the family unit, it manifests itself specifically in communication—the inability of the spoken or written word to grasp the living flux of experience, to convey meaning fully. Yet, the novel clearly establishes the necessity of sustaining oneself, of negotiating wholeness, possible only through communication with another. *Blood Red Ochre* (1989) is concerned with the lethal split in the proud Newfoundland psyche, caused by the white man's destruction of the Beothuk Indians.

However harmful these breaks may be, however prevalent this aspect of "brokenness," Major's novels inspire hope simply because the present triumphs over the past. The protagonists come to grips with the stranger within the unconscious by encountering a chora-like experience, which enables the strange to lose its pathological aspects: "it integrates within the assumed unity of human beings an *otherness* that is both biological and symbolic and becomes an integral part of the same" (Kristeva *SO* 181). "Major heroes" may not always be successful or victorious when confronted with the strange or the different, but their contact with the chora in the unconscious enables them to trust the life process; they become more alive, more hope-filled at the end.

The "chora" is a Platonic term meaning "receptacle." In Kristevan terms, it is the holding place for the drives and their barriers. It is an intermediate space, linking mother and child, and full of potential. Her chora emphasizes the amorphousness, the contradictory nature of the receptacle of the drives, those energy charges within the psyche of the ever-evolving subject. Thus, all discourse moves with and against the chora in the sense that it simultaneously depends upon and refuses it. In her introduction to *The Kristeva Reader,* Toril Moi explains that the semiotic chora "is no more than the place where the subject is both generated and negated, the place where his unity succumbs before the processes of charges and *stases* that produce him" (95).

The language of the chora event may be understood as Kristeva's genotext, which is the non-phenomenal aspect of language and textuality; the phenotext, on the other hand, issues from societal, cultural, structural, and other grammatical constraints (*RPL* 5-6). Kristeva is concerned to affirm that the text is *more* than the punctual presentation of meaning in words—the phenotext—and must be understood to include the engendering of meaning—the genotext—which is semiotically driven as is the language of the chora (Lechte *JK* 127-28). As the psychic repository for the drives, the chora is mobile and "an extremely provisional articulation constituted by movement and their ephemeral stases" (*RPL* 25). In Major's novels, the chora manifests itself through different conductors—play, poetry, letter-writing, music, drama, even drugs and the dream—but all of these are dependent on some form of language for expression. For if the homogeneous subject of consciousness is to be studied, then language must be treated as if it were an object since, as Lechte notes, it is not easy to make the chora comprehensible because it is not, strictly speaking, intelligible. What is representable thus becomes part of the symbolic (*JK,* 128, 99). The symbolic must be used to represent/delimit the unrepresentable chora and thus to alter it to some degree, but at the same time the chora disrupts the symbolic by gesturing to its dissolution. Symbols are used to represent the pre-symbolic, but the necessity to render the semiotic symbolically underscores the eternal tension in Kristevan theory. The chora experience, then, equivocal as it may seem, so educates the protagonists that they have a greater appreciation of what was unconscious in the past and a deeper realization of what was broken or unfinished.

The mobility and fluidity of the drive-propelled chora is reflected in the dynamism of Kevin Major's language—the energetic, charged, physical, pulsating properties of language (idiosyncratic vocabulary, unusual combinations of sounds regardless of meaning), language which signifies the operation of genotext in a chora experience. As the "writing subject," Major casually relinquishes authority over a given work and allows the "speaking subject" within the adolescent psyche, that stranger who is always present in the split subject, to emerge. The "speaking subject" is always split: "divided between unconscious and conscious motivations, that is, between physiological processes and social constraints" or, as Kristeva accounts for the splitting (and as we have examined in another chapter), two types of signifying processes—a "semiotic" and a "symbolic."[2]

It is in analyzing the language of the chora experience that we understand how Major's adolescent heroes recognize otherness. Concentrating on language, then, we can see how characters and events can be viewed psychologically as symbols for pre-verbal, pre-conscious drives that demand recognition. Furthermore, the language spoken by different participants, different narrators in the tale, enforces the non-linearity of the narrative which, like life, is constructed through individual perceptions. Undergoing a chora-like situation, Major's characters regress to a pre-individual, pre-socialized psychological state in order to discover a separateness that makes them strangers, and an otherness that is both biological and symbolic. At the same time, they transcend the constraints of their place in time by a process of interiorization that is distinctly feminine. The subtlety and profundity of Major's use of his native Newfoundland language[3] underscores the interplay between sexuality and death, elements which are usually linked in his characters' very ordinary lives.

Thus, when sent to a strange town, a new locale, Michael, the hero of Major's first novel, *Hold Fast*,[4] becomes the prototype of a Major novel. After a fight, the lonely, grieving adolescent, dismayed by the brutal domination of his uncle and socialized in the symbolic to hide his grief, is suspended from school. (The transitory nature of the boy's suspension penalty underlines the provisional nature of the chora experience.) Together with his cousin Curtis, Michael runs away from home and finds shelter in a campsite that has been closed for the winter. The boys enter into the Newfoundland wildness, an abandoned campsite, which is imaged as the primeval, semiotic mother. Michael had been sustained here before: "it was a good place to hide ... a place to give us some shelter" (175-76). And here the adolescent protagonist must sort out the conflicting emotional upheaval caused by the death of his parents; his revolt against cruel male domination in the person of his uncle; and his enjoyment (*jouissance*) of a burgeoning sexuality, nourished not only by his girlfriend but also by his experiences with masturbation.[5] Michael is the stranger longing for his lost outport home with all the values of maternal comfort and paternal stability that that old home signified. The melancholic lover of a vanished place, Michael exhibits a hard-hearted indifference, a strangeness, that must be pierced and that is perhaps nothing more than a universal nostalgia for a lost innocence. To confront the stranger within himself, Michael undergoes a chora experience wherein he faces his otherness. Recognizing himself as "other," Michael must accept his separateness both from his dead mother and from societal dictates. He must see the difference between the ordering subject "I" and the feeling "me," both elements constrained by social conventions; he is an "other" who exists only in the mirror of his own imaginary, a "creation" constantly changing.[6] Both Michael and Curtis come to realize that identities are never static but are constantly being revitalized by the mutual pulsions of semiotic seduction and symbolic challenge.

The deserted campground, shrouded in swirling snow, conveys the indefinite space of the chora in which Michael and Curtis separate themselves from the world of time with its ordered demands of school regimentation, familial chores, and social repression. Not only do they refuse to succumb to driving blizzards which obliterate space, but also they refuse to bend to static cold, starvation, and death. Mother Newfoundland, calling from the northern rim of the world, encourages the two adolescents to choose life; at the same time, she threatens it, in the blizzards and the cold that are endemic to her climate.

In one moving scene at the abandoned campground, where the boys exult in their new-found regression to a semiotic existence free from social pressures, Curtis wants his autocratic parents to suffer and Mike responds:

> That's what we was doing all right, letting them suffer. Especially Curtis' old man. Good enough for him. He deserved to suffer for a change. Find out what it's like to be getting the dirty end of the stick. Having to take it now instead of dishing it out. That'll make the old man think twice. Make him learn the hard way that this stupid yelling and roughing up don't work all the time. (139)

Those thoughts, and the conversation that spawns them, take place during the boys' first cold night in the camp after they have run away from home. The "dirty end of the stick" not only means that the father's anger is the controlling factor in the young boy's life; in Newfoundland parlance, "dirty," when applied to persons, specifically reinforces the fact that the father is "angry, ill-humoured, vindictive, crooked."[7] But the phallic significance of the stick cannot be ignored. Similarly, when the two lads awake to a snowstorm next day, an early-morning snow fight becomes a form of baptism into pre-social independence. The individuating process of the chora experience, where drives and their barriers are confronted, is described in the authentic, ungrammatical, uncluttered language of Newfoundland's outport communities. The barefoot Curtis and the shirtless Michael pelt each other with snow; all the pent-up drives of grief and frustration are released. Michael exclaims:

> We stopped when we got around and had it out—one dyin big frosty snowball fight.... It was cold all right, but I didn't mind that. All that snow coming down in those big fat flakes. Lodging on my bare head and shoulders and gut and melting. Like I didn't give a shit about anything. And Curtis either and what the hell. It was some darn good. (142)

The language of the passage is dynamic, honest, and pulsates with raw energy. The fecal imagery hearkening back to the "dirty stick" indicates that Michael has reached the mobile, non-physical space of the chora and unloaded the repressed weight of pain and anger. Grief, crammed together with his dependent and subservient state, had constipated his enjoyment of life. He excretes it all, and the passage explodes with the freedom of release from waste. He also exults in the "big fat flakes" which melt over his heaving body, making him oblivious to cold. A note of raw transcendence is struck.

But the experience of the chora is always fleeting and amorphous. As the receptacle of instinctual drives and raw energy, the chora is a provisional space where the subject's repression of the semiotic by the symbolic overlap. Excitement and movement are followed by periods of stasis. As anxious as Michael is "to get away from all signs of having to depend on someone for a place to live"(195), both boys realize that the unchecked freedom of the semiotic is temporal; they can't "run away for good" (200). As Curtis explains in his homespun Newfoundland dialect:

> We both knew that what we was on wasn't no running away from home and never coming back deals. We wasn't on the lookout for no circuses to join. We'd been out to prove something. And by then, maybe we'd done it. (200)

Michael affirms life and his maternal responsibility for the care of his young brother, while Curtis, separating himself from parental domination, articulates his own strangeness, his own individuality: "he was having a chance of being himself" (199). Both boys have learned a degree of autonomy and in doing so have cut themselves off from the instinctual mother-son, parent-child dyad. They accept themselves as separate "Newfoundlanders" living on "the rock." Language itself defines the island rock which has been detached and freed from the cultural pressures of European civilization.

When Michael returns to Marten at last, he finds his grandfather dying. The novel begins and ends with death—first the death of Michael's parents and then that of his grandfather—and the fourteen-year-old Michael reacts to both with tears that cannot be repressed. Major suggests that the process of gaining independence and self-assurance that Michael thought he had won is never fully resolved. He must continue to live in that void which is so necessary for the relinquishment of autoeroticism. Michael concludes his story with a confession:

> I caught myself half on the bawl last night after I was in bed. There's still that time after every day when, no matter how much I've done, everything gets quiet and I'm alone with all that's happened and I feels like bawling. But I drove it out of my system last night and that might be the end of it. It was a hard bloody thing to do, but I think that maybe I got it done. (224)

The reader understands that the "bloody thing" is never over, there is never an end to pain, and Michael has to employ the rigid prohibitions of restraint in order not to collapse totally into the semiotic where he would be unable to "drive it out of his system" but would just "bawl" all the time.

It is the ordinariness of Michael that is duplicated in the characters of Chris, Lorne, Terry, and Jackson—characters in Major's novels who exhibit contemporary teenage interests: rock music, raw language, sports, photography, sex, drugs, alcohol, and, to a lesser extent, the arts, like poetry and literature. Chris Slade, the protagonist from Major's *Far from Shore*, finds semiotic release in music. Describing a "friggin good concert" by a Newfoundland group called The Fish, Chris exults in how the group sends him "right off":

> First, all you heard was the sea, and then real quiet and slow they started playing this old Newfoundland folksong, "We'll Rant and We'll Roar," only they got it going faster and faster until the lead guitar ripped into it and tore it right to shit so that it came out sounding like it could blow your fuckin head off.... Music always sounds ten times better when you're stoned.... We're wrecked right out of our skulls ... it's a wild time ... enough tits flopping up and down that you'd need about ten sets of eyes to keep track of them. (67-68)

Neither Major nor Kristeva suggests that one must become a substance abuser to confront the semiotic. Drugs and alcohol mitigate the symbolic power of reason, but reason must interpret the meaning of the semiotic drives. In the passage above, Chris lays bare the rawness of his own instinctual drives. The word "friggin" is, no doubt, the young Newfoundlander's substitute for "fucking," which he uses readily enough further on in the passage, but the initial sound "frig" also carries connotations of the Norse god, Frigg, wife of Odin, who presided over marriage and domestic life. Later on in the novel, having smoked two joints, Chris almost drowns himself and a young camper in a canoeing accident. Water is a material element, and both Kristeva and Freud describe primary narcissism as "oceanic" in its fluid lack of boundaries. Perhaps this is another moment when the necessary seduction of regression must be met with refusal; for in the water of Ochre Pond, where the accident occurs, Chris assumes the feminine role as nurse and nourisher to an eleven-year-old. He saves young Morrison's life and experiences the chora wherein he confronts otherness.

Although Major uses a multiple narration technique in structuring *Far from Shore*,[8] it is in examining the language of Chris, the main narrator, that the reader discovers not only the duality between drives and duty but also the way mothering is encoded in the text. Again the water imagery suggests the amniotic fluids and reveals Chris's maternal concern for the younger, "waterlogged" Morrison. When the canoe capsizes, Chris strips off his own clothes and tries to undo Morrison's heavier apparel. The stripping is itself symbolic of the layers of self that will be uncovered. Noting that the boy is injured, he soothes and washes his bloodied head. All his energies are directed towards the other, and together they swim to safety: "We push away from the boat and onto our backs. That's the only way I can move because of the way Morrison's got his arms so tight around my neck"; however, the "friggin waves lopping us up and down make it all the worse" (150). The language of this chora experience pulsates with the same energy of the passage wherein he describes the raw ambiance of a drug-fogged rock concert. Only this time it is not the women's breasts that flop up and down but rather the water's waves. Alone, with the unconscious camper, far from shore in that destructive/creative chora experience, Chris perceives his own independent separateness, his dependence on others for rescue, and his responsibility for the accident.

> Come right down to it and it was all my own friggin fault. If I had a mind of my own instead of letting myself get talked into everything all the time, then that friggin accident might never have happened. (161)

Refusing to blame his friend for proffering him the marijuana, Chris accepts his responsibility for taking narcotics; he also faces the lethal consequences of his father's alcoholic addiction and unemployment. He sees his dismissal from camp as just punishment; the "friggin accident" is his own "friggin fault."

But on a deeper level his use of "friggin," a long-used slang expression, becomes a trope for the continuing complexity of his world, a complexity which becomes even more obvious when he returns home and discovers his mother's suitor hiding behind a door. Angry and dismayed, Chris goes again to the succouring waters, this time the waters of Birchy Cove, and sits in his boat for six long hours trying to rationalize his instinctive feelings of loss and revulsion.

> I didn't get much straight in my mind, but at least I was able to settle down a bit. I headed back in when I figured I had enough of being alone. No matter how miserable I gets I'm not much good by myself for very long. (162)

The rhythmic rocking of the waves settles him down. (What kills can also cure.) Like a soothing lullaby, the water calms his spirit and a semblance of reasoned calm reveals to him the knowledge that he is not much good by himself. Chris comes to grips with his "strangeness." He goes back to face his mother, who further clarifies for her son the reality of broken relationships.

A certain ordering of events is evident in *Far from Shore* and *Hold Fast* wherein the chora experiences help to distance the protagonists from their present problems. The distancing, and the subsequent articulation of the experience, is a mark of the symbolic, which in the mother-child-father triad is the domain of the father. While the father's place is clearly defined, that of the mother corresponds to the unrepresentable chora, symbolized here by the maternal connotations of the language of the speaking subjects.

The chora's manifestation on an individual level is also clearly obvious in the language of *Thirty-Six Exposures,* where the camera becomes a metaphor for the hero's perception. With the title's photographic connotation of a section of film exposing a sensitive surface, Major structures his narration on the broader context of the word's meaning—to lay open, set forth, reveal.

Thirty-Six Exposures is significant because it exposes the writing subject as adolescent.[9] The camera and poetry of Lorne, the speaking subject, provide the chora, a womb-like receptacle for experiences in which are encoded the "not yet understood" part of the conscious self. Lorne's strange poem at the beginning of the novel offers a good example of Kristevan poetic language and chora—a semiotic, pre-symbolic receptacle for the drives. Pocked with its blank spaces, the poem is indicative both of Lorne's semiotic groping for the symbolic word and of the empty spaces in his own self-analysis.

> I am best photographed at a distance.
> From there I could look average.
> But as I come closer some   becomes apparent.
> You would probably detect my   by the way
>   I walk
> and if I were to speak, a slight   might be
> noticed.
> It's most likely, though, that I'd walk right past you
> and not say a word.

Lorne's poems are all attempts to come to grips with the reality of his own place in time and space.

In her monumental work *Desire in Language*, Kristeva explains how poetic language, that language learned by each child before it learns a formal language, results from the subtle bodily communications between mother and child ("Place Names" 280). And in her explanation of the semiotic and the symbolic, she presents a possible middle ground between feminine expressiveness and masculine logic, and finds inspiration for this reconciliation in the language of poetry. In poetry, felt experience and logical order are expressed in rhythm and structure. On the one hand, Kristeva explains, we have rhythm; on the other, the "ego," situated within the space of language, no longer merely rhythm but sign, word, structure, contact, constraint. Once "the rhythm has been centred in the fixed position of an all powerful 'ego,' the poetic 'I' thrusts at the sun—a paternal image that is coveted but also feared" (*DL* 29).

In Kristeva's theory we have the rationale for Major's hero and his need to objectify experience in the choric receptacle of either literature, music, or the dream. These media represent the outpourings of the semiotic chora, revealing a subject's search for symbolic meaning. Thus Terry in *Dear Bruce Springsteen* lets loose his frustration at his father's absconding by writing to the rock singer. The letters parallel the chora's relation to language because objective, symbolic language is underlain by the very drives which, by their pre-social nature, paradoxically seek to destroy it. Terry's anger and frustration push up through the structure of the letters, revealing his attempts at finding some meaning not only in paternal absence but in maternal indifference. Major explores how every institutional system—particularly that of the family—is fragile and replaceable. He does not indulge in "father bashing," although the fathers in his novels are often disappointments.

In Major's novels, the plot is constructed so that the haphazard, living immediacy of the hero's experience is shaped as it is experienced. Just as the speaking subjects must work out the meaning of their problems through the chora experience, so too must the reader work out the meaning of the novel as a reflection of modern life. And here one recalls that the aim of a Kristevan theory is not to institute a new view of language but to call attention to language as a social construct. Kristeva rejects unity in the text as a particularly phallocentric fetish and seeks the feminine contribution to language—that quality which is charmed by difference, multiplicity, and inconclusiveness. Thus, the not-so-happy endings of the novels, their fragmentariness, the adolescent language (ungrammatical, informal)—these are the outpourings of the seeker, the learner, and they are identified with the feminine.

So far we have studied the break in the individual psyche from social constraints. In *Eating Between the Lines*, the pain caused by the break in the familial structure is closely scrutinized. The novel also illustrates Major's belief that language/literature is of central importance to recognizing the stranger within the psyche who is never completely unmasked, because adolescence is less an age category than an ongoing state whereby the human psyche restores balance by maintaining a renewable identity through integration with another. Certainly the book is not merely about food but about what Arlene Rae suggests is "the idea of nourishment that all kids need—intellectual and emotional nourishment as well as the edible kind" (16). I would argue even further that the novel illustrates literature's power to sweeten the initiation rite imposed on all adolescents when they come face to face with the split subject, the power of brokenness, the stranger within. By literally eating a "Masterpizza," Jackson submits to the power of language, the written word as found in literary masterpieces, and enters into a chora experience. He becomes what he reads. Playing on the cliché of reading between the lines, eating becomes a metonymy expressing the socializing effect books have in enabling the individual to cope with the split subject both in the self and in the family triad. At the same time, Jackson, the hero of the novel, transcends the constraints of his place in time by experiencing an aspect of time which has no meaning save what a process of interiorization gives it.

As a teen, caught up in the breakup of his parents' marriage, Jackson understands that he was the product of two "flower children" of the sixties who named him for Jack Kennedy, Jackson Pollack, perhaps Jackson Browne. He discovers that his parents do not communicate; they are strangers to each other, strangers to themselves, and Jackson's ego, a stranger to his unconscious self. The father's confession sets the tone of dissatisfaction within the family unit:

> Before I left Newfoundland I wasted years, Jackson, years. Roaming from job to job, listening to Cat Stevens records, steeping myself in the so-called wisdom of the East, looking for answers, thinking I'd found them, only to realize in the end that I was going nowhere. Meanwhile, the guys here were getting the real jobs. And now, you know who they are? They're the presidents of companies, and I'm still slogging away, the johnny-come-lately, waiting for the next promotion. (13)

There is a whining self-pity in the father's confession as well as a childish envy of his peers indicating the child/adolescent is still resident in the adult psyche. That envy is even more insidious when the reader suspects the father resents the fact that Jackson's mother still finds fulfillment and friendship in work as an art-gallery attendant. Literature and art have given the mother satisfaction and stature, whereas the father finds a pseudo-consolation in a book collection which he only looks at, never reads. His mother reads the books but is always careful never to disrupt the impeccable order of his books' "sacred lineup" (15).

Distressed by his parents' inability to express their differing viewpoints, and to compensate for his problems with school work and his own communication problem with Sara, the girl of his dreams, Jackson takes comfort in "Masterpizza," a food franchise newly opened by a former librarian friend who has a passion for masterpieces of literature and who has given her establishment a decidedly literary flavour. Here Jackson finds himself the winner of a gold medal because he is the 028 customer (028 is the Dewey Decimal classification number for reading). By means of the gold medal, he is able to experience the chora and, in an extraordinary manner, to fuse his mother's passion for vicarious experience with his father's love for order. He is both "defiant and practical" when he returns home and takes from its ordered niche his father's gold-bound copy of *The Odyssey,* which he intends to use in preparing an essay on Greek civilization.

> He pulled the book from its comfortable little row. He turned to his mother, the book under his arm, his hands in his pockets. He gave her a smile that was worth a thousand apologies. He said nothing more, just strolled to the foot of the stairs, then climbed them slowly, precisely, as if he were being filled with the power of the written word. (35)

Unknowingly, Jackson does possess an awesome power. When he haphazardly rubs the gold of the medal and the gold of the book's binding, he discovers he has a uniquely compensatory gift: being able to live in each book he is reading. He becomes Odysseus with his men in the cave of those one-eyed monsters, the Cyclops. He allows the poetic text to "smash" his self momentarily, to give up the phallocentric hold on identity to become someone else, and he questions himself. "Had he, by some force beyond all the known laws of the universe, been yanked out of his own century, transported back to Greece, and dumped in the midst of the book he had been reading?" (38). The answer, of course, is yes. He has exceeded his father's superficial love of books, his love of their surfaces; he has gone even further than his mother's vicarious experience of literature (she always returns the book to its proper place); he, the son of both, has explored more deeply than either. He has submitted completely to the power of the written word, albeit only for a time.

Jackson finds himself invincible under cultural pressures. After reading *The Odyssey*, he presents a brilliant class essay (52); he fights censorship at the school board by speaking of Jim's experience from *Huck Finn* (79-80); he finds courage to go after the girl he fancies after reading *Romeo and Juliet* (101); he even serves as a marriage counsellor, repairing his parents' marriage, after he reads his mother's diaries recounting his own birth (117).

Major's narrative of Jackson's journeys into literature begins terrifyingly enough, but as the journeys continue, the text become more comic than fearful. Jackson is a split subject because of the impending separation of his parents. The narrator explains his reaction to this familial tension: "Jackson felt sick. He thought his family was made of tougher stuff. They shouldn't have to take the easy way out, no matter what one half of the population was doing" (31). With the experience of separation without resolution, unlike animals whose only recourse is in behaviour, "the child can find a fighting or fleeing solution in psychic representation and in language" (*BS* 36). For a non-depressive solution to the melancholy dilemma, the child needs a solid implication in the symbolic which is channelled to him through poetic language. Jackson is capable of remarkable symbolic activity. Trapped in his own lonely fear of losing either of his parents, Jackson finds in the gold "Masterpizza" medal a chora episode. The cave of the Cyclops becomes an ideational representation of his own ambiguously confused state. As subject, he is capable of splitting. Jackson does not deny the traumatic force of the breakup in his family, but as the clever Odysseus, quick at solving his parents' one-eyed appraisal of each other, he symbolically acknowledges the trauma's impact and seeks a solution in the imaginary.

Jackson invites his parents into the imaginary when, through the words of his mother's diary, they re-live the birth of Jackson and recover the freedom and joy of their hippie years before they left St. John's, Newfoundland for Toronto, Ontario. The move signified Jackson's father's acceptance of consumerism. "You left Newfoundland," his mother explains, "and you lost sight of something very important" (119). In entering into Jackson's chora world, they recover balance; their marriage is saved and Jackson achieves independence. When his parents go on a second honeymoon at the conclusion of the novel, Jackson "[feels] himself a man ready to savour the timeless, priceless pleasures of this life—love and a good meal" (136); but neither is lasting.

To scrutinize the chora only as a semiotic device distancing the individual from his conscious self and from society is to lessen its full significance within the historical context. In *Blood Red Ochre* we find the richest vein of psychoanalytic study. Here Major reaches far back into history to explore perhaps the deepest form of repression, a repression from which the modern Newfoundlander still suffers and which has contributed to the very fabric of Newfoundland society: the white man's decimation of an entire tribe of native Indians, the Beothuks. It is David, the white adolescent male, always in search of the father, who discovers in a chora experience both the foreigner within himself and the stranger within the Newfoundland psyche. He confronts his own difference as he experiences that adolescent chaos when familiar space is disrupted, when time itself is jostled unevenly between past and present, and when complete understanding and affinity collapse.

Kristeva maintains that the ability to symbolize must always be implicated in the separation-murder relationship a child has with its mother. She reads literature with her own body and shows how profoundly captivating to her is the idea of the son separating himself from the mother and of the mother separating herself from the son. In her essay "Motherhood According to Bellini," for example, she analyzes Bellini's painting of the Madonna and Child and, minutely examining the Son's grip on the hands of his Mother, explains how at times the baby Redeemer attempts to free himself violently from the Mother's probing hands which "prod the stomach and penis of the frightened baby" (*DL* 254-55). Her chapter "The Father, Love, and Banishment" offers another satisfying account of the son's need to free himself from the tyranny of the father (148-158). In *Blood Red Ochre,* Kevin Major enacts the separation of an adolescent from both parents: in David's rejection of his step-father, in his "leaving" his mother's space to seek his biological father, and, most significantly, in the "murdering" of his ideal of Newfoundland as benevolent Mother.

By its complete break with chronological time, *Blood Red Ochre* starkly dramatizes the disrupted parent-child, son-motherland relationships. Past and present merge. This disordering of time can be studied in the language of the dialogue between David, the contemporary white adolescent, and his nineteenth-century counterpart Dauoodaset, the Beothuk Indian. David is split into his present self, the David of the contemporary narrative, and Dauoodaset, David's past self, who recounts Beothuk history. Both narratives give evidence of a repression-induced melancholia, of the pressing up of feelings that can never be expressed in logical time, never represented fully in objective language. Neither does space remain familiar in *Blood Red Ochre*: the climax of the novel occurs on an uninhabited island, set apart from the mainland. Nor can comprehension itself be assured. Complete understanding disintegrates.

The two narrators, both fifteen-year-old males, relate their stories in alternate chapters and tell two stories, one in the present and one in the past. David, the contemporary hero from Marten, Newfoundland, has just discovered that the man he calls his father is not really so. He struggles with anger towards his mother and, on a school trip, seeks out his real father, who turns out to be a devastating disappointment. Dauoodaset, an early Beothuk Indian, struggles with his tribe members to resist the diseases and weapons of the White Mother Newfoundland, who deprives the natives of their lands and livelihood. Dauoodaset is sent forth to find food in order to save his people from starvation and death. The two stories are linked by the character of Nancy/Shanawdithit, loved by both young men, who lures David onto Blood Red Ochre Island where he confronts the semiotic drives of his personal and national selves, and enters more fully into the symbolic, the agency that opens up and reveals the semiotic at the same time that it restrains and prohibits it.

The language of Nancy/Shanawdithit deserves particular examination because she speaks both as the contemporary school companion of David, his first love, and also as the lost lover of Dauoodaset, a Beothuk Indian slain by the white man on an island off the coast of Newfoundland almost two hundred years ago. Nancy, or Shanawdithit, is the novel's stranger and her language epitomizes the element of alienation lurking within the Newfoundland psyche. The reader can never be certain whether she belongs to time present or time past. She not only addresses the dilemma of the woman speaker subjugated to the dictates of a male-dominated society which distorts what she wants to say, but also she illustrates how her Beothuk Indian ancestor, Shanawdithit, is the victim of the same patriarchal oppression that exists in both societies. Separated though they are in time, Nancy/Shanawdithit are one and the same woman working to overthrow a paternalistic social structure by entering into the symbolic order and questioning that order. The modern Nancy, "different, foreign, almost a bit mysterious" (*BRO* 5), occupies the bottom rung of Newfoundland's class structure; she is the foreigner, victim of the whites who, at one point in historical time, killed her lover and obliterated her people. At the same time, the Beothuk Shanawdithit, young, powerful, and still mysterious, is the mother of the Newfoundland psyche and the originator of its guilt. She represents the split between Kristeva's narcissistic mother and her creative mother. Shanawdithit taints the Newfoundland national character with that original sin which is both destructive and inventive. She is the mother of Newfoundland's guilt, but at the same time, the mother of their endurance and resilience.

In falling in love with Nancy, David falls in love with his remote mother, Shanawdithit. In Kristevan terms, David comes to grips with the stranger within by encountering a chora-like experience, which enables strangeness to lose its melancholic aspects. Nancy is a chora-like figure and David undergoes a chora-like experience on Red Ochre Island, the island where Dauoodeset's body was found covered in the red dye used by the Beothuks for burial—hence the title of Major's novel. Undergoing a chora-like experience, David regresses to a pre-individual, pre-socialized psychological state in order to discover the separateness that makes him a stranger not merely to the Beothuks, Dauoodaset and Shanawdithit, but also to himself.

Besides confronting himself as essentially a stranger, David also confronts the guilt/repression from which the modern Newfoundlander still suffers and which has contributed to the very fabric of Newfoundland society. Historically, white invaders, instead of showing an expressive maternal care for the natives, obliterated them from the face of the earth. Mother Newfoundland, in her treatment of the Beothuks (the last one of whom, the historical Shanawdithit, died in 1829), bloodied those boundaries between the self and the other. In a seemingly law-governed society, the unclean, unspeakable crime of genocide penetrated and ruptured the Newfoundland psyche. In leaving his mother and giving his love to Nancy, by means of an almost unbelievable symbolic effort, David transposes the erotic object, Nancy, into the "sublime" mother, Newfoundland.

Nancy/Shanawdithit is a split subject. As Nancy, she is the adolescent David's first love; as Shanawdithit, she is also the mother both of the Newfoundland psyche and of the post-colonial Newfoundlander. Her language is worth examining.

> I tell David ... how it cannot be that way again [the whites killing of the natives], that he must see us as we are, and he must tell others they have to learn to share this island with us. The food of the waters about this island is not for his people alone. (136)

The dialogue does not sound particularly native or aged, but at the same time it is neither artificial, archaic, or stilted. It is deceptively modern, but the direct and dignified tone gives the passage an element of timelessness. The simple words, the compact phrasing, the lack of adornment in the language, all evoke the silent endurance of native people.

Symbolically, David re-lives the killing of Dauoodaset by the white man and the flight of Shanawdithit into history; but semiotically, before her flight into timelessness, Shanawdithit reveals David's guilt as a Newfoundlander. White and Canadian, David assumes the guilt of his people who have displaced the original First Nation. Even though the Newfoundlander distances himself from his crime, its reminder is always present in the modern native, Nancy/Shanawdithit, who speaks in only one chapter of the novel. Shanawdithit's chapter is, primarily, a narrative of reconciliation between past and present, between Dauoodaset and David. That one narration is all-important, however, because Shanawdithit therein establishes herself as the link, the mother of modern Newfoundland. The birth blood is the blood-red ochre with which Nancy/Shanawdithit smears herself:

> I am Nancy no longer. It is the Whiteman's name. I am where I belong, with Dauoodaset. I am Shanawdithit.
>
> I turn to his [David's] shouting, throwing wide the fur coat. I am wearing body furs like those of Dauoodaset and my arms and neck are colored red.
>
> "I am Shanawdithit!" I call to him. I take the red of ochre and rub it over my hands and about my face .... The life of our people will not be frozen away, never to walk about this land. (130)

The language of this passage, with its subtly changed word order, indicates a new order in the First Nation-Canadian relationship. Shanawdithit's scorn of the white man emphasizes her rejection of paternal nomenclature. The primacy of the Beothuk legacy can never be eradicated from the mind of a Newfoundlander, and that new order comes with an assertion of the Beothuks' maternal care for and dependence on nature. The red of the ochre and the furs of the animal are used but not abused. The language indicates a quiet assertion of power, even superiority, in the First Nation's relationship to nature. The spirituality of the native culture is dignified and subverts that of a white, European, ecclesiastic, male-dominated society. Shanawdithit's language also reveals her acceptance of self: "I am Shanawdithit."

When Dauoodaset went forth to the island from the last of the Beothuk camps, he went forth as the saviour of Beothuk influence and as the father of the Newfoundland psyche (89). There is no doubt that the amulet Shanawdithit gave Dauoodaset at his departure is the same amulet given to David by his step-grandfather, who in turn had been given the Beothuk Indian pendant by his own grandfather as a boy (3). The amulet is given back to Shanawdithit by the modern David, after he saves her from fire, and the amulet becomes a sign of reconciliation between Newfoundlander and Beothuk. Shanawdithit speaks:

> David stands up and takes it [the amulet] from about his neck. I rise too from the ground and stand in front of him. He puts the leather strip over my head and lets the bone piece fall against my body furs. I feel in me a warmness I have not felt since I have known him. (140-41)

Major deliberately strives to make the incident resist a rigid interpretation, but the symbolic eroticization of Shanawdithit's language in her "warmness" shows that the Beothuk murder has entered deeply into David's and his province's psyche, providing the condition of his individuation and nourishing the stranger within the Newfoundlander—that stranger forever fleeing his homeland and carrying with him the seeds of his guilt.

What Major suggests, and what Kristevan theory asserts, is that whatever violence the Beothuk genocide entailed, it has also engendered the individuality, the difference, of the Newfoundland character, a character molded by both aggressiveness and endurance. And Shanawdithit's language seems to voice that uniqueness. The historical characters of Dauoodaset and Shanawdithit have nurtured in David (and the Newfoundland character) the Beothuk pride, patience, courage, and stamina. Shanawdithit admits that once David has recognized the sin of his white ancestors, "There is a pride in who he is that I had not seen before" (135). After losing Shanawdithit, whom he last sees in a canoe paddling "straight out into the open sea" (146), David returns to Marten, "gone from the island, back to his home and his family" (147). The chora experience of the dream he had when he fell asleep over a book on Beothuk history has taught him that reconciliation is a possible element in human existence; its acquisition is painful but also useful in providing a different way of viewing history.

In *Blood Red Ochre*, as in all his novels, Major's heroes free a repression-induced melancholia by experiencing the chora. Individual, familial, and historical lesions may be a major contributor to adolescent despair, but Major's main characters recognize that life is both merging and separating, finding and letting go. The Newfoundland writer also believes in the salvific power of love, but love is not something that remains fixed. Through the experience of love for another, his heroes come to accept love's symbolic truth. They become familiar with the feminine space of the semiotic chora, and because they must finally leave the mother and seek the other, their imaginary preoccupations are necessarily amorous. Major fosters no illusions about the loved object being susceptible to loss or about the depressive position being easily reactivated. His heroes, however, refuse to accept loss, and their egos triumph through the fetish of the word, whether that word be written in letter, song, or poem. His novels free the reader (and perhaps the writer himself) to explore the pain of a primal loss, the strangeness, the anomalies, the contrarieties that lie at the heart of human experience. At the same time, his works affirm that ordinary human consciousness can develop a sense of personal fulfillment which can appreciate the simple pleasures life has to offer. Because he lays bare the lethal lesions that threaten any life, because he acquaints his readers with the stranger within, because he confronts the distress of "difference," Kevin Major helps us comprehend the modern crises of ambiguity, of living with the possibility of never being able totally to understand the self or the other. His is an inestimable contribution to both adolescent and Canadian literature.

4

ABJECTION IN THE NOVELS OF KATHERINE PATERSON

ABJECTION—that fundamental, necessary, unrepresentable moment of separation from the mother's body in which subjectivity is first structured and then destabilized—looms threateningly over the gates of identity and the boundaries where meaning collapses. Struggling with the indeterminate nature of the concept, in *Powers of Horror* Kristeva describes it as "the twisted braid of affects and thoughts" (1). Abjection is a "something" unrecognizable as a thing, a "weight of meaninglessness, about which there is nothing insignificant" (*PH* 2). It "disturbs identity, order, system." It "does not respect borders, positions, rules" (*PH* 4). To be understood, the abject must be scrutinized at the borders of subject identity, that ever-fluctuating state which is always in process of formation and deformation. For Kristeva, inner psychic space, so essential to subject identity, is purchased at a disturbingly painful cost because it involves opposition: between the subject and its object, between self and other, between the inside and the outside. It might be said that the abject falls between subject and object differentiation; it is by means of the abject that the subject is first constrained to construct itself, impelled towards constituting itself—in an act of repugnance.

Kristeva's semiotic mother, the first imaged object of the pre-verbal, preoedipal infant, mirrors an image of unity to the child. At the same time, however, the mother is caught between her semiotic, narcissistic desire to keep the child as an extension of herself and her symbolic function, initiated at the advent of speech, to relinquish her power and allow separateness in order that the child may enter into the paternal symbolic, the domain of language, and so become a speaking subject. Because the semiotic drives become repressed by the laws of signs, of language, the abject confronts us with our earliest attempts to release the hold of *maternal* entity even before "ex-isting" outside of her (*PH* 13). Abjection uncovers the ambivalence of drives and the instability of language.

In Katherine Paterson's novels, "the time of abjection is double: a time of oblivion and thunder, of veiled infinity and the moment when revelation bursts forth" (*PH* 9). And for Paterson, as for Kristeva, the tilting with the abject continues all through life: perhaps even into eternity and beyond—into infinity! Joy comes through laughter, since "laughing is a way of placing or displacing abjection" (*PH* 8), and also through learning how to take pleasure in starting something one can never finish. It takes courage and enormous strength to prevent the abject from taking control and assuming ascendancy. When one confronts abjection, one faces a power so strong that in any contest with it, one wins not by being powerful but by exercising endurance. What we can be is more important than what we are—*who* am I more crucial than *where* am I (8).

Katherine Paterson's novels offer analogical counterparts of abjection—counterparts of that which defies description. But in addition to deflating the myth of ideal parenthood, by probing the relationships of her young characters with their parents and by unravelling in her novels the "twisted braid" of the drives and reason, Paterson allegorizes how the pain of abjection both grants and threatens subjectivity. In novels like *The Great Gilly Hopkins, Come Sing, Jimmy Jo,* and *Park's Quest,* Paterson unmasks the parent, specifically the narcissistic mother, who tends to view the child as a phallic extension of herself. Her novels reveal how parents may distort their role as mediators whose non-narcissistic mode should direct the child to the other, to a future apart from themselves. For both parent and child the separation causes violent, seething revolts on the borders of subject identity.

In Lacanian theory, the acquisition of language marks the intervention of the symbolic and the separation from the idyllic state of being one with the mother. Essentially, the acquisition of language enables the child to articulate a pre-symbolic existence, a nostalgic Eden-like state in which the infant had no desires because all longings and desires were completely satisfied within the mother's body. With the acquisition of language and the developing power of reason, every unsatisfied object awakens the sense of original loss which the individual forever regrets. Kristeva accepts Lacan's theory of primary narcissism, but she probes further back than Lacan. She questions those objects outside of us which are *not* objects of desire or displacements for the mother. As Lechte expresses it, "If the objects in the world are a fundamental displacement of my desire for my mother, what is the status of these other things?" Kristeva argues that there must be a prior state before the full intervention of the symbolic begins; "there must have already been moves, by way of the drives, towards expelling/rejecting the mother." The symbolic, however, is not strong enough to ensure separation; it depends on the mother being abjected (*JK* 159). In Kristeva's words:

> The abject might then appear as the most *fragile* ..., the most *archaic* ... sublimation of an "object" still inseparable from drives. The abject is that pseudo-object that is made up *before* but appears only *within* the gaps of secondary repression. *The abject would thus be the "object" of primal repression.*
>
> But what is primal repression? Let us call it the ability of the speaking being, always already haunted by the Other, to divide, reject, repeat. Without *one* division, *one* separation, *one* subject/object having been constituted (not yet, or no longer yet). Why? Perhaps because of maternal anguish, unable to be satiated within the encompassing symbolic. (*PH* 12, Kristeva's italics).

Lechte further explains that "the abject is what allows the drives to have complete and uninhibited reign"; that, with the rules tied to cleanliness, toilet training, eating habits, and other early lessons, the "mother" is gradually rejected through becoming, at the pre-symbolic level, the prototype of what the drives expel (*JK* 159).

Kristeva, an atheist, and Paterson, a committed Christian, seem to make strange literary bedfellows, but both the atheistic psychiatrist and the Christian writer are concerned with the vagaries of human behavior and the mystery of pain. Both are haunted by the meaning of suffering. For the Christian, suffering and pain have meaning in the act of love which culminated in the crucifixion of Christ, the Son of God, the Word made flesh, the supreme Other who was rejected, reviled, persecuted. For the psychoanalyst, suffering and pain can only be relieved through the power of the word spoken by the patient to the analyst. Quoting Freud, in *In the Beginning Was Love*, Kristeva maintains that "the foundation of the cure is 'Our God Logos.'" She continues:

> The analytic subject, or analysand, in substance says the following, "I am suffering from a primitive trauma, often sexual in nature, a deep narcissistic injury, which I relieve by displacing it onto an analyst. Here and now the omnipotent author of my being or malady (my father or mother) is the analyst. The deep meaning of my words is governed by this hidden drama, which presupposes that I grant considerable power to the analyst. But the confidence that I place in him is based on my love for him and what I assume is his love for me." (*IBWL*, 2-3)

The Christian finds God in all people, events, experiences. There is a meaning to pain and abjection which can never fully be understood, but suffering is somehow made bearable because it was shared by the Son of God, who suffered because he loved humanity. The psychoanalyst knows that suffering has no scientific explanation but she recognizes that, because it is a lack of love that sends people to the psychoanalyst in the first place, it is only through psychoanalysis that confidence in, the capacity for, love can be restored. Through the transference of love in the psychoanalytic process, the analysand is enabled to distance herself from the analyst with a renewed identity (3). Both Paterson and Kristeva understand that only love can heal the painful rupture that separating from the mother's body entails; however, that rupture, both inevitable and painful as it is, must be confronted so that an identity may form.

In Powers of Horror, Kristeva studies how the emotional states of horror, love, and melancholia, so characteristic of the modern psyche, are capable of structuring subjectivity; yet they must be encountered. She explains how the power of horror, the abject, becomes greater if it is not confronted—if it remains hidden, unrecognized, repressed. Refusing to confront the abject limits development not only of the individual but also of society, because to ignore the power of horror is to ignore "the other facet of religious, moral, and ideological codes on which rest the sleep of individuals and the breathing spells of societies. Such codes are abjection's purification and repression" (*PH* 209). Recognition of the repressed makes up the individual's "apocalypse," the willingness "to have a face-to-face confrontation with the abject" (209). All literature, Kristeva maintains, is a version of the Apocalypse, rooted on the fragile borders where identities do not exist or only barely so—double, fuzzy, heterogeneous, animal, metamorphosed, altered, abject (*PH* 207). It is precisely because we are drawn back to that abyss of non-separation from the mother that identities become clouded and we find ourselves lost—dejects "on a journey, during the night, the end of which keeps receding" (*PH* 8). The one in whom the abject exists is thus a *deject*, a situationist, more interested in *where* she is than in *who* she is (*PH* 8). And, like Kristeva, Paterson gives place a prime position in the imagination.

As lucid as are the geographical landscapes in Paterson's novels, so, conversely, the psychic landscapes of her young characters are darkly turbulent, lowering, and frightening as they deal with abjection. And no matter what the locale—whether the novels be set in the East, like *Of Nightingales That Weep* and *The Sign of the Chrysanthemum*, or in the West, like *Jacob Have I Loved*, *Come Sing, Jimmy Jo*, or *The Great Gilly Hopkins*—the parental figures hover near, perhaps not corporeally, but always imminent. Paterson's novels possess such physicality of place—of the cherry blossom festival in *The Sign of the Chrysanthemum,* of Rass Island in *Jacob Have I Loved*, and of the Appalachian region in *Come Sing, Jimmy Jo*—that the reader is able to smell the flowers' fragrance, to feel the cold of oyster fishing in the Chesapeake, and to watch the sunset dust settle on a tired old mountain in Appalachia. But deeper, darker than any external scene is the internal view of abjection which the reader apprehends in Sarah Louise's biting of her fingernail so as to bring blood, for example; or in Gilly's vomiting when she understands the lie of her mother's love; or the searing of Takiko's flesh when her step-father accidentally brands her with a hot poker. Paterson's characters face abjection, are cast off, dispirited, and degraded, principally and often unintentionally by parents who exploit their children, starve them emotionally, and stifle their creativity. Paradoxically, however, it is Paterson's forthright exposition of abjection's might and her decision to treat it both playfully and seriously that give her fiction its joyful dynamism. Paterson never forgets that abjection, a dirty player, *is* powerful. Abjection "does not respect borders"; it is "the traitor, the liar" (*PH* 4).

Abjection deals out disgusting hands in Paterson's fiction. In *Bridge to Terabithia*, for example, abjection brings maternal favouritism and death; in *Jacob Have I Loved*, unreasonable jealousy; in *The Sign of the Chrysanthemum*, illegitimacy; in *Of Nightingales That Weep*, shades of incest and physical impairment; in *Come Sing, Jimmy Jo*, maternal desertion and drunkenness; and in *The Great Gilly Hopkins*, lovelessness. Paterson looks directly at abjection and respects its power; but because she knows she is playing a continuous game with narcissism and realizes that the contest between good and evil, hope and despair, will go on long after she is gone, she puts her trust in an infinite order which demands that human life prevail. Therefore, she can laugh at the hand abjection deals because she has learned to understand, as we all must, that abjection counteracts narcissism at the same time that it makes it seductive (in the sense that the clinical narcissist is often looking to replace the mother with his own self-image); that the dangers in thus regressing to the first stage of sexual development, in which the self is the sole object of sexual pleasure, are insidiously real; that there is hope and peril in continuous processing; that the concept of family is always evolving and devolving; and, above all, that there is exhilaration in infinite play, of continuing the game that has no ending.[1]

This study will focus chiefly on an analysis of abjection as it is revealed in one novel, *Jacob Have I Loved*, a title which raises quintessentially ambiguous questions. Why does God love Jacob more than Esau? Is it merely because Esau sells his birthright as the elder son for a bowl of red lentil soup and bread (Genesis 25:29-34)? Exegetists may parry the existential question, but the mystery retains its enigmatic secret. Likewise, the first person narrative in *Jacob Have I Loved* promises revelation and invites a sympathetic response from the reader. But it also raises questions to which no answers are ever given. The narrator tells us of her return to Rass Island and comments that when her mother dies, there will be no Bradshaws left on the island; they—her sister Caroline and the narrator—"couldn't stay" (3). Why not? the reader wonders. The interaction between reader and narrator is immediately established, but the initial question gives rise to others, more perplexing, more profound. Why couldn't Sarah Louise share her troubles with a mother whom she loved dearly? Despite all the proofs of her parents' concern for her, why did she persist in her jealousy for her twin sister, Caroline? Is her depression a mask of anger at her sister's success? Why was she so angry at her mother's final revelation? Will Sarah Louise replicate her mother and "waste" a life, throw it out, allow it to become odious and vile? *Jacob Have I Loved*, like its biblical progenitor, still retains its secrets, but some of these questions may be answered in the light of Kristeva's theory of abjection.

The speaking subject in *Jacob Have I Loved*, Sarah Louise Bradshaw, could only begin to discover who she was when she separated from her mother and Rass Island. The two objects are mentioned in the novel's first sentence: "As soon as the snow melts, I will go to Rass Island and fetch my mother" (1). The separation has already taken place; the narrator will recite for the reader her recollection of past events. At the same time, however, the "will go" of the novel's first sentence indicates a return again to her mother. The separation is never over. By reviewing her repressed past, Sarah Louise will re-enact those painful conflicts which separation from her mother and from Rass Island have entailed. More importantly, though less obviously, by probing the unconscious, Sarah Louise Bradshaw will confront her own abjection, her unrecognized narcissism, which Kristeva describes as a regression "to a position set back from the other, a return to a self-contemplative, conservative, self-sufficient haven" (*PH* 14).

Sarah Louise's primary repression of the "loss" of her mother is a "curious primacy, where what is repressed cannot really be held down, and where what represses already borrows its strength and authority from what is apparently very secondary: language" (*PH* 13-14). That is why language in *Jacob Have I Loved* is so revelatory of abjection's in-between, amorphous state; images like "Wheeze," "sook," and "mud" become powerful manifestations of Sarah Louise's abject state. In order to enter into the process of subject identity, Sarah Louise must pass through a period of defilement, of a painful breaking away from the mother. This breaking away "is a violent, clumsy [process], with the constant risk of falling back under the sway of a power as securing as it is stifling" (*PH* 13).

Thirteen years old in 1941, the narrator, Sarah Louise Bradshaw, "[t]all and large-boned, with delusions of beauty and romance" (5), begins to reveal the tragedy of abjection lying at the heart of her "wasted" adolescent years.

Sarah Louise, who as an infant grew "fat on tinned milk formula," resents her twin sister, Caroline, who nursed at their mother's breast. That deep resentment is repressed, but the feelings of anger, jealousy and hate resurface again and again, making Sarah Louise an abject victim of self-loathing and disgust until they are finally confronted.

> There is a rare snapshot of the two of us sitting on the front stoop the summer we were a year and a half old. Caroline is tiny and exquisite ... her arms outstretched to whoever is taking the picture. I am hunched there like a fat dark shadow, my eyes cut sideways toward Caroline, thumb in my mouth, the pudgy hand covering most of my face. (20)

The connotative power of those images associated with the very young child—"thumb in mouth," "hand covering my face," "fat dark shadow," "eyes cut sideways"—are all descriptive of Sarah Louise's unconscious, abject state—deprived of the breast and so resorting to the thumb, hiding an identity she is already afraid of, disagreeably dark and fat, with eyes furtively, jealously cast at her golden-haired, gifted sister's image. In infancy an intense jealousy took root in her unconscious; it took root at the moment she was ejected from the womb. Because her twin sister, born afterwards, "refused to breathe," Sarah Louise, the first born, robust and healthy, was "washed and dried and [left] lying in a basket. Clean and cold and motherless" (19). Her grandmother had bathed her while all the mother's attention was directed to the sick infant. No wonder Sarah Louise felt "cast aside and forgotten" (18): she will be eclipsed by Caroline for the rest of her girlhood. Not only will the immaturity of the "thumb in her mouth" continue, it will also be intensified by a blind jealousy which will isolate her and retard ego formation. The thumb-sucking child will become a stunted "sook."

The physical description of crabs (sooks) moulting becomes a recurrent metaphor parallelling Sarah Louise's developmental process of identity consolidation and transformation, since the human's abjection-resolution is a discarding-integrative process. As a teenaged speaking subject, Sarah Louise describes the process of the crab moulting:

> Shedding its shell is a long and painful business for a big Jimmy [crab], but for a she-crab, turning into a sook, it seemed somehow worse. I'd watch them there in the float, knowing once they'd shed that last time and turned into grown-up lady crabs there was nothing left for them. They hadn't even had a Jimmy make love to them. Poor sooks. They'd never take a trip down the Bay to lay their eggs before they died. The fact that there wasn't much future for the Jimmies once they were packed in eelgrass didn't bother me so much. Males, I thought, always have a chance to live no matter how short their lives, but females, ordinary, ungifted ones, just get soft and die. (184)

Paterson's descriptions of crabs in the process of shedding, of taking a trip down the Bay, of mating, of laying eggs, all emphasize disintegrating boundary situations parallelling Sarah Louise's own soft, indefinite, amorphous, in-between state of "letting go" and "entering into" a new phase of subjectivity which involves abjecting the mother, leaving the island, and coming to terms with her own sexuality. Abjection feeds on these isolating boundaries of in-betweenness where "now" only whispers of "then."

Sarah Louise's "now" is clouded by Caroline and by God. "There was something about the thought of God being with me that made me feel more alone than ever. It was like being with Caroline" (38). Caroline "was so sure, so present, so easy, so light and gold, while I was all gray and shadow" (39). Caroline's "perfect" state, like God's, is an impossible, unattainable "then." All Sarah Louise possesses is a consciousness of a self, isolated from her mother, an abject "now"—*per omnia saecula saeculorum*—doomed to incompleteness. She seems fascinated by the horror of her own vindictive, jealous thoughts, but at the same time, her unconscious fear is that she may become a sook, a lady crab who never mates, or worse, one whose love turns to hate like her grandmother, old Mrs. Bradshaw.

Rass Island, with its shifting boundaries, is itself isolating. Paterson herself seems attracted to the amorphousness of boundaries, where identities barely exist or are, at best, fuzzy. There are no girl playmates, nothing for her talents. Sarah Louise's vocabulary is learned from books; she can't connect with the semiotic; she has a fertile imagination but can't develop her unique gifts for writing. She may love Rass Island but she is being suffocated on it. Her struggle isn't always conscious, but her feelings of frustration, anger and incompleteness are. She's trapped in her own difference, the source of her abjection. Age, sex, religion, education are so many factors in consolidating an identity, but moulting from these boundaries necessitates feelings of abjection. If there is to be any identity, it is at that point where self must merge and conform, separate, then individuate. But Sarah Louise cannot get outside her own shell of abjection long enough to share her pain. With her childhood companion, Call, she metes out part of herself in humour—telling jokes, which he is too literal to understand. However, she keeps straining against the sides of her tight-fitting shell until she finally breaks through, leaves the island and only tentatively consolidates a sense of who she is and can be. The vulnerability of the moulting crab, like a human being's own growth to adulthood, can be delayed; and in Sarah Louise's case the delay approaches the psychotic.

Sarah Louise's ambiguous identity, her abject "in-betweenness," is imaged in the contrasting figures of mother and grandmother, both of whom were active participants in the birth scene. Her mother represents the woman who has serenely "moulted," who has controlled the twisted braid of affects and thoughts bottled up within. On one occasion Sarah Louise, recognizing the hatred her grandmother had for her mother, admits it was driving her "to the brink of insanity," but her mother, "kept her silent course." It would have been easier for the daughter if the mother "screamed" or "wept, but she didn't" (222-23). The mother would not give the drives uninhibited reign. On the other hand, her grandmother exemplifies the "sook" whose psychotically delayed growth (tragically caught in her own perverted religion) transforms her into a bitter, cranky old woman intent on keeping Sarah Louise in bondage. It is Grandma Bradshaw who mirrors Sarah Louise's jealousy and tauntingly quotes Romans 9:13 to her: "Jacob have I loved, but Esau have I hated" (178).

Sarah Louise is rarely given her full name but usually called "Wheeze." The nickname literally means breath with audible friction and evokes an irritating unpleasantness. It suggests a state in between the relief of taking in air and noisy abrasiveness; it essentially captures Sarah Louise's vexing, ambiguous state, which rests primarily in the belief that she is detestable, laughed at by her peers, hated by her family and by God. In a recurring dream Sarah Louise sees herself saying to her family, magisterially, "Call me no longer Wheeze, but Sarah Louise." She would cast off that debilitating nickname by which she had been diminished since she was two years old (40). Sarah Louise is trying to recapture her pre-infant stage, an Eden-like existence of complete union within the mother's body. Her resentment at being fed tinned milk while her sister was nursed at the breast indicates her unwillingness to let go of the mother, to accept her own corporeality; it also attests to the fact that her resentment is festering into jealousy, and worse—into hate: "Hate. That was a forbidden word. I hated my sister" (74). The source of her fear of God is in this hatred: "I who belonged to a religion which taught that simply to be angry with another made one liable to the judgment of God and that to hate was the equivalent of murder" (74).

Wheeze clings to that dark void of abjection, re-lived at those critical moments when she feels herself most cast off, derided by her peers; as when, for example, she suggests that the Christmas concert be cancelled during the war (World War Two), and her classmates "snorted," then "broke into open laughter" (30). Was there not an unconscious motive in Sarah Louise's making the suggestion in the first place? Although she confesses, "I was proud of my sister" (25), when at thirteen her life turns upside down, in her unhappiness she fixes the blame on Caroline, on her grandmother, on her mother and herself (25). Since Caroline was the singing star of the Christmas concert, it is reasonable to suspect that in Wheeze's suggestion to have it cancelled there is more than an intimation that she wanted her sister's giftedness eclipsed. She wished her sister dead:

> I often dreamed that Caroline was dead. Sometimes I would get word of her death—the ferry had sunk with her and my mother on board, or more often the taxi had crashed and her lovely body had been consumed in the flames. Always there were two feelings in the dream—a wild exultation that now I was free of her and … terrible guilt. I once dreamed that I had killed her with my own hands. I had taken the heavy oak pole with which I guided my skiff. She had come to the shore begging for a ride. In reply I had raised the pole and beat, beat, beat. In the dream her mouth made the shape of screaming, but no sound came out. The only sound of the dream was my own laughter. I woke up laughing, a strange shuddering kind of laugh that turned at once into sobs.

Her tangling of reason and emotion is evident in the aftermath of the concert cancellation scene. Derided, Sarah Louise runs to her refuge at the tip of the island. There she sees that "the mud had a frozen brown crust and the cord grass was weighed down by ice" (31). Mud blurs the distinction between dirt and water as Sarah Louise's reason and emotion are mixed, encrusting her in her abject state. Even more revelatory, the mud imagery suggests that mixed boundary between life and wished-for death, the epitome of horror and abjection. Mud is that insignificant dust to which all life returns and Sarah Louise is both attracted and repulsed by death's waste of life. In her confusion she confesses that it would be "a very comfortable feeling to remove myself from the world I imagined was laughing at me" (33). At other times, however, the thought of death terrifies her as when she cannot finish her night-time prayer, "Now I Lay Me Down to Sleep." She concedes, "'If I should die' didn't push back the emptiness. It snatched and tore at me, making the hole larger and deeper" (38). Trapped in this chaos of abjection, Sarah Louise will not allow the emptiness to be filled; rather it grows until she enters that nightmarish world of unfilled holes and silent screams and wakens with a "shuddering kind of laugh" (75).

Even more evocative is the imagery of abjection associated with the smell of cats in Auntie Braxton's home when Sarah Louise faces the actual reality of death for the first time. Auntie Braxton, a recluse who defies the rigid social code of Rass Island society, has had a stroke and is lying motionless on her kitchen floor. Sarah Louise, intent on returning one of her wild, stray cats which had come into Captain Hiram Wallace's house, tries to reach her, but "the overwhelming essence of cat stood like an invisible wall between me and the front door" (98). The stench of cat invades the porous membranes of Sarah Louise's psyche and prefigures another confused emotional state when she falls in love with Captain Wallace, a man old enough to be her grandfather, but the only one who always addresses her majestically as Sarah Louise. In Kristevan parlance, the captain represents the father of individual pre-history—the rescuing father who both saves the subject and catapults her into otherness.

Experiences of abjection expose to the emergent ego its own precarious hold on identity. In both incidents recounted above, Sarah Louise realizes she must leave Rass Island, which is itself an abject image with confused boundaries "losing part of itself each year to the sea" (202). But how can she leave the island when, as she admits, "there was no place for me to run. How could I share with my mother the wildness of my body or the desperation of my mind?" (142).

A climax is reached when her sister Caroline leaves Rass Island for Baltimore and Captain Wallace pays for her schooling. It is World War Two, and Sarah Louise finds some relief for her abject jealousy in a new and fluid boundary situation—on the waters of the Chesapeake Bay (beautifully evoked in this novel). She finds the time spent fishing with her father on board the Portia Sue the "happiest of my life"; she is "deeply content" with what life is giving her (187). She confesses that part of her contentment is due simply to being with her father. But is he not another father of individual pre-history—the combination of the mother and her desire? He who saves the child from narcissism? (*TL* 46-48) Her father's ego, like her mother's, is consolidated—so much so that "[my] quiet, unassuming father, whose voice could hardly be heard in church ... sang to the oysters" (187). Part of her contentment, too, results from the fact that she is no longer fighting. Her sister is gone, her grandmother, a fleeting Sunday apparition, and God, if not dead, is far removed from her concern (188). She could afford to maintain her separateness.

Sarah Louise has begun her moulting, but she still strains against the boundaries of her own shell through her resentment at Caroline's "snatching other people's rights without even thinking" (135). It becomes apparent that what Sarah Louise fears are the very parts of her own identity that are reflected in Caroline—assertiveness, imaginative fancy, intelligence, laughter—gifts that are clearly evident to the reader throughout the novel. There is no evidence that Caroline resents her sister, who is a decided asset in lessening the family's poverty. And yet, when Caroline uses some of Sarah Louise's hand lotion (which the latter intended to use in smoothing and whitening her hands for the Captain), Wheeze's anger explodes like the jar of Jergen's she hurls against the bedroom wall. Quietly, Caroline questions, "Wheeze, ... have you gone crazy?" (148-49). What Sarah Louise does not face is the abyss of abjection in her own jealous drives which are truly threatening her very sanity—drives only too evident in Grandma Bradshaw's jealousy for Sarah Louise's mother, a jealousy which parallels Sarah Louise's jealousy for Caroline.

Abject again and disintegrated emotionally when Caroline marries her old friend Call, Wheeze once more asserts her individuality when Captain Wallace assures her that she can make her own choices. But it is her mother who most helps Sarah Louise break through her shell because, as strong as the attraction to her mother is, Sarah Louise's reason dictates that she must leave her. She will be saved only "off the island" (77), detached from her mother. She must abject the mother.

To compensate for Caroline's leaving Rass Island to pursue her studies in music, her mother proffers that the family borrow money and send Sarah Louise to school on the mainland, in the nearby town of Crisfield. Sarah Louise refuses and interprets the action as hateful, as "trying to get rid of me" (182). Yet the ambiguity of her desires is evident when she vindictively tells her mother to "get out and leave me alone," while in reality she wants her to stay. If she stayed, she confesses, "I would have taken it for a sign, not only that she cared about me but that God did" (182-83). This oscillation between loving the mother and hating her, between drawing close and withdrawing, is evident in other incidents—the menstrual staining of her Sunday-best dress, for example. Menstrual blood, finger-nail clippings, dead skin, and feces are all abject in that they remind the subject of its own bodily limits, the body that will itself someday be waste. This was Sarah Louise's first menses, "almost a year after Caroline's, of course." She draws closer to her mother when the latter covers up her embarrassment, allows her to stay home from Sunday school, and shields her from her fear that Grandma Bradshaw would discover the reason for her missing church and she'd get "prayed for out loud" by a "bunch of old sooks" (89-90). Moreover, in this scene, menstruation provides the ambiguous logic of maternal abjection since the act of menstruating (a mature, maternal act) is also the cause of embarrassment since, in Kristevan terms, bodily fluids are specifically, repulsively abject.

Another time when Sarah Louise draws closer to her mother is evident during the night of the great storm on the island. In the safety of her parents' bedroom, the adolescent realizes that she "wanted to snuggle up on her [mother's] lap like a toddler, but she was fourteen, so she sat as close to her body as she dared" (122). This drawing close to the mother is often countered by periods of angry withdrawal. Her drawing away, her loathing, is at its most intense in that scene, already described, when the mother offers her a means of escape and Sarah Louise rejects the offer. She "bit down savagely on a hangnail and ripped it so deeply that the blood started" (182). She spits herself out at the same moment she claims to establish herself. She is in the process of becoming an other at the expense of shedding her own blood. This oscillation between drawing close to and retreating from the mother indicates the continuing, shifting miasma of Sarah Louise's turbulent emotional state.

Lechte notes that "the abject may be understood as the dark side of narcissism; it is precisely what Narcissus would not want to have seen as he gazed into the pool" (*JK* 160). In her mother and grandmother as objects, Sarah Louise's unconsciously registers aspects of herself. Her mother is the clear water while her Grandma is the mud in Sarah Louise's pool. Grandma openly quotes from the Bible and yet hypocritically flouts its principal rule of loving one's neighbour. Grandma Bradshaw hates both Sarah Louise and her mother. Sarah Louise must confront that same abject hatred in herself.

Kristeva calls the abject "the moment of narcissistic perturbation" (*PH* 15). In Sarah Louise's case, the moment of narcissistic perturbation, or the decisive illumination of abjection's chaos, comes on a very ordinary house-cleaning day. While washing windows (the glass allows Sarah Louise to see herself reflected in the mother), the angry adolescent uncovers the mystery of abjection in her mother's life. The scene is a crucial one, because it is the mother who initiates the climactic illumination in which the mother sees her daughter seeing her "self" (subject) in the mother's "self" (object). As mother and daughter each wash a side of the window, the grandmother is also seen through the glass "poking anxiously about the living room." Sarah Louise feels a "perverted pride" but also a "nagging guilt" in taking pleasure in her grandmother's apparent discomfort as mother and daughter work in harmony. But her guilt turns to "a growing anger that my clever, gentle, beautiful mother should be so unjustly persecuted," which, she acknowledges, "was transformed, heaven knows how, into a fury against my mother for allowing herself to be so treated" (223). She asks how her mother ever came "here" to this place, this island. In the ensuing conversation she learns how her mother confronted the abject by controlling her own rising fury at her mother-in-law's virulent jealousy for her, the woman, she feels, who had taken her son away. The younger Mrs. Bradshaw, a writer of poetry, had given up her own home and the idea of going to Paris; instead she had come as a teacher to Rass Island and calmly bore the miserable hatred of her husband's "sooky" mother. Her mother had accepted abjection; she had become the prototype of what the drives expel. Sarah Louise, shaking with tearful fury, pounding the wall at the "stupid waste" of a life, perceives her mother as abject. Her touch would "taint," her weakness "infect" her. When her mother assures her that she is what she wanted to be and that she freely chose, Sarah Louise finds the idea "sickening" (226). The daughter abjects the mother. The abysmal fury at her mother's wasted life fuels Sarah Louise's decision to leave the island: "I'm not going to rot here like Grandma. I'm going to get off this island and do something" (226).

But Sarah Louise's withdrawal is complicated by the fear she has of being "different." For all her bombast, she realizes she is afraid of leaving, of moulting, fearful that "I would find myself once more cold and clean in a forgotten basket" (228). She is afraid of envisioning a future apart from her family. Wisely affirming the power of choice, her mother tells her that she will be missed, and Sarah Louise asks the ultimate question, "As much as you missed Caroline?" "More," and with that assurance, Sarah Louise realizes that one word "allowed me at last to leave the island and begin to build myself as a soul, separate from the long, long shadow of my twin" (228).

Perhaps the novel should have ended there. But the final anti-climactic chapters reveal that Sarah Louise follows her mother's footsteps and not those of the bitter Bradshaw grandmother. Like her mother, she too marries for love—an "outsider," a Lithuanian Catholic widower, Joseph Wotjkiewicz with three children; like her mother, she comes to a strange place in the remote hill country of West Virginia; and like her mother, she lives on an island—"a mountain-locked valley ... more like an island than anything I know" (232). Through her brooding recitative, in remembering her moulting process, the mature, married Sarah Louise lives again the pains of abjection and finds her own soul.

But that soul is still questing and questioning, particularly her own sexuality. Why could she not have been a boy? She "would have given anything" to have been the son in the household (21). Why couldn't she "be a woman on [Rass] island?" (216). Why should "a bright girl" like Sarah Louise have "practically non-existent" chances of entering medical school? (231). Sarah Louise accepts that desires are never fully satisfied. To let the drives that propel desire gain control can embitter one's life, as Grandma Bradshaw illustrates. The elder Mrs. Bradshaw is the phallic/narcissistic mother who refuses to lose her son to another woman. In contrast to Sarah Louise's loving mother, Grandma Bradshaw allows her anger to poison her life. Sarah Louise accepts the incompleteness of the human condition. In the on-going conflict to construct the self, she knows that the ideal image she has of that self rests on an abjection that shatters the image just as soon as "repression, the constant watchman" (over the drives) is relaxed (PH 13).

If the apocalyptic power of grasping identity from the horrors of abjection is most obvious in *Jacob Have I Loved*, it is not missing from Paterson's other works. Her first three novels, *The Sign of the Chrysanthemum* (1973), *Of Nightingales That Weep* (1974), and *The Master Puppeteer* (1975), are set in medieval Japan, and already abjection's wing with its whisk of despair has begun to brush her readers' imaginations. In her very first novel, *The Sign of the Chrysanthemum*, the tale of a young Japanese boy, Muna (the nameless one with no identity) is in search of his samurai-warrior father, marked with the sign of the chrysanthemum on his left shoulder. This first novel presented what was to become a major theme in all Paterson's novels—the ordeal of entering into the symbolic and finding one's identity as a speaking subject. It is an ordeal, painful and ecstatic, for both mother and child, and it tears the veil from the mystery on which love of self and others is based. It involves a glimpse of the abyss of abjection, noted principally in boundary situations and in the cryptic portrayal of the mother figure.

Just as *Jacob Have I Loved* presented some aspects of Kristeva's trinity of psychic life—the *symbolic*, the *imaginary*, and the *real*, all of which love ties together (*IBWL* 43)—so do Paterson's other novels.[2] Muna, the young hero of *The Sign of the Chrysanthemum*, is a deject who never stops demarcating his universe with its fluid confines. When the thirteen-year-old boy's mother dies at the beginning of the tale, Muna's identity, consequent on the breaking of the instinctual dyad between mother and child, seems assured. He thinks he has relinquished the comforting but inhibitive relationship with his mother and has begun the symbolic identification with the father. Saddened, yet happy to be free from the peasant task of rice planting, of bending "ankle deep in the mud like a water buffalo" (*SC* 2), he decides to find his father and an identity he thinks his mother has denied him: "I am going to find my true name—the name of my father's people" (9). The quest is essential to psychic maturation and, in Kristevan terms, there is tremendous pleasure in assuming "the father's power and elevation to the summit of authority" (*IBWL* 40).

Two "fathers" present themselves: Takanobu, the ronin—a renegade samurai with no lord to serve—and Fukuji, who rescues Muna from a disastrous fire. Muna betrays his "father" Fukuji in stealing a sword for his "real father," Takanobu. Afterwards, repentant and chastened in Abjection's Valley of Humiliation, he returns to Fukuji and resumes his servant status. Muna chooses to accept his abjection. That he has owned his abjection and has clearly moved away from the mother is seen at the New Year celebrations when, at fifteen, Muna asks Fukuji to give him a name, and the wise sword maker-father replies, "It is your name, and it must please only you" (129). He keeps his own name—the nameless one. As Kristeva reminds us, "There is nothing like the abjection of self to show that all abjection is in fact recognition of the *want* on which any being, meaning, language, or desire is founded" (*PH* 5).

All three aspects of psychic life—the symbolic, the imaginary and the real—operate in *Of Nightingales That Weep*, in which the adolescent heroine, Takiko, ends up marrying the object of her abjection—her step-father. The novel provides a fascinating study of Kristevan theory of Freud's oedipal complex; more importantly, it reveals Paterson's belief that in the confrontation with abjection, one's most powerful ally is the imaginary. Although the imaginary and the symbolic are closely allied, theirs is a nervous alliance. Kristeva describes the link between Thing and Meaning as "tense," and carefully scores what becomes the fundamentally sympathetic chord between herself and Paterson—the imaginary's potential for hope. The imaginary, writes Kristeva, is "the very universe of the *possible*" and in it "there is the infinite possibility of ambivalent, polyvalent resurrections" (*BS* 101). The real child might be fragmented, but the image the child sees in the mirror is whole. Paterson's characters learn how to face abjection and are aided chiefly by the ability to sustain an imaginary unity. In *Jacob Have I Loved*, Sarah Louise, realizing that poetic language lies and that "[i]n poems you can't say plain out what you mean" (79), still finds expansion and sustenance of the self in poetic language. Muna, the protagonist of *The Sign of the Chrysanthemum*, finds a haven in his imagination—his vision of the tree which was "his place for sorrow and anger and dreams" (42). In *Of Nightingales That Weep*, Takiko seeks refuge in the imaginary unity of music; music "was inside her" (2). She plays the koto with amazing dexterity and control. And through the power of her music, at the New Year celebration, she is able to apologize to her step-father Goro, whom she considers abject: "for my rudeness of the past year, I beg my father's forgiveness" (26). Goro then instructs his step-daughter in the value of signs; he teaches her "not only Japanese script but nearly a thousand Chinese characters as well." She "was thus the only female she had ever known who could write Chinese characters" (33). Step-father and daughter are thus bonded by art: she as a musician, he as a potter—an expressive art which he also passes on to his daughter. Takiko has now entered more fully into the symbolic.

The symbolic is always associated with the development of a sign system. It is the domain of reason and judgement and, genetically speaking, comes into being later than the semiotic. But synchronically, the symbolic is always present, even in the semiotic disposition which cannot exist without constantly challenging the symbolic one (*DL* 19). But if the symbolic is active in the semiotic, the reverse principle is also operative. Thus Takiko's libido, associated with the semiotic, is activated at the court of Princess Aoi where she charms the Child Emperor with her music. Here the maturing girl is made aware of her mistress's lover (61) and learns from Princess Aoi that "Love is too cruel" (63). The symbolic domain of reason and judgement seems to desert Takiko as she herself falls in love with the Princess's lover, Hideo, and finds that love indeed is painfully cruel. Betraying her own people and her family, Takiko returns home, abject.

In a terrible accident Goro brands his step-daughter with a hot poker across the cheek and scars her beauty permanently. Takiko, now as abject as Goro in her deformity, is scorned by Hideo—politely: "What wise god created etiquette as a haven for lost souls?" (160). But Takiko owns her abjection in marrying Goro and bearing a daughter, initiating again maternal love as the source of hope as well as of life: "Man overcomes the unthinkable of death by postulating maternal love in its place" (*TL* 252).

In nearly all of Paterson's fiction a triangular structure of abjection may be discerned. At the apex is a child or adolescent seeking identity—who to be and how to be. On one leg of the triangle is the parent who has not accepted the pain involved in earning an identity, and on the other, the parent (or authority figure) who has come to terms with the pain of abjection, accepted it, and achieved wholeness. When Paterson switches from an oriental setting to a North American one, as she did in *The Great Gilly Hopkins* (1978), she continues this patterning of the child caught between opposing adult figures. With insight and intelligence, she studies the true nature of parental love, which is not necessarily a biological imperative—an abject truth that Gilly/Galadriel Hopkins must learn even though it literally splits her in two.

Gilly, the emotionally abused, abandoned, neglected child who has been bounced from one foster home to another, covers up the sensitive Galadriel's anger, hopelessness, and loss of self-esteem by bravado. Gilly is abject: "I am not nice.... I am famous across this entire country. Nobody wants to tangle with the great Galadriel Hopkins. I am too clever and too hard to manage. Gruesome Gilly they call me" (3). She forces people to take notice of her with her rather monstrous behaviour, and hers is not a stage act. She must act outrageously to survive as Galadriel, the hurt, abandoned, fearful child. She finds comfort in an imaginative creation of her biological mother, Courtney. Thus the triangular structure is set up—Gilly at the centre caught between her birth mother, Courtney Hopkins, and her foster mother, Maime Trotter.

Maime Trotter is "a huge hippopotamus of a woman," whose very name "m'aime" indicates her as object: "love me." But she is a "maimed" object with a "Before" body and an "After" smile (5). Furthermore, "her house was crowded with junk." But Gilly does not mind: "She could stand anything ... as long as she was in charge" (6). Gilly must control everyone—especially Galadriel, who is always in pain, not knowing why her mother has abandoned her. Although Gilly and Galadriel are one physical, thinking person, they represent two psychological states as witnessed in one incident when Gilly, looking at a picture of her mother with her beautiful black hair and perfect teeth, reads the inscription, "For my beautiful Galadriel, I will always love you" (9). Gilly must come to grips with this cruel lie. The idolatrous icon of the envisaged "mother" must be shattered; the boundaries between the imaginary and the real, collapsed. The "beautiful" Galadriel, daughter of the beautiful Courtney, and the insufferable Gilly, with the "straw-colored hair," are two personalities in the same individual, but uniting Galadriel/ Gilly demands that Gilly face the abjection of her biological mother's rejection. Gilly shoves the picture (and her feelings) out of sight in a drawer and goes downstairs to resume her obnoxious Gilly existence (9).

Only when Gilly merges the boundaries of her Gilly/Galadriel selves will she be capable of ownership and acceptance of a co-dependent/independent ego state, intact with intelligence and feeling. Such wholeness is never fully attained and never possible without the pain of abjection, which is eased in Gilly's case with the help of wise adults like the foster mother, Trotter. But Gilly will not allow Maime Trotter to invade Galadriel's isolation, her deject situation, until her maternal grandmother takes her to live in Virginia. Her mother visits, and Gilly is forced to face her abjection, her "reject" situation. Her mother did not want her. She "wasn't going to take Gilly back with her. 'I will always love you.' It was a lie. Gilly had thrown away her whole life for a stinking lie" (146). Her mother was "a very ordinary flower child gone to seed" (145). And Gilly faces the pain with the nausea and disgust of abjection. She vomits that ideal of motherhood she has harboured inside her, only to be comforted once more by Trotter whom she phones for help: "All that stuff about happy endings is lies" (147). In her final "therapy session" Trotter tells Gilly that she is home: "Your grandma is home." And Gilly, content to be who she is, remains with her maternal grandmother and accepts the denial of wish fulfillment. Gilly and Galadriel are one. "No clouds of glory, perhaps, but Trotter would be proud" (148).

Another demythologizing of the ideal mother is found in Paterson's *Come Sing, Jimmy Jo*. Here Paterson's sense of place, so marvellously explicit, re-creates Appalachia in Blue Country, West Virginia, with its mist-drenched mountains, raw, naked poverty, a pipe-smoking old woman, bean soup, porched cottages, and the world of country music. The hero is eleven-year-old James Johnson, the youngest member of the Johnson Family country singers. Grandma is the wise old woman on one side of the triangle, and on the other is Olive Mae, Jimmy's young mother who has jettisoned her child from his rightful place in her affections, yet refuses to let go of him completely.

Grandma reveals her down-to-earth, practical acceptance of abjection when she debunks the ideal mother in speaking of her own mother: "She was a falling-down drunk what beat the tar out of ever'one of us nine kids. We was glad to see her go, tell the truth" (6). Later, Grandma herself is cast off. She quietly steps aside when she realizes the ravages of time on her own voice. Grandma is perceptive, patient, and loving. She yields serenely to age, puts the family's needs before her own, and is always capable of exercising control over her strong-willed and sensitive nature.

On the other hand, Olive Mae (or Keri Sue) is eager to assume fame, fortune, a new identity. She would sacrifice anything and anyone, even her child, to achieve stardom. Jealous of her son's talent, she is the narcissist, completely focused on herself. Unlike her son, she refuses to separate her stage self from her real self. Content and obsessed with her "Barbie doll" existence—fake, plastic, cheap—Olive cannot confront the pain of abjection, but her son Jimmy Jo does and in doing so experiences its desperate jubilation.

In Paterson's novels, subject identity is not a matter of chronological age; it is achieved through abjection, and abjection is usually experienced within the familial construct. Thus Jess Aarons in *Bridge to Terabithia,* who wants only to be the best runner in the fifth grade of Lark Creek Elementary School, understands the meaning of life and his place in it before he has reached his twelfth year. That he is abject is noted in the first scene of the novel when Jess' "smelly" self is barred from the breakfast table. From this "smelly" piece of familial disharmony, Paterson creates a hero who must bear the partiality a mother shows to her four daughters (6, 67), the hard work that falls upon the only boy in a family of five, the drudgery of school, and the loneliness that comes to an artist whose sole delight is his escape into the imaginary through drawing. Jess is a lonely exile, a deject, until the day he meets Leslie Burke (16-18). It is Leslie, with her writer's imagination, who leads Jess into the "dark places" in the woods of Terabithia where "it was almost like being underwater" (39).

Crossing the boundary into Terabithia, Jess begins his journey away from the maternal bond because he finds himself caught between the love of two women—his teacher and his girlfriend, Leslie Burke. Leslie, the exceptional child who receives maternal nurturing and intimacy more from her father than her mother, shows Jess that maturation and identity integration do not depend on chronological age. She comprehends, for example, the secret abjection of the terrible Janice Avery who was beaten by her father (75); she also comprehends the coexistence of pain and love. Leslie, whose family are atheists, accompanies Jess' family to church one Sunday. Jess tries to explain the mystery of the Crucifixion: "It's because we're all vile sinners God made Jesus die" (84). Leslie disclaims the explanation: "It's crazy, isn't it? ... You have to believe it, but you hate it. I don't have to believe it, and I think it's beautiful" (84-85). Leslie understands the ambiguity of abjection.

Jess' life is totally shattered when he discovers that Leslie has died. The rope bridge to Terabithia breaks and Leslie, striking her head on a rock, drowns in the swollen creek. In his grief-crazed state, Jess confronts his anger and cruelty after he lashes out at his little sister May Belle and hits her in the face, "as hard as he had ever hit anything in his life" (115). Over the painful months following Leslie's death, Jess realizes that the love of his friend had changed his life in helping him understand the enigma of abjection. She had taken him from an abject, smelly "cow pasture" and in Terabithia had made him see the world "huge and terrible and beautiful and very fragile" (126).

It would be impossible to do justice to all of Paterson's novels in this one study. *The Master Puppeteer*, *Rebels of the Heavenly Kingdom*, *Park's Quest* and *Lyddie* are yet to be considered; all of these novels offer unique experiences. They are all completely different, and all, underscoring the many faces of abjection, demand that the imagination put form to it. Perhaps *Park's Quest*, more than the other three novels mentioned, should not be ignored, simply because it so clearly constructs a new vision of the family after the chaotically destructive Viet Nam War. It is a modern, sad, hopeful, and sometimes funny, book. Park/Pork/"Gareth"/Parkington Waddell Broughton the fifth/"Sir Gawain"/"knight"/"the young lord"/young Park/"our little man"—these many identities are separate in Park. He is different things to himself and different things to others: "Park's son," "city boy," "useless city kid," "fat kid," "bruzzah." Raised by his single mother who is strangely reluctant to tell him anything about his father except that he bears his name (a name bestowed on the first-born Broughton son for over five generations), Park's quest is both to seek the truth about his father who was killed in Viet Nam after returning there and to "kill" his mother's secret by forcing its revelation. Like a true medieval knight, he wants to journey to the Viet Nam War

Memorial where he will touch his father's name on the stone when he has proved himself worthy of being a Parkington Waddell Broughton (not the baby "Pork" or "Gareth" the kitchen knight).[3] But before Park can discover the truth of his identity and consolidate the different parts of himself into a "Park" he can accept, he must pass through the brokenness of abjection.

Parkington Waddell Broughton V must accept the truth that his father has crushed the boundaries of the marriage contract: that he sired a Vietnamese child. He must also realize that by divorcing Park's father, his mother shut the "golden airman" (107) out of her life, allowing her psychological wound to suppurate and letting the hurt infect her son. She could not or would not forgive; her angry grief "festered unhealing all these years" (136). Her husband, Park IV, returned to Viet Nam and was killed. His death contaminated relationships in three families, and the would-be knight is quick to blame himself for his grandfather's paralysis, his father's death, and his mother's pain. Like a medieval knight, Park undertakes a crusade to break the evil curse of his parents' choices, but before he can do so, he must see himself as abject—as "fat" (58), a "giant splinter under the skin" (61), a "useless city kid" (78), a "nothing" (127).

Park's quest takes him to his father's old Virginia home, where, in the familiar triad of young boy, dead father, and uncle who becomes the new father, Park separates himself from his mother and enters into a new, larger, more life-giving family. In the separation process, however, he confronts his abjection. The image of his uncle (the father's brother) in overalls milking cows pollutes the imaginary father—a dashing, romantic figure that Park had created. His father, a bomber pilot, who flies "high above the world," wouldn't go round "watching for shit." No wonder the sight of his uncle makes Park want to "vomit" (60). Park is also offended by being thrown together with his unknown half-sister Thanh, whose racial difference he detests and whom he promptly names the "geek." Park's first chore at his father's old homestead is at the milk-separating machine. That he doesn't understand how to run the machine parallels his inability to comprehend his own workings. The milk separator (with its natural, semiotic connotation of maternal, comforting nourishment and unnatural separation into milk, cream, butter, skim milk) becomes an ironic indicator of Park's own separation from his over-possessive mother. He is about to enter into his paternal, symbolic inheritance, fed to him by the imaginary which provides him with a pseudo-identity as knight.

Only at the end of the novel, however, does Park finally accept the suffering that all humans, even knights, must face. He finally understands that both his paralyzed grandfather and his mother share the same open wound of guilt, blaming themselves for causing the death of his aviator father. In discovering the Broughtons' guilty secret and by exposing the pain of the present, Park breaks the evil spell of silence covering his parents' past mistakes. In his "war" with his Vietnamese half-sister, which culminates in his shooting of a black crow, Park re-enacts the tragedies of Viet Nam. But he also brings peace and healing. The black crow and his paralyzed grandfather, though maimed, are both healed. In delivering his mother and grandfather from their paralyzing guilt, in accepting the new racial bonding with his uncle (who married Than's mother), and in realizing that secret, disintegrating wounds can heal, Park actualizes the deeds of the imaginary: "The King has sent me to be your deliverer" (23).

The Viet Nam memorial is not only a monument to wasteful carnage, the proliferation of corpses, the epitome of abjection; it is also a monument to the desperate need we have to tolerate difference. Only in exposing the psyche's secret abrasions can they be healed. But Paterson does not dwell on the past; she stresses the importance of remembering the past but not being haunted by it.

Paterson's heroes and heroines struggle through repeated experiences of abjection, of being forsaken and separate while undertaking the great journey of existence. The journey reveals a few moments of ecstasy—not only in completion, in wholeness, in oneness with the Father but also in resurrection, in beginning again, in trusting another human being, in loving and caring. Paterson recognizes the power of abjection, but she is content, psychically at least, to be an infinitesimal part of that mysterious supernova that erupted fifteen billion years ago. She realizes that everything in the cosmos is abject, separated, and seeks oneness with that original unity of being we sometimes call God. Like the old prophets she understands "though [she] thought [she] had toiled in vain, and for nothing, uselessly spent [her] strength, yet [her] reward is with the Lord, [her] recompense is with [her] God" (Isaiah 49:4). A grateful America has recognized the giftedness of this doyenne of adolescent fiction and rewarded it. Besides two Newbery Awards (*Jacob Have I Loved* and *Bridge to Terabithia*), two National Book Awards (*The Master Puppeteer* and *The Great Gilly Hopkins*), an American Library Association Notable Book Award (*Come Sing, Jimmy Jo*) and a Phoenix Award (*Of Nightingales That Weep*), Paterson has been recognized with honorary degrees from institutions in both the United States and Canada. What power does abjection have against this woman's pen?

5

THE DILEMMA OF MELANCHOLIA

AIDAN CHAMBERS

ONE OF THE FOREMOST British writers of adolescent fiction, Aidan Chambers, winner of the Farjeon Award (1982), admits that he doesn't "feel at home in the world."[1] He feels cut off, estranged, disoriented—an exile. The admission echoes the Kristevan view that some people choose to be exiles "because they have never felt at home anywhere" (Kurzweil 216).[2] In Chambers' case, the springs of his distinctive creativity hide in this simple confession; an awed perplexity and a muted melancholia pervade all Chambers' writing and reveal his discomfort in a world where language, love, and even life itself seem debased. He is forever searching for an "at homeness," an "at-one-ness," and at the same time his novels continually assure us that wholeness and completion are modern obsessions best controlled by accepting multiplicity and difference. But feeling like an exile has had a positive influence on his art because it has prompted him to study the link between his own feelings of estrangement and the constitution of the subject. His novels allow not only the reader but also the author himself to enter into a process of becoming.

Aidan Chambers' private research lab is his own mind, specifically the quiet inner world of his creative imagination, wherein he carries out all sorts of innovative experiments to demonstrate the transforming power of the word, of literature, whose primary purpose, he maintains, is "to recreate the texture of life, to explore and seek for meaning in human experience" (*The Horn Book Magazine* 48: 131).[3] At the same time, Chambers suspects there is no meaning in life save what the free individual gives to it. The struggle to attain meaning in existence might be the cause of his own uneasiness in this world; it is certainly responsible for Chambers' uncanny ability to probe the twisted coils of language and sex—topics which characterize his fiction wherein author and reader grope for meaning. Chambers intimates that his own subjectivity is constituted by his fiction as much as his fiction is constituted by him.

When he began to write for young people, Chambers consciously created a "second self" to entice his readers to give themselves up to the book, to become part of it without relinquishing their own subjectivity.[4] He was omnipresent in his fiction and extremely adroit in shifting his own "voice." In an essay entitled "Ways of Telling," Chambers explains that the novel is a "contemplative medium" and that the use of both first and third persons is not arbitrary: it intimates the human habit of self-reflection. The first-person voice creates an effect of immediacy and intimacy, while the third person (and this might be associated with the semiotic self) creates a sense of distance, of being an observer rather than a participant (characteristic of the symbolic). This juxtaposition allows the reader to hear the linguistic shifts more keenly, to stand now within the character's mind, now without (*Booktalk*, 114, 104). At one time Chambers is the first-person narrator; at other times he is the omniscient third-person seer or commentator on the actions, attitudes, and events in the novel. Subtly or flamboyantly, by examining the many conflicting emotions operative in any one human experience, Chambers merges both internal and external worlds. In this way he suggests that the author as subject never entirely exists as an entity. The writer re-examines and re-creates his own self in an "open" process—a fact that Chambers admits in "Ways of Telling" when, in discussing the writing of *Breaktime*, he says, "I sometimes think that what I was doing ... was shaping—or rather re-shaping—my own youth, re-examining it in the light of the years since then" (*Booktalk* 105). However, he denies his fiction is autobiographical; rather, he bears witness to Julia Kristeva's thesis that all art is constitutive of the subject.

Kristeva maintains that in language, in writing, the self is re-constituted, re-shaped. Rather than emphasize that the writer creates a work of literature, she believes that the work helps re-create the writer. In an important interview with Perry Meisel, Kristeva noted how the work of art—for example, the novel—extends beyond and reshapes subjectivity.

> It's necessary to see how all great works of art ... are, to be brief, masterful sublimations of those crises of subjectivity which are known, in another connection, as psychotic crises. That has nothing to do with the freedom of expression of some vague kind of subjectivity which would have been there beforehand. It is, very simply, through the work and the play of signs, a crisis of subjectivity which is the basis for all creation, one which takes as its very precondition the possibility of survival. (Meisel 131-32)

Chambers' honest depiction of adolescent depression and melancholy gives his novels their distinctive note of authenticity for, as Julia Kristeva has written in *Black Sun*, "there is no imagination that is not, overtly or secretly, melancholy" (6). But how is the connection between melancholia and subjectivity depicted in a Chambers novel?

The writing subject usually begins with a slightly pathological experience: Ditto's acute feelings of guilty repugnance towards his father; Hal's dancing madly, excitedly on his friend's grave; Nik's vomiting in his bath when he comprehends the finality of death. These are all disruptive, disintegrating experiences illustrating that the subject feels alienated, alone, lost. The ability to see life as having any meaning collapses. In a Chambers' novel, however, the pathological state of depression or melancholia is connected with a developing sense of self. A new "self" contributes to the re-creation of a world view wherein human experience has meaning.[5] But it is the pathological dimension of an experience, usually an experience of loss, that initiates the search for meaning through some sort of aesthetic medium. Thus creativity, particularly in the use of language, is a response to suffering, melancholia, and a loss of meaning which themselves are all related to crises of relationships. Aesthetically, language has the potential to resolve the melancholic crisis.

In describing the language of those afflicted with melancholia, Kristeva notes that it is "repetitive and monotonous ... they utter sentences that are interrupted, exhausted, come to a standstill..." (*BS* 33). There is a splitting within the self: a withdrawal from the symbolic, the law of the father, and from life. As Kristeva notes, the sadness of the melancholic stems from "the most archaic expression of a non-symbolisable, unnameable narcissistic wound, so precocious that no outside agent (subject or agent) can be used as a referent" (*BS* 12). There is no object for the melancholic—only a 'Thing,' a vague, indeterminate something "that does not lend itself to signification" (13). The "Thing" is a denial of the signifier. The melancholic has lost the desire for meaning.

Because language, however wounded, ensures a way of re-entering into relationships, of re-connecting with others and the world, writing provides the means by which the self assumes some form of control over the varied aspects of loss. It allows a period of mourning the loss and of accepting the symbolic. Kristeva explains the melancholic dilemma in the form of a question: "will the traces of the lost Thing sweep the speaker along, or will he succeed in carrying them away—integrating them, incorporating them in his discourse, which has become a song by dint of seizing the thing?" (*BS* 146). In Chambers' case, language is salvation from despair because, unlike a true psychosis, his protagonists' melancholia does not result in the complete collapse of the symbolic and the loss of the use of signs. Thus, language in a Chambers' novel is multi-levelled, fragmented, divided into different voices, all of which try to throw some light on the truth of experience. It is with his alienated, melancholic, adolescent heroes—Ditto in *Breaktime* (1978), Hal in *Dance on My Grave* (1982), and Nicholas Frome in *Now I Know* (1984)—that we find characters who serve as "contemplative media" for the emergent self made possible through the use of signs—of language (*Booktalk* 114). By means of language, they break through the melancholia that first initiated them into a search for the meaning of self and of the world.

Chambers first explored that loss-induced melancholia in *Breaktime*, in which Ditto's loss of his father is made repulsively palpable and where his melancholia becomes an opening towards transformation. Coming home from his comprehensive school one day, Ditto, the adolescent hero, tries to avoid his convalescent father who is watching television in the living room. A sense of duty, however, compels him towards that place where the air "was greenhouse stuffy, smelt of rancid snot, stockinged feet, and overheated television set" (14,7). The odour of the room, the deadly suffocating atmosphere, the supplicating position of the seventeen-year-old before the father—these are all tangible witnesses to the decomposing relationship between father and son.[6] Communication between father and son has been lost; it is dead.

By the end of the novel, however, that lost father-son relationship has been transformed: the son recognizes the father as son, and the father sees his son as father. When the father passes on to his son two medals he had won in motorcycle racing—the passion of his life when he was eighteen, the same age as Ditto—the son accepts them, recognizes the adolescent in the father, and forgives him. He receives from his father the hope of fulfilling his own dreams of becoming a writer, a creator, and a father. Thus Ditto is initiated into the symbolic; the father allows his son to have his dreams as his own father had not done for him.

Chambers is fascinated by the complex changes in human relationships, particularly those in sexual relationships, that take place in adolescent passages—passages both terribly exclusive and at the same time wonderfully inclusive, intensely private and exasperatingly universal. His many-layered voices respect the slow process of becoming that links the worlds of adult and adolescent. Ditto's burgeoning creativity as a writer, a worker with words, parallels his burgeoning sexual experiences. In a psychic sense the father has "died," as has the "child;" in Kristevan parlance, "By the quirks of biology and family life we are all of us melancholy mourners, witnesses to the death that marks our psychic inception" (*IBWL* 41).

But there are other multi-levelled transformations of meaning in the language of *Breaktime.* Chambers makes the novel a comic debunking of all the modern stereotypes associated with adolescence. Even the title "Breaktime" has concentric levels of signification—breaktime as a recess from class, work, or school, as a breaking away from the mother-father dyad, and as a surrendering to the power of the symbolic sign in language. But in a real sense the title suggests that the hero has broken the chain of time. The book delivers a cleverly orchestrated defense of the "art for life" thesis in Ditto's response to Morgan who "thinks art or (lit-er-arr-tewer) is crap" (8). Furthermore, there is a carefully crafted, sometimes irreverent play on "breaking" and "entering," of integrating and disintegrating as part of the Kristevan "open" process of "becoming."

Ditto's name emphasizes the universality of that process just as his narrative of his breaktime experiences dittoes life. In another sense, the reader must break open the words in the text in order to enter into meaning. Is Ditto's narrative report to Morgan real or is it simply fiction? Does it matter?

The answer to these questions is as ambiguous as is the author's use of words. Chambers' interspersion of variations on the "break and enter" theme continues in the break between father and son, the break in Ditto's thought patterns, the experimental breaks on the canonical printed page; and perhaps most obviously in Robby's "break and enter" incident (113-116) which serves as a prelude to Ditto's "breaking" and "entering" into Helen (126).

Helen's name itself serves as an example of Chambers' debunking of clichés—it "dittoes" Helen of Troy, that immemorially beautiful heroine of male fantasies. Chambers weaves into the novel those other clichés—such as the boy meets girl plot, rebellion against parents, adolescent engagement in dares, thrills, rivalries, and first sexual experience (*Booktalk* 96). But Ditto's account of his first sexual experience is unique in fiction. Chambers, as implied author, has re-created a Kristevan moment in time whereby the semiotic/symbolic experience is narrated in a three-fold narrative voice. The first-person narrative—rational, masculine-nuanced—is printed in regular type with every half-page line interspersed with the feminine, more dynamic, semiotic drives reflected in italicized typescript. Counterpointed with this double presentation, on the right-hand side of the page, is the third dimension of patterns of love-making—practical, prosaic—elucidated by Dr. Benjamin Spock's *A Young Person's Guide to Life and Love.* The reader, inside Ditto's memory and his present consciousness, experiences total involvement in the complexities of falling in love.

However, *Breaktime* cracks yet another cliché—that of the Romeo and Juliet myth of youthful, eternal love. Helen, Ditto's first sexual partner, writes afterwards that her "word-child" lover has been a "help" but that she doubts they'll ever "meet again." On his part Ditto experiences a "loss sweet with gratitude," but his is a resigned, educative loss. Both young people realize they are "not ready" (126-27) for the serious commitment of love—and perhaps never will be because of differing, sometimes conflicting, biological and social programming. Their sexual experience is merely a "break" in time—an irruption, an experience observed. Ditto's melancholic sense of loss, so evident in the early pages of the novel, is transformed at the end. He becomes acutely aware of the kinetic and potential energy of his being; he savours what he is at a singular, particular, never-to-be-repeated moment. Perceiving the inter-connectedness of his being, he is alert to the stimulations of the nervous system and its influence on different parts of his physical, psychic, and emotional being. He knows he cannot change who he is because of social/cultural strictures, but he can change *how* he is—how he responds to a given moment in time.

It is with *Dance on My Grave: A Life and a Death in Four Parts* (1982) that Chambers' melancholia, his fascination with death and language, surface most clearly. In this novel the hero escapes a melancholic psychosis through language. Indeed, the melancholia begins the social-cultural reflective process that enables the protagonist to structure himself as subject, creating meaning out of chaos. Self-understanding and self-development are integrated within the aesthetics of language. Chambers highlights the often muted layers of meaning in words to illustrate how strangeness and melancholia can be unperceived components of identity. The subject is recognized not by language but through it. Thus the title suggests the grave as a memorial to life after being in time, while the dance indicates the imperative to carry on with life, celebrate it. Or, as Chambers describes it, in *Dance on My Grave* "Hal writes [re-creates] himself into an understanding of his experience [now dead and gone] with Barry Gorman" (*Booktalk* 112).

The hero, Hal (Henry Spurling Robinson), admits to being struck "by the foreverness of time" (58). Even more dramatically, in one of the earliest entries to his journal, the protagonists more than hints at the borderline state of a melancholic psychosis. Hal acknowledges his fascination with timelessness, death—and with Barry Gorman. From the outset the death drive and the life-giving sex drive are inter-related.

> I must be mad.
> I should have known it all the time.
> If your hobby is death, you must be mad.
> . . . . .
> I have no interest in dead bodies. What interests me is Death. Capital D. Dead bodies scare me.
> <u>Correction</u>: One dead body [Barry Gorman's] did terrible things to me. (9)

Hal's terror revolves not so much from the death of a body which was once his friend, but from that friend's seeming betrayal and the confusion surrounding Hal's own identity. Hal (and the reader) questions his sense of identity and meaning by seeking answers to such questions as Am I a homosexual? Can love last? What is love? Chambers raises some profound questions with his readers, and the argument that he is conscious of the readers' needs to find their own selves in his works is clearly revealed in the Kurt Vonnegut quotation that precedes Part One: "We are what we pretend to be, so we must be careful what we pretend to be."

The book opens with a newspaper clipping headed "Grave Damage," which describes vandalism in a cemetery. As the novel unfolds, the reader recognizes the pun in the title and the "grave" damage done to the hero's psyche, part of which lies buried in the "grave" of his beloved friend Barry. Chambers' authorial voice encompasses different functions of language: newspaper clippings, private journal entries, and a social worker's report. The tri-levelled narrative seethes with a dark energy. In the final analysis, it provides a robust texture for a Kristevan thesis, which asserts that the writer must bear "witness to what the unconscious (through the screen of the mother) records of those clashes that occur between the biological and social programs of the species" (*DL* 242).

Sexuality is always related to entering into the symbolic power of the word. The "child" in a Chambers' novel must relinquish the mother—must be abandoned, so to speak—in order to be accepted by the father, enter into the symbolic and become an "adult" capable of mastering language. Language-learning begins in sadness and the pain of loss. Separation from the mother and identification with this third party, the father, project the child into symbolization where language unfolds and where, after relinquishing the father, the "other" is discovered. But, as Kristeva explains, "the abandonment by the father—the symbolic 'other'—triggers a melancholy anguish that can grow to suicidal proportions" (*IBWL* 41).

Resisting the father's powerful symbolic function, indicated at the beginning of the novel when Hal admits "my father decided for me that I should take a summer job" (14), Hal finds an other in Barry Gorman. But Hal, fraught with disintegrating fusions of semiotic drives and symbolic functions, loses Barry at the novel's climax with Barry's death (suicide?). The novel's power emerges from Hal's study of those dissected evasions and confrontations which, after he anatomizes his sexual ambiguities, lead to his eventual transformation into a calm interiority—all the more compelling because it is the result of confusion, pain, and death.

The social worker's report tells us that Hal is "pretty" rather than "handsome," looks younger than his sixteen years, and dislikes his name: He "thinks Harry is even worse. He asked me to call him Hal. I gathered he had made the change only this summer, but he was cagey about telling me why" (25). Hal's confusion about his name augurs a deeper confusion about his gender preference, which he questions seriously after he has been rescued from drowning by Barry but which he had been questioning since he was seven. Friendship, for Hal, has long been an ideal and is equated with the can of magic beans of the "Jack and the Beanstalk" tale (42-44). When Barry, who is under the domination of a too-powerful mother, brings Hal home after the boating accident, Hal is subjected to her unusually maternal ministrations. Mrs. Gorman is the voyeuristic mother who violates the young male's privacy-in-nakedness.

Kristeva maintains that the mother is "a thoroughfare, a threshold where 'nature' confronts 'culture,'" but Barry's mother devalourizes her son (and Hal); she refuses to allow either to become "a gift to others ... an object destined to be a subject, an other" (*DL* 238-9). Before his sensuous, endometrial bath, Hal describes being stripped naked by Barry's mother who

> tugged my jeans and underpants down with one swift (and obviously practised) movement, finishing with an expert flick of the hands that slipped them under my feet...
>
> Mrs G. straightened up and stood back, appraising me as if I were a piece of sculpture she had just finished. (31)

The languages indicates Hal's awareness that he is in a transitional stage between understanding and not understanding: between being both subject and object at the same time. In his self-reflectiveness Hal is subject, but in Mrs. Gorman's appraisal of him he becomes an object.

Mrs. Gorman has her antecedent in Kristeva's Mrs. Da Vinci. In studying the typical configuration of a homosexual structure, Kristeva focuses on

Leonardo Da Vinci and his relationship with his mother: "His was a forbidden mother because she was the primordial seducer, the limit of an archaic, infantile joissance that must never be reproduced." She establishes Leonardo's diffident narcissism and his making a cult of the male body. As a painter in such works as *Madonna with the Carnation* and *Virgin and Child with St. Anne*, Leonardo makes the male infant the "real focus of pictorial space and narrative interest" (*DL* 244-45). The maternal figure is completely absorbed with her baby—much as Mrs. Gorman is totally obsessed with her "Bubby," her nickname for her son. And like his medieval counterpart, Barry never stops looking for a maternal phallus in the bodies of young men. He finds one in Hal who, after sharing a meal with Barry, records the beginning of his homosexual relationship:

> Afterwards I know Barry is sizing me up while I dress in his room. I know I am sizing him up too. And the more I see the more I like him. Which is one of the great conundrums: how do you *know* that you like someone in just a few minutes? How does it happen with this person so quickly and not with hundreds, thousands of other people who cross your path every year? I've thought about that a lot and still haven't a clue. Because it isn't just that you like the look of a face or the shape of a body or even how someone lives that makes them attractive. It's something else.... (55)

More than wondering whether the semiotic magnetism is one-sided, Hal tries to unravel the mysteries of sexual fascination and is stymied.

But Chambers does not trivialize the "something else" that attracts lovers, whether homosexual or heterosexual." *Dance on My Grave* dares the reader to come to grips with love's elusive "something else." Although the book has a distinctly sexual undertone, revealed chiefly in Chambers' exploration of the intimacy of private places—bedroom, bathroom, and borrowed clothing, especially underwear—Hal constantly questions the intimacy into which he has been drawn, always looking for an ideal friend—the "something else" beyond sex.

One night Barry surprises Hal by rescuing a suicidal drunk who is being robbed by a cab driver. Barry becomes the ministering mother, and Hal watches his friend bend down and carefully comb the abandoned, unconscious drunk's hair. As he does so, Hal realizes that the dishevelled intoxicant was "handsome," his face "well fleshed. Tender in sleep." He knows in the way Barry takes such obvious pleasure in tidying the sleeping man's hair, "why he had rescued him and why he had rescued me" (96). Hal is Barry's "Bubby."

Throughout the novel the reader, like the protagonist, is left to ponder that strange ingredient of "something else" which constitutes Hal's love. It is not only Hal's finding an ideal friend in Barry, or Barry's seeking escape from a powerfully possessive mother, in his tender, maternal care for the victimized; neither is it the two young men's love-making after a row with a motorcycle gang (148). The "something else" seems most problematic in the compelling perversity of Barry's request: "Whichever of us dies first, the other promises to dance on his grave" (151). For Barry the "something else" seems to be that short-lived but deathless moment of submission, when the lover does the loved one's bidding. Hal's promise to dance on his friend's grave is made solely to satisfy Barry. It is the only request Barry ever makes of Hal—the fleeting moment of love's total giving—and Barry seems to have lived only for that moment. Hal promises. "At that moment there was nothing I wouldn't have done for him." Then he adds, "it was a split lip on a bruised mouth that sealed the oath" (152).

Recognizing Hal as an intelligent, earnest student who tries intensely to understand the mysteries of life, love, and death, Barry counsels his friend not to be so inward but rather to learn to "laugh" at life (150). But the reader wonders if Barry, so conscious of the moment, laughs to escape from past memories. Is his fascination with time—especially the present moment, his compulsion for speed, for change, for crises—merely a cover-up for his guilt in not being able to escape from being his mother's Bubby? Why is Barry so attracted to the noise, power, and excitement of motorcycles? Speed is his being, his mania; he lives too fast for the simple physicality of his own being. He is energy, passion, feeling, entirely feeding on itself, frantically chasing experience in time; his is semiotic energy gone crazy. Charging through the self causes its destruction. Barry cannot be confined to time but, rather, must break through it to infinity. He must die. Perhaps that is why he asks Hal to dance on his grave.

The more controlled Hal, although puzzled by his friend's obsession with speed and time, intelligently sums up Barry's disregard for time past and time future when he reflects that "he [Barry] had no memory either.... He lived for the moment all the time, so memory was something he didn't need" (113). Hal is growing more conscious of time's effect on life. In his mental video, "[e]ach time the me that is me detached a little more the me that was me from the me that is me" (101).

New excitement lures Barry to a recent acquaintance of Hal's, a young Norwegian girl named Kari. Barry dates Kari, and Hal, realizing the consequences of his own infatuation with Barry, becomes insanely jealous; he knows that he has experienced "the awful daring of a moment's surrender." The realization causes him to explode in anger because he thinks he might be losing Barry's love. He had been warned of over-possessiveness: "You don't own me, kid" (175); furthermore, Barry tells the younger lad that he is "bored" with him.

> It's not what we do together that you want. It's me. All of me. All for yourself. And that's too heavy for me, Hal. I don't want to be owned, and I don't want to be sucked dry. Not by anyone. Ever. (179)

In a furious tantrum, Hal smashes up the Gormans' music shop where he is employed—thanks to Barry's good graces—and leaves on his bike. Fifty minutes later he learns that his friend Barry is dead, killed in a motorcycle accident.

In his disintegrating, melancholic state, Hal must work out the terrible burdens of sorrow, guilt, anger, and jealousy. He dances on Barry's grave, tears at the earth, trying to get at his dead friend, and is charged with interfering with a grave. In the special inquiry which is launched, Hal is urged to write the journal that proves to be his therapy as his words give materiality to experience. Writing his journal allows an objectification which by its distancing effect allows Hal to grasp its significance. Through the power of the word, his sexual dilemma is expressed—pressed out of his unconscious. Hal thus comes to a deeper understanding of his love for his friend.

Perhaps even more therapeutic than his journal is his friendship with Kari, who helps Hal explore his dependency. Because Barry's mother refuses to allow Hal to see her son's dead body, Hal, dressed as a girl under Kari's direction, visits his dead friend in the mortuary chapel posing as the devastated girlfriend of the deceased. The incident exposes Hal's melancholia and his confused subject/object transitional state. It also initiates Hal into transvestitism, a mode of acting whereby Hal can assume a feminine to Barry's masculine role. To be more precise, it allows Hal to reverse not only the Romeo-Juliet roles but also those of the mother-child. He, as Juliet/child/subject, gazes on Romeo's/the mother's/the object's dead body. Hal can now assume a maternal role to Barry, who was not so much an *other* as a *mother* to him. In this scene too, Barry has become a Thing—a dead corpse and Hal, as the melancholic mourner, has lost meaning:

> I am looking, staring. I am wishing. I am wishing for the body to move, the eyes to open, the mouth to speak, the hands to reach and touch.... I stare down from the cliff edge of my life at the shore of his death and feel the seductive tingling urge to plunge down through the separating space and join him. (219)

When Hal hurls himself at the body, the mortician, pulling at his dress to restrain him, discovers the boy in the girl's guise. The macabre humour of the incident allows Hal to see himself as he really is—dependent on the love of his friend. In his next entry his words indicate a new awareness of himself: "I have become my own character. I as I was, not I as I am now. Put another way: Because of writing this story, I am no longer now what I was when it all happened" (121).

Kari's assistance is even more profound when she wipes away all Hal's illusions about his attraction for Barry. She makes him recognize his dependency—that he had become Barry's child. In the recognition comes release.

> He decided everything for you, didn't he? Everything important. Where you should go, what you should do, how you should do everything. He even told you what to wear, how to comb your hair, what to eat. When he wasn't with you, you waited for him to be there again. When you were with him you did whatever he wanted. (244)

Kari helps Hal to see that Barry had been right when he accused him of being too possessive. Hal tried to make Barry into something he never was: a superior being able to take charge of Hal—a mother. In reality, Barry was just as dependent as Hal. "Perhaps," Kari remarks, "we even invent ourselves. Make ourselves appear to be what we want to be" (246). The "something else" that attracts us to the significant other insures that the self shared is never diminished. Kari, not Barry, gives Hal a sense of his real self, which allows him to get on with his life with an enlarged vision and a deeper appreciation of his own, mysterious process of becoming. Hal is transformed. We make ourselves what we are, but, as Chambers suggests through Hal, the tragedy is to think that we are already made.

> I have written all this so you can see how I got to be what I am. But that is not what I am any more because what I am now is someone who is making sure that he is no longer influenced by what made him what he has become.
>
> The only important thing is that we all escape our history. (252)

These are the last words in the book. But how can we all escape our history? Is it simply a matter of learning from the lived moment because we know that it can never be repeated exactly? That one's personal history maintains an extraordinary particularity? That we are always becoming something that we were not? Or does history, as a record of time, allow us to distances ourselves from experience, to objectify it and so to understand it? Or perhaps the history referred to by Hal is our sexual history? As Kristeva reminds us, our sexuality is "perverse"; we are "narcissistic, incestuous, masochistic, sadistic, patricidal, and naturally attracted to or repelled by physical and moral types different from our own, hence aggressive toward others" (*IBWL* 48). We may not always be able to escape our history, but we can finally recognize it as a construct. Chambers, like Kristeva, believes that we can "make do" with human nature as it is, and that love is a "more effective, profound, durable treatment than electroshock therapy or psychotropic drugs" (48). Hal seems to have escaped his history. He accepts his homosexuality. It is not to Kari but to Spike, another male friend, that Hal turns at the end of the novel—still looking for his elusive childhood dream of the "can of magic beans."

Chambers' novels are timeless and do not have tidy endings. As the author remarks, "None of my writing, whether fictional or critical, is either an end in itself or ever comes to an end" (*Booktalk* 115). *Dance On My Grave*, like *Breaktime*, dares the reader to come to grips with the elusive "something else" that is beyond sex. Both novels have lives of their own and force the reader to search out the meanings of unanswered questions. In both *Breaktime* and *Dance on My Grave*, Chambers' melancholic characters create their own meanings. His works are revelations; they are like guideposts for scared, isolated, socially inept teens who need to be reassured that feeling deeply, experiencing sexual attraction, and even feeling suicidal are simple manifestations of humanity's on-going process of becoming. Through imaginative intelligence, his characters tell stories about themselves: Ditto in writing his breaktime experience and Hal in his journal about his homosexual relationship.

Chambers continued the search for insights into subjectivity in *Now I Know* (1987), wherein the protagonist, Nik Frome, is transformed by what he believes. As in his other two novels, the author is implicated, and Chambers extends beyond and reshapes his own subjectivity. As Kristeva maintains, "the work of art is a kind of matrix that makes its subject" (Meisel 131).

The novel's introduction captures the mingled awe and terror of that moment when the meaning of death is first realized. Nicholas (Nick, NIK [Now I Know]) Frome, who believes in himself but not in God, is taking a bath one night when the thought of his mortality dawns on him; he is seventeen years old and "no fool." Realizing he is "a separate, individual, unique and self-knowing person who would one day snuff it" (9), he vomits in his bath at the thought of his own extinction. With this incident the reader is plunged into a macabre tale of death, pain, rebirth, and faith.

Like Chambers' other novels, *Now I Know* unfolds in a three-fold manner: Nik's notebook (a repository for words), Julie's tapes, and the narration itself, which tells a simple detective story. According to Kristeva, all these forms of expression are valuable as a semiological activity, for the opportunity to screen one's ideas from another's appraisal, and for the production of novelistic fiction. On a first reading, the novel may appear to be religious fiction; it is certainly the author's clearest statement of a secular Christianity. The word is made flesh not by the power of a Creator God through the action of a Holy Spirit in the flesh of Jesus Christ, but rather by the power of the human creator (poet, artist, sign crafter) using his imagination to bring forth a word or sign. Kristeva notes, "Whatever phylogenetic relations there may have been between the sexual function and the development of language, it is clear that the two are closely dependent on one another; symbolism has a powerful influence on sexuality…" (*IBWL* 46).

Clearly, sex and language are linked in the relationship between Nik and Julie. Nik loves Julie, the mystic, who is angry at the destruction of the earth by the threat of atomic power. When she is injured in a demonstration, Nik enters into the mystery of pain and acts out the crucifixion. Through Julie, Nik also learns to understand the mystery of faith. "Now I know," Julie murmurs in a tape she makes for Nik from her hospital bed and in which she quotes Nina from Chekhov's *The Seagull:*[7]

> now I understand, my dear, that in our calling, whether we are writers or actors, what matters most is not fame, nor glory, nor any of the things I used to dream of. What matters most is knowing how to endure. Know how to bear your cross and have faith. I have faith and it doesn't hurt so much any more. (214)

The reader is not certain whether Nik lives out his faith. But what is certain is Nik's growing absorption with language, especially the relationship between the language of story and reality, a relationship which is intensified by the way Chambers (in Nik's notebook) spells the word "crucifiction." Chambers connects all life, all time, with the meaning of the word, the WORD made flesh. Fiction is the divine flesh of individual existence.

Thus, as enchanted as Nik is with Julie and his strong sexual need of her, he is also enchanted with story and with words. Words are alive. "They have bodies," he remarks. "You can see them, and you can like the look of them or not, just as I like the look of Nik.… the two tall letters protect the little eye" (57).[8] The word *selah*, for another example, has an endless fascination for him and he uses the word repeatedly throughout his story. *Selah*, Nik explains in his notebook, is

> A Hebrew word of unknown meaning … I do like words of unknown meaning, because they can mean anything you want them to mean. The dic. does say, though, that *selah* probably had something to do with an instruction in music. Like saying: Pause here. Which makes it very suitable for this songandance. (25)

Further on, he continues his speculation on words—how words produced on the word processor are different from words you write on paper. They are "different," "not so much your own," "less dangerous." His thinking on words leads Nik to reflect on the bombing at which his girlfriend Julie is almost killed, and the only way he can think "without breaking into a sweat" or "bursting into tears," is to record it, "look at it in words held away from me," not mine, but themselves—OTHER.

> Words words words. I like words. Begin to like words more than people. Not like: LOVE.
>
> Love: that which cannot be done without; wish always to be with, be part of, belong to, know intimately inside and out, entirely, WHOLE-LY, for ever and ever amen.
>
> Shining bright words in amazing patterns of endless variety. Drawings of the inside of my head. Selah bloody selah. (115-16)

The word *selah* thus serves as a pause, a breathing space in the novel's song, because the narrative flow constantly shifts from Nik's notebook to Julie's tapes and letters, and thence to the narrator's recitation. In this way we get a kaleidoscopic view of a past, present, and future which are somehow all interconnected, as we have seen in the cruciform depiction of the plot at the beginning of the novel.[9] Nik's narrative maintains a sequential chronology, while Julie's is more dependent on how the past shapes the present and the future. At one point she remarks,

> I'm beginning to think we only know who we are, only know ourselves, through our memories. I mean, think what it would be like if we couldn't remember anything. We wouldn't be able to learn anything. We wouldn't even be able to learn from the mistakes we

> make all the time, because we wouldn't be able to remember our mistakes no matter how painful they were. (38)

Memory feeds on the past, but because time is omnivorous, it consumes the present too, so that we are all children of the future in a never-ending process of becoming.

With Aidan Chambers, love is the Great Enabler which allows lovers their selfhoods. Whether it is parental, fraternal, or sexual love, all those in love must be the enablers of the other. Not the surrendering of bodies but the surrendering of love's enemies—possessiveness, jealousy, greed in passion—these are the poisoners of love. As Julie tries to explain it:

> In the love you wanted of me, Nik, two people come together and make themselves one. Whereas it seems to me the love Jesus is telling us to have for one another is the love of two friends: the love of distinctness, of separateness. Neither wants to dominate. Neither wants to be dominated. The desire in the love of friendship is the desire of the other's freedom.
>
> . . . . .
>
> You want your friend to be as perfectly herself as she can be. (205)

Perhaps echoing Chambers' own uneasiness with twentieth-century existence, Julie "wants to change our way of life for the better of poor people, and the sick, and the oppressed." She is "against those who keep all the power and wealth to themselves" (138). And like Chambers, she is uncomfortable in this world: "However much I love the life I know, I've never really felt that I belong here. I mean I've never felt that the world is my home" (139). No wonder Julie (and Chambers) lives in the world of the imagination, in a distinct separateness, and why she re-creates old words like "belief" which Julie, breaking it up into "be" and "lief," defines as the "will to give all your attention to Living with loving gladness in the world you think really does exist" (231).

At the beginning of the novel, Nik retches in his bath at the thought of his own death. At the end, having already lost his old life through his "crucifixion/crucifiction" in a garbage dump (214-217), he experiences transformation, a "resurrection," the saving of his life, by his renewed attention to living joyfully in the world—as it is. Through Julie's pain, and re-enacting the mystery of pain, Nik learns compassion—the ability to feel solidarity with a fellow human being, to accept his place in time—past, present and future—and to allow its rhythms to harmonize life's experiences.

In the silence of their sacred separateness, Julie and Nik become friends, not lovers. They continue re-creating their own worlds through the power of the word: Nik's poems appearing under the enlarged title "Making Light of Leafing" (an obvious play on Julie's "lief") which contains two poetic attempts, "Eye Saw," harking back to his fascination with the letter "I" in his own name and enabling him to create meaning from his own experience in time.

Illustrations of the word surprise the reader throughout Chambers' fiction. If Hal is typing up a report, the report appears in typed script; if Ditto receives a letter from his father, it is legitimately reproduced in cursive writing. If Nik draws a picture of two cones kissing, the pen and ink illustration appears.[10] But like any creative artist, Chambers is re-making the world in his own image and likeness. He "balloons" scraps of script, breaking ordinary linear sequence on the page in order to generate messages like "Every I is a You; every you is an I," or "Think afterward on the story" (235). Thus, on the human level, the word is made flesh again by the power of its creators to use their imaginations to bring forth healing wisdom and hope. In a sense, melancholic, depressive writers, as seen in Chambers' novels, become their own therapists.

In her last essay of *In the Beginning Was Love*, Kristeva affirms what Chambers has made obvious. Psychoanalysis, she claims, wherein the analysand tells a story to the analyst, "is the modest if tenacious antidote to nihilism in its most courageously and insolently scientific and vitalist forms" (63). Chambers seems to have caught on to the analysand's story in combatting despair, and Nik gives expression to the hope found in the power of the word in the conclusion of his poem significantly entitled "Birthday Song."

Now I know
But
for
the poet
living in

ourselves
we
wouldn't
learn anything
end without end. (236)

Chambers doesn't hesitate to admit, however, that the word is made flesh through the influence of a woman. Helen in *Breaktime*, Kari in *Dance on My Grave*, and Julie in *Now I Know* are the agents who release within Ditto, Hal, and Nik respectively the freeing power by which they become (more fully) themselves. After communication with their girlfriends, whether sexually or verbally, the protagonists make straightforward decisions to re-orient their lives in favour of hope. They understand their present and believe that their future can be good. The woman figure liberates by unlocking within man that deepest energy for self-making, an energy that is, in the final analysis, irresistibly hopeful.

Chambers' belief in human freedom and the never-ending process of becoming insists on the necessity of hope. Life, confused as it is, is a joyful affair. So, like John Bunyan, the author of *The Pilgrim's Progress*, Aidan Chambers, the melancholic, confused Christian goes "not forth alone; for there [is] one whose name [is] Hopeful ... who joined himself unto him; and, entering into a brotherly covenant, told him that he would be his companion."[11] And Chambers has shared that companionship with us, his readers.

6

ROBERT CORMIER AND MONUMENTAL TIME

NO WRITER OF FICTION is less surprised by present-day malevolence, brutality, and the resultant hollowness of adolescent consciousness than Robert Cormier. With the publication of *The Chocolate War* (1974), originally intended for an adult audience,[1] Cormier destroyed forever the myth of an innocent childhood, which had been dictated by the adult's Rousseauistic, nostalgic perceptions. Uncovering the "bland face of evil" (Veglahn 12) and the corruption of power (Rees 156), Cormier forever obliterated the boundaries between the child's innocence and the adult's guilt. He faced what Kristeva terms "the real stakes of a discourse on childhood within Western thought"—stakes which involve "a wandering at the limits of the unthinkable" (*DL* 276). Cormier's fiction, bleak and ambivalent, dares to explore the despairing disposition arising from those imponderable questions: the child's "Where did I come from and where am I going?" and the adult's "What binds me to my past and what blinds me to its implications for the future?" Cormier has uncovered the violence and the void of human existence, but at the same time, subtly, almost imperceptibly, he reveals life-giving hope by unveiling the enduring, if enigmatic, figure of the mother and studying the ever-recurring pattern of escape from and return to her womb. Cormier's intertwining of escape and return, of hope and despair, of time past and time future has splendid reverberations with Julia Kristeva's weaving of linear with monumental time, an insight she explores in the essay "Women's Time" (1979).

In this essay, Kristeva analyzes three generations in the advancement of women; as Toril Moi explains in her introduction to the essay, the term "generation" has for Kristeva less a chronological than a spatial signification (Moi 186). In the first phase of their movement, women adapted to the male mode for mastery and entered into linear historical time; in the second phase, while recognizing the need for equality by synchronizing themselves in a history that was heretofore denied them, women rejected that linearity in favour of a cyclic temporality associated with female subjectivity. In the third phase, Kristeva combines the "insertion into history" mode with "the radical refusal of the subjective limitations imposed by this history's time on an experiment carried out in the name of irreducible difference" (195). Linear time is the time of history, time as project, teleology, departure, progression and arrival. Monumental time englobes the supra-national, socio-cultural ensembles within even larger entities; monumental time refers to eternity (187-189). Linking female subjectivity to both cyclical and monumental time, Kristeva underscores the complex but transformative power of mothering. For her the mother's body provides the point where breast, light, and sound "become a *there*: a place, a spot, a marker" (*DL* 283). At the same time, because the mother denies the breast at weaning, the child's relation to the breast operates both as a form of identification and negation. It forms the nexus for a pattern of escape and return to the maternal body. Initially, however, the mother's face becomes the privileged receiver of laughter, and it is she who is forever active in leading the child from narcissism to time-and space-transcending love.[2]

Cormier's fiction also opens up a timelessness whose essence is love—essentially a forgiving love which consents to cancel out the bad times when the young are victimized by betrayals, by the vagaries of chance, and by death. His motif of loving forgiveness becomes ahistorical and regenerative. Like Cormier's, Kristeva's forgiveness is essentially regenerative. In *Black Sun*, Kristeva explores how, "staying the historical quest in the name of love, forgiveness discovers the regenerative potential peculiar to narcissistic satisfaction and idealization, both intrinsic to the loving bond" (205). But unlike Kristeva, Cormier's forgiveness partakes of the divine covenantal love, and that covenant between an all-forgiving God and His people echoes in the name given to the setting for all Cormier's novels—Monument. Not necessarily modelled on Leominster, Massachusetts (his actual hometown), Monument becomes a metaphor for Cormier's view of time and place, and for the centrality of forgiveness in transcending both. Because we live in two worlds—an inner, private, expressive world and the external world of time and place where we are impelled to repress, or at least control, natural impulses, emotions and desires—language sustains our living in both worlds. But even when we insert ourselves in the external language game, success in attaining self-identity is never assured. And for Cormier, as for Kristeva, perhaps place, more than time, exerts greater influence in determining identity.[3] Thus the recurrence of the mythical Monument carries its own ironic testament, since all Cormier's young protagonists seem to have no fixed place of abode save that which they occupy internally. From the particularity of that inner space, however, his protagonists fashion for themselves through language what Kristeva has termed "monumental" time (to distinguish it from mere linear time).

By limiting the role of the father figure in most of his plots and subtly but profoundly interjecting that of the mother, Cormier creates protagonists who learn to live both inside and outside of time. The journey motif of the exile baited by time becomes a remarkable device for taking on the modern world of the adolescent whose own proper place in that world is constantly shifting. The shiftable nature of time is also connected to the mutability of space so that the world of Cormier's characters changes in size—sometimes shrinking to the size of a bed or of a ping-pong ball. The fictional world of Monument necessarily becomes a paradigm of eternity, a legacy to one for whom language has become another womb which the subject returns to and escapes from in a life-long quest for a little more truth, a little more meaning.

Believing that we have no permanence in either time or place, and supported by a strong Catholic heritage, Cormier fashions an honest, if terrifying, vision of the world for his young audience. His paradise is beyond history; his exiled hero is the poet who creates a personalized salvation in searching for a goodness founded on love and whose summit is achieved in forgiveness. All his characters must learn how to forgive: parental and institutional failure, fate, disease, even death itself.

Forgiveness is central to Cormier's works. Forgiveness thwarts time's destructive power; it enables the self to be reconstituted by becoming accommodated to one's place in time. *The Chocolate War* (1974), for example, in the persona of the young protagonist Jerry Renault, poses an existential question: why should the individual "disturb the universe"[4] when paternal figures—his father and the brothers who teach him in school—all fail him? But the creative marvel of the novel is that through the figure of the dead mother, occupying no real place or time in the novel, Cormier's young hero experiences a salvific presence that enables him to forgive and so become accommodated to his temporary, impermanent place in time.

Jerry Renault dares disturb the universe by refusing to sell fifty boxes of chocolates to raise funds for his school, Trinity High. His idealism, blazoned in a poster thumb-tacked to his locker, shows a wide expanse of beach, a lone star, and a small solitary figure walking on the beach. At the bottom of the poster is the caption: Do I dare disturb the universe? (97). Thus, when the devious Brother Leon, an assistant master at Trinity, whose voice "like a whip" asks whether he will sell the chocolates, Jerry answers, "No. I'm not going to sell the chocolates." At that moment linear time explodes: "Cities fell. Earth opened. Planets tilted. Stars plummeted. And the awful silence" (89). With his declaration of independence, Jerry confronts evil as represented by Brother Leon, who perverts the use of academic time for personal greed; by Archie, who manipulates time to aggrandize his power; and by Janza, the arch bully, who realizes that tyrannizing the weak provides the maximum interest on time. In the novel's climax, after Archie stages a fight between Janza and Jerry in which the latter is severely beaten—spiritually as well as physically—Jerry, in his agony, whispers to Goober, his football friend, "It's a laugh, Goober, a fake. Don't disturb the universe, Goober, no matter what the posters say" (187).

What makes *The Chocolate War* so riveting is that at the end goodness endures but does not triumph; forgiveness is just being learned. Jerry Renault has only begun to understand that chronological time is indifferent. It breeds both the corruption of his mother's cancer and the beauty of his ideal—to dare disturb the universe; it generates the golden-haired girls of his adolescent fantasies and the black-hearted, blackguard personae of Brother Leon and Archie. Loveliness and ugliness, virtue and vice—these abstractions are actualized depending on how one lives out one's place in time. Only through language, through the inner dialogues in which they are impelled to question themselves as thinking, speaking subjects, do Cormier's heroes learn how to transform mere chronological to monumental time—not as measured by the logical passage of the minutes and hours of everyday life, but rather by the space of those personal experiences which involve the making of choices.

Monumental time does not ignore actual time; indeed, *The Chocolate War* contains innumerable references to specific, chronological time. At the beginning of the novel, the football coach tells Jerry to "show up tomorrow … three o'clock sharp" for football practice (9). Archie, the brains behind the Vigils and Jerry's arch enemy, has only until four o'clock to think of two more names and two more assignments (16). Goober, Jerry's friend, begins his frightening, Vigil-assigned work at three in the afternoon (45). Jerry is summoned to the Vigil meeting for two-thirty (122). After his beating Jerry gets the first terrifying crank call at 3:00 p.m., next at 11:00 p.m. and then 2:00 a.m. (139). References to relative time are likewise evident, as when Obie realizes that Archie was "keeping him here, stalling, killing time" (11). The Goober rightly views the Vigils as "a midnight word" (116). Likewise, Jerry's mother had died in the spring, "suddenly, at three-thirty in the afternoon" (48). Cormier rarely forgets that we are all the puppets of chronological time. But even when he slips into an obvious cliché, for example, the "moment of truth," the cliché clearly has particular significance to other episodes or images which oftentimes signify a period of birth or rebirth to goodness. His heroes are doomed to virtue—expressed by grace-filled acts of either self-sacrifice, generosity, or courage—as if to prove that, no matter what the suffering, goodness does exist and that each generation must replenish its store. Though occupying linear time by living in a definite historical era and belonging to a particular socio-cultural milieu—white, urban, North American, Christian—Cormier's young people have their own particularity. It is nonetheless obvious that they are placed in a diagonal relationship to similar adolescents all over the world. In so far as they belong to monumental history, they not only act as North American adolescents but also echo the universal traits of their structural place in the ever-enduring process of reproduction and representation ("Women's Time" *DL* 190). These ubiquitous traits result from universal choices common to humankind.

Thus, the choice between good and evil results from our reading of the people and events we encounter in specific times and places. Carter, one of Jerry Renault's colleagues at Trinity High School in Monument, illustrates the difficulties involved in making choices that transcend time. As the nominal head of the Vigils (itself a school society whose name ironically suggests time—the eve of a holy day or the night during which a young man spent long hours in prayer prior to taking his knightly vows), Carter is not evil, but he recognizes evil's manifestations in Archie who "repelled him in many ways but most of all by the way he made everybody feel dirty, contaminated, polluted" (175). Carter thinks of himself as one of the "good guys," yet he is controlled by Archie. And Jerry himself recognizes his own contamination, that he is becoming "another animal, another beast, another violent person in a violent world." Even more disturbing, Jerry realizes that "he had allowed Archie to do this to him" (183). He has reneged on one of those casual choices proffered by chronological time.

Only when Jerry lies beaten on the football field, which becomes the actual battle scene of the chocolate war, does he begin to understand, painfully, the relationship between linear and monumental time. The incident carries with it the birth of a new consciousness which Jerry is reluctant to accept. Chronological time does not matter here. There is no mention of a specific date or hour. That is why, when during the fight Goober calls to his friend, "Come on, Jerry," the emphasis is directional, in the adverb "on." Place supersedes time. But "Come on where?" Jerry has escaped from linear time and has taken refuge and found peace in the womb. "He liked it here, in the darkness, moist and warm and wet" (186). Here, as in a previous incident when Jerry fought with Janza, the imagery describing the aftermath of the violence also supports the birth motif. Then, too, he was cocooned in a womb-like, semiotic existence: "Sweet, sweet in the dark, safe. Dark and safe and quiet." Jerry came to consciousness realizing that he had been "crooning softly as if he were singing himself a lullaby. Suddenly, he missed his mother. Her absence formed tears on his cheeks" (156). In both brutal incidents Cormier suggests with birth imagery, the dark, private place of the womb where once Jerry struggled downward into chronological time; now in his suffering, he lies defeated seeking a return to the mother, the same soft, secret place where he will feel safe. From that warm security will come more pain, and blood, and suffering, yes, but also his regeneration and renewal—his birth into monumental time. Jerry is called into a world where forgiveness is the ultimate proof of adulthood, a thetic stage which is itself impermanent.[5]

In his suffering Jerry becomes a salvific figure both for the Goober and for the reader; and the imagery throughout the novel suggests, perhaps too obviously, the suffering Saviour who counselled forgiveness as a corollary to God's forgiveness of sinful mankind (Mt 6:14; Mk 11:25; Lk 17:3). At the beginning of the novel when Jerry reports for tryouts for the football team, "The shadows of the goal posts sprawled on the field like grotesque crosses" (14). And at the end, when surveying the field where Jerry had been "crucified," Obie again "looked at the goal posts and they reminded him of something. He couldn't remember" (188). Clearly Brother Leon, standing "at the top of the hill, a black coat draped around his shoulders," is a creature of darkness, a Judas figure whose "face was like a gleaming coin" (184). And Goober, like the weak Pilate, "washed his hands of the school and its cruelties." He couldn't bear to witness Jerry's daily humiliations; he couldn't accept another's pain and the agony of his own betrayal and defection (179). Goober's space has shrivelled to the size of a bed (190).

But just as the representation of Christ's crucifixion represents a guilt that is visited upon the Son by the Father, so does Jerry's cruel passion, in which he is unaided by his father, signify a new awareness of the pain of human existence and the symbolization of language. Commenting on the sadness of young children prior to the acquisition of language, Kristeva notes that the child's renunciation of the maternal paradise in which every wish had been gratified is a condition of being accepted by the father and of beginning to talk. If it is true, she explains, that language begins in the mourning inherent in the evolution of subjectivity, the abandonment of the father triggers a melancholy anguish—such as is experienced by Jerry Renault at the end of the novel when he is "crucified"—abandoned and defeated. Kristeva sees in the "scandal" of the cross not only the embodiment of the psychic and physical suffering that irrigates our lives, but also, and even more profoundly, the essential alienation that conditions our access to language and symbolization (*IBWL* 40-41). Thus, although suffering and death appear in all his novels, Cormier does not deny hope. Indeed, the art of his novels represents the triumph of language and of hope—both of which are birthed in either pain or blood or both. Art does not seek to change present or past suffering, but rather to challenge it, to transform it. Choosing to dare is a dreadfully personal affair and entails enormous risks and fears. But to Cormier it is just as fallacious to have a hope without fear and dread as it is to have faith without a nagging doubt. Jerry Renault experiences a new birth at the end of *The Chocolate War*, but his is an excruciating travail, and the pain prevails.

Not until the sequel to *The Chocolate War* do we learn that Jerry has learned forgiveness and accepted his place in his Monument world. Although *Beyond the Chocolate War* (1985) was written more than ten years later, it seems to enflesh the original exploration of the relationships among place, time, and evil that was gestating in Cormier's mind even as he wrote the first novel. It certainly raises deeper, more complex issues than the 1974 work. Even the title sparks a question: why did Cormier call the book "beyond," not "after," *The Chocolate War? After* refers more specifically to linear time: "later" or "following"; whereas *beyond* carries the idea of monumental time—it is uncircumscribed: "outside," "farther." Certainly Jerry Renault has moved beyond the sordid events of the war that was waged during the early months of his first year at Trinity. He has rejected the power-hungry, violent world of Brother Leon, Archie Costello, and Emile Janza. He has understood the time- and space-transcending power of forgiveness.

That sort of timelessness is encapsulated in the little country church of Quebec—solitary, tranquil, separated from Monument's "dull and ugly [mills]," its "drab tenement houses and grim factories" (3). Jerry has found rest in the symbolic "Talking Church" (107). Perhaps it is the "relentless" space-defying wind which speaks to him in a Pentecostal fashion and makes the church seem timeless. The walls and windows chattering to each other make him smile (his first smile in ages). In his escape to solitude he returns to that semiotic space of his childhood and "the old French prayers his mother had taught him long ago—'Notre Père,' 'Je Vous Salue, Marie'—the words meaningless but comforting somehow" (107). While sitting quietly there, aware of "the afternoon sun [losing] its warmth," and "the church [growing] colder" (108), he has gone "beyond" the linearity of time's inexorable progression. The period has been healing: "So the winter passed, a succession of peaceful days and evenings, Monument and Trinity existing in another world, another time, having nothing to do with him" (108).

Once back in Monument, Jerry wishes he could return to the timelessness of the Talking Church but knows that would be impossible (109). Nor is it necessary: he can endure "the goons" and Archie Costello not by fighting them but by outlasting them. He has survived the birth pains of entrance into a deeper level of the symbolic; he can live not only within time—doing what "the goons" want—but also outside it (224). One of the reasons Jerry goes back to Trinity, feeling stronger morally as well as physically, is his new awareness of forgiveness, which does not come easily or quickly. It needs time.

When Goober first asks Jerry to forgive him for his betrayal and admits, "I let you down. Let you face Archie Costello and Emile Janza and the Vigils by yourself" (60), Jerry can't talk about the chocolate war; he has not had enough time to absorb the pain. But later in a telephone conversation, when Goober again brings the subject up and asks, "Do I get another chance?", Jerry has obliterated the incident from chronological time. He has discovered forgiveness: "You don't need another chance, Goob. You're my friend" (150). When he hangs up, he is "weak with relief, breathing his thanks. His thanks to whom? God, maybe, thinking of the Talking Church in Canada," where he understood the relationship between measured temporality and perpetuity, between linear and monumental time (152).

Forgiveness is not a passive surrender to things as they are; rather, it is an active resistance to the thing that destroys love and peace in one's place in time. Jerry remains exceptional because he asserts the particularity of his own place in his epoch. His colleagues at Trinity have yet to learn that integration. Even the Goober must be counselled by Jerry to study time: "Wait a minute, Goob. You're going too fast … sit and wait awhile." (191-2). Goober plans to leave his place at Trinity; Jerry will remain there. For Cormier, space, as well as time, is entirely mutable, without definition, until given direction, boundaries. The Goober sums up the human dilemma as he muses: "Who am I? What am I doing here, on this planet, in this city, in this house?" (160). Jerry and Goober will define their places in the interval of their lives and continue to struggle in a totally corrupt and corrupting world.

In *Beyond the Chocolate War*, it is in the students at Trinity, itself a microcosm of the world, that Cormier most deeply explores the relationship between time and space, evil and the void. Thus Carter, stereotypically macho and proud of his athletic achievements, has no sense of appreciation of personal space nor any appreciation of personal history: he "felt a void within himself, an emptiness." He has no escape except "Archie Costello and his terrible words" (69). David Caroni, another Trinity High student, refusing to accept the realities of time and space, senses his life as a "sunless, airless desert" (71). An excellent student, David chose to be manipulated by Brother Leon, who threatened him with an F grade if he did not reveal Jerry Renault's reasons for not selling the chocolates. David buckled under the pressure of the moment and became an informer. Now he can't forgive himself. He will not accept his own weakness and failure and, as a result, his life has no meaning. He "had found the secret of killing time by filling up the minutes and hours of his life with little actions" (138) and thus withdraws from his place in time. He ceases to exist to himself, even avoiding his own reflection (73).

For David, life has become a waiting game, merely a means of revenge. His one source of satisfaction comes when he confronts Brother Leon and puts a knife to the headmaster's throat: "this is what he had been waiting for all this time." When Leon begs to talk, David says, "It's too late for talk" (235). To Leon nothing was "irrevocable." But to David, "some things were" (238). Suicide offers the ultimate escape from "his utterly useless place" in a despicable world where even teachers are corrupt. As he stands above the railroad tracks, David thinks, "This was the best way, the clean way, a flight through air, like a dive from the high board … and then beautiful blessed oblivion" (257). Jumping from the bridge, destroying space and time, a "sob escaped him … But it was too late now to cry" (258). In that last second of time, he asked the universal question, "What am I doing *here?*" (258). And in that split second of illumination Cormier suggests that David "did not mean" to destroy himself (258). Up to that point, he could not transcend the linearity of his physical existence; that is, he could not actualize his ideal. His motto, "After the Rain, the Rainbow" was "[s]tupid…. Words. Meaningless. Vowels and consonants. Letters." (72). So was the verse he had memorized: "Look thy last on all things lovely,/ Every hour" (72). Despite moments of startling surfacings "as if he were emerging from deep waters into sunlight," David surrenders to that sterile place which knew "no sun, no sky, nothing" (71). He could not go *beyond* the chocolate war; he could not comprehend monumental time. Thus, David and Jerry offer reverse apprehensions of time and space. Jerry will sell the "damn chocolates" when he returns to Trinity, because he has understood that ideals are never fully actualized. Like David, he will continue to long for escape from the dullness of ordinary linear temporality. "It would be nice," he muses, "to avoid the world ... to leave it and all its threats and unhappiness." But at the same time he understands that good people are needed "to fight the Archie Costellos and even the Brother Leons of this world" (160). These two are the arch villains in both *The Chocolate War* and *Beyond the Chocolate War.*

Archie and Leon's fascination with evil, their deliverance to it, results from their manipulation of those garments of eternity, time and space. And caught between these victimizers and their victims—Jerry, David, and the Goober—are Obie and Carter who, until they themselves are victimized, do not understand the face of evil as revealed by Brother Leon and Archie Costello. Of these two, Archie, although younger, is the more vile and violent, perhaps because he is the more intelligent, as is evident when he explains, both to Carter and Obie, the true nature of evil. There is some hope that these adolescents will reject it because they have seen its effects in the lives of Brother Leon and Archie.

Brother Leon, by his very vocation, would have been counselled to surrender to the divine will as it manifested itself in his situation as a religious Brother. In fact, he is time's manipulator, avid in his pursuit of power. Leon, "of the swift short steps," masters past, present, and future at Trinity by acceleration. He confesses to Archie, "I don't want to dwell on the past" (44), and events prove that he hypocritically tries to control the future. He is always associated with speed. With his quick and sudden classroom movements, in which a student was usually the loser, Leon's pointer or a piece of chalk could fly (through space) across the room faster than a speeding bullet; so could his eyes flash with malice or quicken with a cold intelligence and without an ounce of pity or mercy. (37). Yet Leon fears not being able "to keep up with the times"—not being "moderately mod" (38). Only Archie upsets Leon's sense of control when he has the Vigils plan to sabotage the Bishop's visit (79). In a confrontation with Archie, Leon is a master of words which "snap and crackle" through the room (78). But Archie knows that Leon's bombast screens his cowardice and jealousy. In his exercise of power Leon belittles others—especially students. Certainly he completely destroys David Caroni by obliterating his future with a failing grade. But when Leon is pinned against the wall with David Caroni's knife to his throat, he is immobilized, "paralysed by fear" (234). In another revealing episode, Archie uncovers Brother Leon's jealousy—"the hook" used to bait Leon. Jealousy had dictated Leon's removal of the "good" brothers—Eugene and Jacques. The final chapter, however, reveals Leon losing control, unmasked as the hypocrite he really is. When discussing the tragedy of David Caroni's suicide, Brother Leon takes no responsibility for the death; he blames the students for their neglect and indifference. He makes a mockery of forgiveness by not acknowledging guilt. Unctuously, he intones, "I have searched my heart and have sought forgiveness for my ignorance and found it," but the students recognize his hypocrisy and guilt in making everything and everyone at Trinity miserable (271). "Those who ignore history are doomed to repeat it," Leon continues (272). Ironically, and precisely because his cowardice and jealousy blind him, Brother Leon learns nothing from the lessons of time.

Vile as Brother Leon is, he is no match for the cold, passionless, inhuman Archie Costello, who knows his own power as a manipulator. Archie completely dominates time because he has eliminated its effects by anaesthetizing his feelings. Archie has no passion. He seems to be a walking bomb—a human detonator of time and space. When he enters the Vigils' meeting place, "All conversation ceased ... everyone was waiting for an explosion to occur" (112). His "leadership of the Vigils was a thing of delicate calibration, and he knew instinctively when to call meetings, to adjourn them, or to allow the Vigil members to go their way" (174). Even when Archie has sex with Jill Morten he is in full control: it is "a moment they abandoned so swiftly that they barely had a memory of its existence a minute later" (146). Archie enjoys the disruption—even the destruction—of any ordered progression. A sudden heat wave, distorting the spring, causes him to love the heat because "other people were so uncomfortable" (173). In Archie's presence, time "falls apart" (204). Obie expresses his admiration for Archie's command. "That's what was intriguing about Archie—you never knew what was coming next" (10); he "never forgot" (115). Archie regulates time to such an extent that he "never said hello or goodbye" (69): he has no beginning nor any end.

Thus, the real evil influence in both *The Chocolate War* and *Beyond the Chocolate War* is Archie Costello, the author of deceit, who "always envisioned lurkers, predators, watchers in the shadows or around corners, peeking out of windows, waiting behind closed doors." He is fully convinced that it "was a rotten world, full of treachery and evil, and you had to be on your toes at all times, ready for combat, to outfox, outwit, outdeal everybody else" (*BCW* 40). In this sense only, Archie is an admirable character because he recognizes that only human virtue or vice can control time. Archie thinks vice is more powerful. His philosophy is summed up in a graffiti motto: "*Do Unto Others, Then Split*" (40). That may be why the dominant image associated with him is that of a knife. Getting out of his space-controlling car, his "thin body" appeared "knife-like and lethal silhouetted against the rays of a spotlight above the garage door" (206).

The Archies of this world endure, as both Carter and Obie, the victims of Archie's manipulations, come to realize. He transforms both young men from perpetrators of violence into its victims (11), and he delights in letting "the victim be his own torturer" (174). Carter realizes that through Archie's manipulations, he has become an informer, a traitor (101). At one point Archie deigns to sum up the secret of evil's power: "Everybody likes the smell of his own shit.... That's the story of life" (69). Obie, too, recognizes Archie's power, which has driven him to the point of attempted murder (261). Archie insists that Obie must take responsibility for his own actions. Then follows one of the eeriest illuminations in the book, for Obie comes to recognize the truth of Archie's words, the timelessness of evil in the world as well as of its universal ubiquity. "But what about you?" Obie asks. "You just go on and on. What the hell are you?" Archie's response is both honest and chilling:

> "I am Archie Costello. ... And I'll always be there, Obie. You'll always have me wherever you go and whatever you do. Tomorrow, ten years from now. Know why, Obie? Because I'm you. I'm all the things you hide inside you. That's me—" (264)

Perhaps this is the darkest moment in *Beyond the Chocolate War*. Carter, like the reader, recognizes evil's devastating impact and power. But Carter had thought graduation would be the end of Archie Costello, the Vigils, and everything rotten in this world (208). It won't be, as Archie Costello intelligently explains:

> That was the secret of the world's agony, and the reason crime—and, yes, sin—would always prevail. Because the criminal, whether a rapist or a burglar, loves his crime. That's why rehabilitation was impossible. You had to get rid of the love, the passion, first. And that would never happen. (45)

Archie loves not another but his crime. He can't love another because he is too narcissistic. Nor is his narcissism directed toward the mother, because, according to Kristeva, the mother's love, rather than calling the child back to the maternal body, moves it toward the maternal desire, "toward the symbolic of an other" (*TL* 31). Archie is completely passionless—totally without love for another. He can go neither back to the semiotic mother nor move forward to the symbolic father. That immobility is the reason he is so evil.

But the final chapter of *Beyond the Chocolate War* proves that ordinary humanity still recognizes the power of choice, offered by the circumstances of time and place. Henry Malloran, an ordinary student, shows his obstreperous disdain for the evil and deceit perpetrated by the Leons and Archies of this world in a remarkable scene in the school's assembly hall. Discussing the tragedy of David Caroni's suicide, Brother Leon utters all the usual platitudes associated with time and space: "Thus, remembering the past, let us go to our future.... The future counts..." (273). Listening to the hypocritical jargon, Henry Malloran, apparently more interested in his chocolate-chip cookies than in the platitudes, pitches a tomato which bursts open fully on Brother Leon. In hurling a juicy, ripened fruit, Henry signals that Trinity's students have had enough of manipulators like Leon and Archie. Jerry Renault's daring to disturb the universe has taken hold; he has become a "symbol," as Obie admitted (32), even though Archie's evil-doing will continue in Janza and Bunting. But the throwing of that ripe tomato has an element of Kristevan jouissance about it.[6] It signifies the total enjoyment—physical, sensual, spiritual—which erupts when evil is surmounted and corruption exposed. What better image of triumphant jouissance than that full, ripe tomato exploding on Brother Leon!

Cormier leaves the reader with no illusions; evil has enormous power and is never defeated. However, the young have an amazing ability to appropriate the worst mysteries of the human heart. Perhaps that is why so many of

Cormier's heroes, sensitive and intelligent, aspire to be writers. Cormier realizes the "fundamental importance of idealization in the sublimational activity of writing." And Kristeva reminds us that the ideal "authorizes destructive violence to be *spoken* [written] instead of being *done.* That is sublimation, and it needs *for-giving*" (Kristeva, *BS* 200). Cormier's Jerry Renault is an excellent student in English, while Adam Farmer, the young hero of Cormier's 1977 novel *I Am the Cheese*, wants to be a writer (55) because he realizes the magic alchemy of words to fill in the "empty spaces," the "terrifying blanknesses behind and before him in the darkness" (80).

Space and time are terrifying to Adam because he has no place in either. Adam's past is a blank because his father, a victim of organized crime's revenge (144), has been given a new identity—that of an insurance man named Farmer—and a new place to live—the family is moved from Blount to Monument. Young Paul, now Adam, has no real identity, no permanent place. He is on a perpetual bike ride getting nowhere. As far as officialdom is concerned, Adam's existence is measured by psychiatric reports indicating progress, or the lack thereof. Adam is merely the cheese who stands alone in that ageless singing game, "The Farmer in the Dell."

Government agents, supposedly the protectors insuring a just society, operate *in loco parentis* and are the terrible villains in this novel. Certainly Mr. Grey, or Mr. Thompson, or the de-humanized, desensitized Agent 2222 has deprived Adam's mother and father of their place in time. As the Director of the Department of Re-Identification, he plays God in the lives of the Farmer family. He is their "creator" (172) and their "terminator" (221). Worse, he has condemned Adam to madness—to a bed in a psychiatric ward, a "suspended, isolated inhabitant of an unknown land, an unknown world" (92).

Adam begins and ends his story with an account of his trip from Monument to Rutterburg, Vermont in search of his father. The book, structured on the boy's narrative of his bike ride interspersed with taped reports of a pseudo-psychiatric nature, carries the circular images of wheel and reel as if to enforce the insane, merry-go-round nature of Adam's world. It becomes a journey into his past as he reveals how federal agents have "terminated" both his parents. The juxtaposition of the two narratives, interspersed with authorial commentary, represents two views of time: the spatial, maternal quality of Adam's life-sustaining, nursery-rhyme world, and the sterile linearity of the psychiatric narratives. In Adam's case, space exerts more power. Significant also are the protagonist's two names. The "Paul" of his original Delmonte identity, after the Paul of the great New Testament epistles, suggests the boy's symbolic function, his consciousness of the necessity of words, testimonies, reports, and telling to help him understand existence. "In the talking, the blank spots were filled in" (78). "Adam," the "farmer" of hope in a totally corrupt world of "murders and assassinations" (18) of insidious betrayals, intimates the new, modern man more conscious of the spatial power of the womb, who must rely on time as space, maternal space, in order to survive. His mother as well as his father led him back to the secret of his past; his mother, even more than his father, had been a "rebel" against Grey's intrusions into the intimacy of their lives (176). In their shared fear "love had been forged" (175), and in that love Adam found hope—not in a future dictated by mere chronology but in monumental time, eternity.

As soon as he confronts the horrors of his parents' deaths, and of not knowing "whom [he] can trust" (Bixler 16), Adam withdraws into an abnormal, psychotic state wherein he finds relief and begins the painful recitation of his bike-ride ordeal again and again and again. Three successive years have elapsed, but for Adam, since his mind has been destroyed, time has no meaning. The "rats" of logical, governmental expediency have eaten the cheese. His own termination is certain, as is encapsulated in the bureaucratic language of the final tape:

> Advisory #3:
>
> > Since subject A is final linkage between Witness #500-6 and File Data 865-01, it is advised that (a) pending revision of Agency Basic Procedures (Refer: Policy 979) Subject A's confinement be continued until termination procedures are approved; or (b) Subject A's condition be sustained until Subject A obliterates.
> > END TAPE SERIES OZKO16. (232-33)

Contrast this to the emotionally charged, courageous language of Adam's last entry, where the boy has transcended the mere linearity of chronological time by entering the emotionally charged jouissance of a language that lives on courage—an affair of the spirit.

> I am riding the bicycle and I am on Route 31 in Monument, Massachusetts, on my way to Rutterburg, Vermont, and I am pedalling furiously because this is an old-fashioned bike, no speeds, no fenders, only the warped tires and the brakes that don't always work and the handlebars with cracked rubber grips to steer with. A plain bike—the kind my father rode as a kid years ago. It's cold as I pedal along, the wind like a snake slithering up my sleeves and into my jacket and my pants legs, too. But I keep pedalling, I keep pedalling.... (234)

Hope has not died as long as Adam keeps pedalling.

Adam's will to live comes from the memories both of his girlfriend Amy and of his parents—particularly of his mother. On his never-ending bike ride he sings the song his father taught him when he was just learning to speak.

> I remember how he'd pick me up when I was just a kid and swing me almost to the ceiling, singing
>
> The wife takes the child,
>
> The wife takes the child...
>
> And then he'd gently place me in my mother's lap where she'd be sitting, knitting or reading, and I would curl into her body feeling warm and safe and protected from all the bad things in the world. (24)

Only by recapturing the scent of lilacs, which he associates with his mother and the springtime, does Adam re-experience the safety of the maternal womb. Through that memory he is exalted. As he sings the old nursery rhyme bicycling along Routes 119 and 131, Adam discovers that the day has become "suddenly glorious" (25). He realizes that nothing is more important than life, even though he must confront a horrific violence. Dark as this novel is, there is a radiance in the love for his parents, and for his girlfriend Amy, that allows young Paul/Adam to triumph over his enemies. His very madness and eventual death testify to the spiritual bonds of love that transcend time. In losing his life, as his parents have lost theirs before him, Paul witnesses that love which, though marred, broken, defeated, still generates the devotion linking generation to generation. And even in his hallucinatory bike ride, wherein the asylum's caretaker, Mr. Harvester, and other inmates become actors in his imaginary ride from Monument to Rutterburg, Adam does not lose his capacity to love and forgive. For the obese, ever-perspiring Mr. Hayes, who in Adam's view is a sexual pervert, he feels a generous sympathy: "For some reason, I look at the massive man and find myself saying, 'I'm sorry'" (156). No wonder Amy has given Paul/Adam still another name, "Ace." And his generosity of heart would once more elicit her comment, "[T]here's hope, Ace ... I see the possibility of laughter in your baby blues" (51).

Two other novels, *The Bumblebee Flies Anyway* and *Fade*, should be examined briefly to prove the centrality of forgiveness in Cormier's work. Kristeva reminds us that "Forgiveness is ahistorical" (*BS* 200); it transcends time. Because Cormier's writing produces a new awareness of the other's suffering, an awareness which necessitates a loving forgiveness, his work transforms time. "Is it not," Kristeva asks, "by *signifying* hatred, the destruction of the other, and perhaps above all his own execution, that the human being survives as a symbolic animal?" (*BS* 181). In *The Bumblebee Flies Anyway* and *Fade*, hate, once signified in writing, is made bearable. Barney Snow, in his re-creation of the "Bumblebee," helps Mazzo face the handiwork of the "Ice Age," hated death, and Paul Roget finds in writing his novels an understanding of the evil both in others and in himself. And he can forgive.

Critics have noted that Cormier demands his readers' response to ironies (Iskander 8); and no irony is more tragic than the sentence of death on a child who has just begun to live. The central irony in *The Bumblebee Flies Anyway* is that Barney Snow, confined to an experimental hospital for terminally ill patients, is prevented from knowing that his time in life is limited. By means of drugs, he lives under the illusion that he is not like the others—terminally ill, the victim of time. His credo is expressed "In the Name of the Tempo" (241). He believes in "[k]eeping time. Establishing a rhythm and letting it carry you. No matter what you did, it went easier if you placed your actions to rhythm. Like putting words to music. One-two, one-two-three" (6). What words are to music, meaning is to existence and Barney Snow, the seventeen-year-old protagonist, along with his young fellow patients—Ronson, Mazzo, Billy the Kidney and Allie Roon—are all victims of the Ice Age, death.

(Barney's surname takes on added significance because he doesn't realize his close affinity to the Ice Age.) For all of them, a fake red MG, the "Bumblebee" of the title, which Barney first sights in a junkyard as he is sitting on a fence defying space "between earth and sky" (8), becomes the symbol enabling them to surmount the tragedy of youthful death. In taking apart and rebuilding the fake MG, Barney is really restructuring his own psyche.

Love, fostered by Mazzo's sister, Cassie, has allowed Barney to break through "compartmentalized" space. That straitened existence had been counselled by the Handyman (doctor) who lectures the young cancer patients on the importance of living in a "separate compartment," of avoiding becoming "intimate with each other," and forgetting "about the past and future" (9). Barney uses the model MG, the Bumblebee, to fulfill a promise to the dying Mazzo, who has begged Barney to "pull the plug" and "let me die" (137). But Mazzo's murder and Barney's suicide are prevented by Barney's sudden realization of his love for Cassie. She makes him see "the sweetness of living ... gives him a sense of life going on, from one person to another, from trees to flowers, from one season to the next." His love for Cassie sings "inside him." And even though it is "a hopeless love," it brings "music to his life." The Bumblebee, "this impossible object he had stolen and taken apart and re-created with his own hands," makes him realize "he didn't want to die. He wanted to cling to life and breath" (233). Before the Bumblebee flies, however, Mazzo dies in Barney's arms, exhilarated by his triumph of getting to the rooftop: "we got here ... didn't we ... Barney?" (233). Barney himself, "tired of unknowns" (232), seems resigned to give up his place in time. Almost ecstatically he realizes that the effort expended in accepting the circumstances of one's life is its own reward: "getting there had been the important thing" (233). On the rooftop, seeing "the sweep of sky spinning with stars, the moon radiating silver, turning the sloping roof into a glittering ski slide, the lights of Monument center glowing in the distance," Barney Snow has outstripped linear time and come to recognize "monumental" time. He goes out, peacefully, "In the Name of the Tempo" (241).

In considering Cormier's treatment of monumental time, it would be remiss to exclude *Fade* (1988), which Patricia Head maintains is "arguably the most metafictional of Cormier's novels to date."[7] Undoubtedly intended for a more mature adolescent audience, it represents Cormier's most ambitious attempt to look at time and space philosophically, to unravel both the physical and symbolic functions of the "here" and "now," and to explore the determinative role of language in enabling one to understand and to forgive the self. By allowing his protagonist, Paul Roget, to "fade"—to escape from time and to become invisible in space—Cormier exposes the "constructed nature of reality" (Head 30).

The book doesn't provide a chronological structure of events, but rather a five-part account of Paul's experiences of fading and a commentary on these experiences. Before he died, Paul gave directions that the incomplete manuscript, outlining the family's secret power of fading, be sent to his literary agent after his death. The narratives of Paul, his cousin, and his agent alternate and provide a subjective and objective analysis of the meaning of the fade. To Paul the fade is real; to his cousin, it is illusionary; to the literary agent, and the careful reader, the fade becomes an amalgam of the real and the imaginary—Paul's expression of violent memories that have been repressed.

At the outset, then, Cormier establishes the ambivalence surrounding one's response to the limitations imposed on linear time and bounded space. Very much a participant in linear time and space himself, Paul reveals his growing awareness of time-governed experiences. He is particularly aware of the tensions of his adolescent years: his falling in love with his Aunt Rosanna (surely a mother figure), his problematic sexuality, his wanting to escape from a factory existence and become a writer. These conflicts, the incidents of ordinary time and place, form the nuclei of guilt and repression which determine Paul's fading, his obliterating of time and space. Paul, describing his discovery of his love for Rosanna, relates how, seeing her in his grandmother's kitchen, it was one of those "moments that stop the heart, that catch the breath, that halt the beat of blood in your veins, and you are suspended in time." His oedipal love climaxes when he "was in her embrace, her arms around me, her perfume invading me, spicy and exotic, and [he] was aware of her breasts crushed against [him]" (10). Aunt Rosanna recalls for Paul her own "mothering" of the boy: of "picking you up as a baby kissing you all over" (11). Guilt and repression are compounded with his ensuing masturbation and guilt-ridden sexuality. Paul begins to understand love's ambiguity—the pain involved in being both possessed and negated. He never loves another woman; neither does he marry. But he is able to forgive himself and rely on his own strengths, which are "made available by the ability of language to reach even the most inaccessible traces of instinct and the most troubling representations of desire" (*IBWL* 56). His novel-writing recounts the painful confusion accompanying the separation of the jubilant semiotic self with all its imperative physical drives and its entrance into the symbolic, the domain of language. Over the years he discovers that words alleviate the growing terror associated with repressed sexual desires.

Paul's first experience of fading parallels his first experimentation with poetry. At enormous physical cost, the fade makes the possessor see more of the violence and the void in human existence. While in the fade, wherein one is "caught in that strange place between darkness and light" (90), Paul sees more of darkness than of light and becomes more and more dismayed by pure, naked evil; he realizes that there are some things that are best left unseen, unknown—like the incest between Emerson and Page Winslow (128-29) or the murder of Rudolphe Toubert, which Paul himself might have perpetrated (150-53). But Paul's strength is his creation of a world of words, a world pressed out of his very being in the writing of his first novel entitled, paradoxically, *Bruises in Paradise.*

This unpublished manuscript recounts Paul's life experiences centring on the fade. His cousin's narrative presents a "rational" objective examination which summarizes Paul's manuscript as "fantasy of the wildest kind" (168). The literary agent, providing still another interpretation, recognizes the primacy of the imagination in interpreting the "here and now" truth. By this point it becomes increasingly clear that the fade is real in that it is a function of the imagination, intended to make us aware that through fiction we create the fiction that is the self. In speaking of analytic discourse (or fiction), Kristeva insists that it springs from "the web of the imagination. It works with enticements, shams, approximations, 'truths *hic et nunc,*' to arrive at truths that become absolute only because they first find their exact meaning in the evanescence of the imaginary construct" (*IBWL* 18). Paul, a subject destabilized by a guilty adolescent love, seeks stabilization in recounting his experiences with the fade. Through his manipulation of time and place, by creating fiction and escaping from obnoxious events—literary awards, parties, and such—the fade helps him become stabilized in his own time and place. He no longer seeks security in institutions but grows in compassion for "all the secrets" his family has kept from each other, his own "dark secret"—his love for Rosanna (202)—and worst of all, his murder of his "evil" nephew. But even in this, the most sombre of his novels, Cormier's hero transcends time and place by a loving forgiveness, essentially a forgiveness for the darkness he sees within himself.

In Kristevan terms, the literary agent understands that the "historical reality" of a fictional language is of little importance. All that matters is the meaning of the relationship (the re-telling) that is established between writer and reader (analysand and analyst). Whether or not Paul has actually experienced what he writes is of little importance if through the illusion of the fade, his lie, or even his madness, readers are able to grasp the impact and the logic of his fantasies (*IBWL* 20). The agent expresses her literary credo (and it is reasonable to suspect it is Robert Cormier's also), when she describes the inter-relationship between language and the symbolic:

> On paper, between the first and last pages of a manuscript, nothing is impossible. But in the reality of sunshine on a carpet, furniture you can touch as you pass, faucets that spout water, headaches, loneliness on a Sunday evening, the illusions created by nouns and verbs and similes and metaphors become only that—illusions. Words on a page. And *fade* becomes, then, just another word. (303)

When the literary agent submits Paul's incomplete narrative for publication, she experiences "a feeling that (she) had paid off a debt, as if [she] had completed a mission" (307). And she has. So has Robert Cormier in his novels completed a mission that intimates that of Julia Kristeva. In her Preface to the English edition of *Desire in Language*, Kristeva makes a "confession of humility" which elucidates her belief that, considering the complexity of the signifying process of language, "no belief in an all-powerful theory is tenable." Notwithstanding, "there remains the necessity to pay attention to the ability to deal with the desire for language." By that she means paying attention to the art and literature of our time, which "impel us not toward the absolute but towards a quest for a little more truth, an impossible truth, concerning the meaning of speech, concerning our condition as speaking subjects" (ix). Robert Cormier has paid passionate attention to his art. By presenting his readers with speaking subjects whose quiet heroism reveals an inner paradise that transcends time, he has initiated countless young people on their quest for a little more truth about the regenerative potential of a love empowered by forgiveness.

7

CHUCKLING WITH THE CHIMAERA

Jan Mark's Subject-in-Process

More than any other recent writer for young people, Jan Mark creates a uniquely different blending of tragedy and farce to help her readers confront the chimaera of the divided self. Mythology's fire-breathing monster, the Chimaera, possessing properties of lion, goat, and dragon, may well serve as a representation of the many "selves" in the human psyche—selves which must be recognized, tamed, and controlled. Thus, in her fiction, Jan Mark obliterates the "happily ever after" ending of young adults' fiction when subjects perceive and understand their true selves; instead, she celebrates the reality of the fragmented self. The totally unified self, identity as object, may well be a modern paragon just as threatening and dangerous as the ancient, mythical chimaera. Realizing the perils of impossible ideals, Mark writes novels and short stories that apparently can be divided conveniently into the comic and the tragic, yet there is never any pure comedy or pure tragedy in any of her works.[1] Mark's is a complex dialectic between reasserting the values of the past, shattering them, and bringing forth a new synthesis. And basic to that synthesis is the experience of love. Her vision, uneasy but not unsteady, is fused by an unorthodox blending of ancient Platonism with modern psychological theory. Her amalgam of the comic and the tragic, the conscious and the unconscious, the real and the imagined, is perhaps best understood in the light of Julia Kristeva's psychoanalytic approach to literature. Like Kristeva, Mark forces her readers to confront the unhappy truth that self-identity is never an object, never something to be grasped once and held onto forever; it is an on-going process of reconciling life's expectations with its too-frequent disillusionments. Reconciliation of the differences within the same person can be achieved not so much when we find the self in the other as when we find the other in the self.

Kristeva maintains that psychoanalysis investigates a series of splittings: at birth, at the mirror stage, at the separation process of adolescence. All these splittings are necessary for an individual to work out an identity, and all cause anxiety and loss. "Analysis," she writes, "is apprenticeship in separation as both *alienation* and *loss*." Kristeva sees contemporary humanity as suffering from a crisis of values; it feels itself orphaned. Humanity must discover the "Other is in Me: I am an Other. This humanity lives in and on separation" (*IBWL* 55). As Oliver explains:

> Rather than love the other as himself, the ethical subject-in-process will love the other in herself. She will love what is different. She will love alterity because it is within but not because it is homogeneous. She can imagine an ethics of love because the ethical relation is interior to her psyche. (186)

Thus, psychoanalysis unfolds the unconscious "other" that hides in every apparently unified subject. The individual must recognize difference; it is an other to itself. We are all strangers to ourselves, subjects in process/on trial.[2]

We observe Jan Mark echoing Kristevan theory when we read her first children's novel, *Thunder and Lightnings* (1976), or her later collection of short stories, *A Can of Worms* (1990), perhaps the finest collection of bittersweet short stories ever written for adolescents. Mark's fiction celebrates difference without breaking down identity. Her young heroes and heroines, while avoiding conformity, all operate within a given social milieu, no matter how different or difficult that milieu may be. Exploring the double bind of balancing one's need to belong to a group with the need to be different becomes a recurrent theme in all her fiction. And Mark's ethics place the competitor outside the winners' circle. There are never any big winners or losers in her fiction; rather, all her characters are both winners *and* losers. As a result, there is no total despair because the quest for a completely unified self is never finished; there is always the possibility of renewing the self through love. In Kristevan terms, psychoanalytic theory offers "an infinite quest for rebirths, through the experience of love" (*TL* 1). Furthermore, "[t]he psyche is one open system connected to another," always in process, capable of reorganizing itself (*TL* 15). Identity consolidation becomes an "open system." Only in discourse, oral or written, is the subject able to sort out the manifestations of these three elements and to reorganize his or her own reality. Transference love (in a psychoanalytic perspective, the love that exists between the analysand and the analyst) is the optimum form of interrelation germane to any stabilizing-destabilizing amorous experience (*TL* 15). Mark's young protagonists, however, are not completely destabilized, although the threat to stability is often evident; they do not need psychoanalysis because they are capable of trusting relationships, particularly friendships. This ability to risk for love, to find the other in the self, to balance an unbalanced subject, is evident in Mark's earliest novel, *Thunder and Lightnings.*

Jan Mark won the Carnegie Medal for *Thunder and Lightnings.* It is here that a unique voice, investigating the dissociated self, is first heard. What makes Mark so striking is that she can make her young readers chuckle at the chimaera of that monstrous fantasy so they can completely unify the fragmented self. However, even in the laughter, Mark never sweetens the biting truth that the child's quest for unity is thwarted by separation, alienation, and *loss.* Mark's characters suffer from a contemporary crisis of values which are continually being jeopardized—by human institutions that breed corruption, by individuals who aggrandize themselves by using others, and even by love which, although the only way of finding self-identity in the other, may yet contain within itself the poisonous seeds of possessiveness, jealousy, and selfishness. The only hope for survival in an absurd world, which hinders achievement of a totally integrated self, lies in accepting and even welcoming those trials and perturbations caused by the differences in others. In absorbing those crises of alterity into the psyche, one strengthens the capacity to love. As Lechte explains, "the greater the capacity for love, the less other becomes a threat and becomes, in his or her very individuality, a participant in an identity as 'a work in progress'" ("Art, Love, and Melancholy" 33).

In *Thunder and Lightnings,* for example, young Victor Skelton, painfully thrust aside by his mother, accepts his isolation, in the family and in society, and withstands disillusionment by his realization that perfect love is impossible and that things can never remain as they are. The hero of the novel is ostensibly Andrew Mitchell, who, with his baby brother Edward, his computer technician father, and his ex-librarian mother, has moved into an old house in Norfolk. The Mitchells are a very ordinary family, and Jan Mark looks fondly, even comically, on the tiresome trials of a new family in an old house—trials like discovering a rat or dealing with a stray cat. But Mark's rat, like so much else in her fiction, is different: he is "clean and genial-looking: a country rat" (2). The stray cat is imaged as an old dishcloth which "unfold[s] itself" and stands up on "muddy feet" (18).

Counterpointing this very ordinary family, however, is the fractured, alienated, dysfunctional Skelton family whose youngest member, the dyslexic Victor, becomes the real hero of the novel—not because he achieves true self-identity but because he realizes he might never achieve it. His dyslexia precludes him from mastering language and becoming a fully integrated social being. Andrew first meets the alienated youth at school where the latter appears "hideously swollen about the body but very thin in the face." It turns out that Victor, who "was not so much dressed as camouflaged" wears clothes—layers upon layers of them—to disguise his thinness, to protect his thin, fragile, unformed "self" (33). Victor has much to contend with in his young life. Separated, particularly from his mother, he is the son of a no-nonsense, pigeon-hunting father who sits in morose silence at the evening meal reading the paper "with a frown that went up and down his forehead like a venetian blind" (58). His mother, a compulsive cleaner, keeps a house that "had an unpleasantly shiny look about it and smelt like a dentist's waiting room" (58). Victor must walk upstairs bowlegged to keep his feet off the rugs (54). An outsider in his own home and an outsider at school, where his dyslexia clouds a keen intelligence, Victor's psyche survives because of its ability to expand itself in his love of airplanes, especially the Lightnings, which he admires as the fastest planes in the world (63). When Andrew first visits Victor's house and the sanctuary of his room, he marvels at "how someone who pretended to be such an ignorant slob could possibly know so much [about airplanes] or reel it off with such ease" (60).

This love for something outside himself keeps Victor in the "open system" in two ways. Firstly, he recognizes his own difference, which leads him to accept his mother's alterity—even when he knows that she actively dislikes him. Secondly, he accepts the real in the actuality of loss—that his beloved Lightnings cannot forever remain the fastest planes in the world. Perfect love and permanence are chimaeras. Nothing remains the same. That Victor has realized these profound truths, that he has learned to handle illusions, to accept freely the rules of the survival game, makes him one of life's rare, true "victors," as Andrew's mother attests in a moving scene. Andrew watches, appalled, as Victor's mother "without saying anything smacks him hard three times across the side of the head" after he accidentally soils a clean sheet (159). Victor says nothing, and Andrew is shocked by the silence of it all. When Andrew complains to his own mother about the unfairness of the incident, his mother, in a wisely casual way, replies:

> "There's no such thing as fairness. It's a word made up to keep children quiet. When you discover it's a fraud then you're starting to grow up. The difference between you and Victor is that you're still finding out and he knows perfectly well already." (161)

Victor entered into the identity process long before Andrew because he has been able to absorb his mother's difference and the pain of separation.

Jan Mark generates excitement and suspense in this novel not so much with external events but from internal choices. She pays passionate attention to life's "nows"—those tiny moments of decision which irrevocably change things and wherein eternity hides. Her main characters' decisions and choices are made from an internal awareness, where the fragile self struggles to absorb alterity into the psyche and so to become more supple in the giving and receiving of love. Victor, oppressed as he is, wants his individuality and difference to be accepted by Andrew. His interior sense of his own difference is imaged in the novel on several levels: by the multiple layers of clothing Victor wears to shield his knowing heart; by the dark, warm, safe cocoon of his own room, where unfriendly intruders are forbidden entrance and only his friend enters; by his very handwriting, which "was a sort of code to deceive the enemy" (36). Victor, wary and afraid, "doesn't like people to see him as he really is"; his fragile self, which he recognizes as his and his alone, must be well guarded (153). But he is open to Andrew perhaps because Andrew too feels his difference, isolated and alone in a new school. In their shared love of airplanes, Victor can enter into a loving relationship with Andrew.

Thus, when Victor realizes that his beloved Lightnings are to be replaced by Jaguars at the Coltishall Airfield in Norfolk, he has the courage to face the truth that everything changes—nothing remains the same. Lightnings will be replaced by Jaguars; Jaguars will be replaced by something still to be invented. But Victor can triumph in the splendour that was the Lightning—the "now" that has melted into "then." For one last time, Victor and Andrew glory in the departing flight of a Lightning as it makes its 40,000-foot climb in two-and-a-half minutes. "What a way to go out, eh?" cries the exultant Victor (174). He chooses to retain his innocent belief that the future can be good. Mark respects the emphasis on courage as an affair of the heart. At the core of the process of personality integration is the courageous, never-ending discipline of learning to absorb pain and disappointment: there is neither life nor love without them. As Kristeva warns, "love never dwells in us without burning us" (*TL* 4). To bask in the belief of a totally unified self that can overcome the anxieties and disappointments of human existence is a delusion. But the fragmented self is always kept alive with "heart," the passionate belief that love (in this case the loyalty and friendship of Andrew), although never perfect, enables one to endure.

Always there are risks. Risks and explorations are consistent themes in Mark's fiction, just as they are implied constants in her narrative techniques. She constantly challenges the male position of the speaking subject; she blurs sexes, nationalities, and, in particular, time periods to shatter established assumptions and create new ones. These time periods may be only temporal and tentative, but they are stable enough to sustain youth in their moving place in time. For example, time is deliberately mooted in her major trilogy, *The Ennead, Divide and Rule,* and *Aquarius*, perhaps because "fragmentation of the self entails the disintegration of time" (Makiko-Minow-Pinkney 170). Thus individuals and families are uprooted from one locality to another, children plucked from one school and set in another. One event does not necessarily lead fluidly into another. A quiet walk with a friend ends with a violent blow from a mother. Mark thus emphasizes the disjointedness of time in every person's unattainable quest for the harmoniously balanced self. She respects the separateness of her young reader's world, but she also recognizes that child and adult take part in the same life-long process of seeking a unified self. Psychic maturation is never fully reached, despite the adult conceit that places so much emphasis upon maturity. Her practical vision accounts for the intelligent, unpatronizing, impersonal voice of Mark's narration and might limit her readership to the more intellectually gifted of her youthful audience.

Although this study concentrates on novels whose protagonists are older adolescents, it should be remembered that Mark began writing for a younger audience. When her second novel, *Under the Autumn Garden*, was published by Kestrel in 1977, she launched protagonist eleven-year-old Matthew Marsh on a search using the controlling metaphor of archaeology. The novel is not about a quest, however, although there certainly is one. It is not the story of a misunderstood boy's punishment for an unfinished history project, but rather, a tale about relationships, their fathomless complexity, and how one preteen begins to dig into his own consciousness to discover his relationship with self and with the other. Matthew's history assignment turns out to be an exploration of the self.

Disjointedness in this novel is suggested at the novel's beginning by the turmoil of a house renovation, with all the confusion such a project engenders. Matthew's family home is being remodelled at a time when the boy is supposed to be doing a history project on some aspect of his town's local history. While he is digging in his garden, hoping to find an artifact, he is also excavating into an inner world where he "drifts away" into future and past times. There he contemplates, for example, what Martian visitors will think of his town's police station, erected in 1973, or what the significance is of the game "Sheep and Shepherd," which the younger children at his school play, although few of them have ever even seen a sheep (75, 81-82).

Matthew also begins to probe the strange confusion of own psyche and his deliberate rejection of alterity. His teacher, who had legitimately scolded him for dawdling, later tries to be kind and Matthew discovers "he got an angry sort of pleasure from walking away" from her (126). Recognizing the violence and separateness of different moods—his own as well those of others—becomes apparent when Matthew concludes: "I don't seem to like anyone much.... No one likes me either" (171). Thus Matthew's history project teaches him how to cope in a corrupt and broken world. He is aware of the "number of lies he had to tell" to cover up his obsession with digging (155). His lies are seen to be survival tactics, necessary to balance conflicting drives and social mores. He is still guileless enough, however, to believe that "a time would come when he could stop lying, stop pretending and stop digging"(155). And through the fragmented splinters of time, Matthew becomes increasingly aware of the dangers of his drives. He learns, for example, that the monks who lived in the long-gone, fourteenth-century abbey and whose environs now comprise the Marsh's home, became so driven by the power of wealth and so dissolute that they had to abandon their abbey. Old codes and customs must be shattered, but they must also be put together again, just as the identity of the subject is often broken only to be re-formed.

Matthew, depressed as he is by the discoveries of his own difference, wants his individuality and difference accepted by others. He must, however, first confront the fragmented nature of all human relationships. One scene demonstrates particularly effectively Matthew's putting together his own negativity, rebellion, and self-assertiveness with the needs and pain of another. Paul Angel, the son of the contractor-renovator, unearths an old bottle in the Marsh garden (134). Paul unjustly keeps the bottle and Matthew is afraid to object, even though he discovers the importance of "making a point," if only to himself. He rebels inwardly, but his protests explode in silence so that Paul Angel "should not hear" (145). Matthew needs the bottle for his history project, and when the artifact is accidentally broken and Paul orders the younger Matthew to clear up the mess, Matthew explodes: "I'm not clearing that up.... Get your mother to help you" (161). Unknown to Matthew, however, he has unearthed the Angel family's personal tragedy. Mrs. Angel had recently abandoned her husband and three sons. What is a broken bottle compared to a broken family? Matthew is able to absorb Paul's suffering and understand the tragedy of the recent family break-up, which reveals to him the unreliability of all human relationships—those between parents and their offspring, adults and children, husband and wife, friend and friend. Any illusion Matthew may have had about the permanency of such bondings is beginning to fade.

Jan Mark subtly explores the dialectic between individual desires and social standards, between the fragmentation of time and the synthesis of purpose. These shifts unerringly shatter established modes to bring forth a new awareness and Kristeva's basic dialectic between the semiotic and the symbolic. Matthew eventually does find his treasure, an old ring. But there is no vindication for Matthew's uncompleted history essay; he must bear the pain of failure. Yet the reader understands that the words of an essay are inadequate, even unnecessary. Words, like both bottle and ring, encompass nothing but space. Some things cannot be expressed: they are either too deep or too definite for words.[3] The real jubilation comes from Matthew's solitary discovery of the symbolic ring of history. The sign of the ring, rather than words, signifies his discovery of his own relationship to self and to the circularity of time. "There was no need to trade that in for a good opinion" (175).

In her review of *Under the Autumn Garden*, Ethel L. Heins comments on Mark's "figurative language, offhand wit, and oblique characterization" as well as her clear, direct writing and evocation of people and place (415-416). But at the beginning of Mark's career, critical attention shied away from the starkness of her thinking, although it recognized her demythologizing of the Polyanna syndrome in children's literature. Mark's sifting of cultural sentimentalities began to be noted seriously by 1984 when David Rees noted:

> Scarcely anyone writing today presents youth with a more somber picture of life than does Jan Mark.... [but] the harsh truths of her vision of the world are infinitely preferable to the cosy pap that is sometimes served up for the young. (73)

Rees also comments that some readers might feel her novels go to an extreme beyond which it is not possible to venture in books for children and teenagers (73). However, Mark did dare to go beyond the sombreness of her first two novels in a remarkable triad, *The Ennead* (1978), *Divide and Rule* (1979), and *Aquarius* (1982). She seems to have worried that contemporary young people are being deprived of traditional values—much like Kristeva who sees crises of love in our modern world, covered, as it is, "with so much abjection, because the guideposts that insured our ascent toward the good have been proven questionable" (*TL* 7). Mark set about to study how cultural values arise and then decline. These novels also represent her deepest exploration of separation, alienation, and loss. Only by recognizing the power of love and accepting difference can both individuals and humankind survive. With each of these novels Mark's vision grows darker, yet at the same time her belief in the power of the human spirit to endure grows progressively stronger.

The Ennead may be a pun on the *Aeneid*, Virgil's ancient epic of quest and exploration, but more than likely refers to the *Enneads* of the Neoplatonist Plotinus (205-270 AD). His six sets of nine treatises (*ennea* is the Greek word for nine) contain the most complete expression of Neoplatonic thought. Alternatively, the word may simply be intended as an allusion to the nine major planets or the nine Muses, one of whom, Erato, presided over erotic poetry. Certainly Mark's trilogy contains the fullest expression of her own philosophy. Like Kristeva, Mark believes that love is a good and positive reality, that time is the true life of the spirit, and that choice in the motion of time is the means by which we activate our difference. Thus, in her *Ennead*, Mark concentrates on three members of a group, separated and oppressed on the far-distant planet of Erato, where tyranny has resulted from the repression of individual human freedom. In this future galaxy, beyond the present confines of time, their personal choices actualize the power of their individuality.

The protagonists—Eleanor, Moshe, and Isaac—would prefer what is almost certain death than to submit to the regimented mores of Erato; they place their struggle to exercise the power of choice above the strictures of a dead society. Even the most conservative of the three young people, Isaac, chooses to sacrifice himself, to exercise his right to put Eleanor's well-being before his own. Eleanor's speech before she is transported to almost certain death may be an echo of Mark's own philosophic conviction that vigilance in preserving difference is the price of true freedom and that an endurance that puts others before the self is ennobling in itself, even though destiny (or the gods) might dictate death.

The darkness in the novel comes from the fact that humans know the evil that is done in the dark and choose to ignore it. Indifference and a lack of movement stultify. What is even more numbing is Mark's conviction that we can't change the indifferent. In her essay on the short story, Mark quotes Miss Marple in an Agatha Christie novel as saying, "People don't change, that's the tragedy" (*The Horn Book* 64 [Jan.–Feb. 1988] 44). The unchanging indifference of humans, the hardening of the heart, destroys not only the individual but also civilization itself. Humankind must beware lest Earth becomes Erato—erased, blotted out.

Divide and Rule is an even darker novel. Mark consciously creates ambiguity both in the geographical location of the setting and in the historical remoteness of a pre-Copernican civilization which has barely passed beyond the stage of offering human sacrifice. Likewise, Mark is deliberately vague as to her intended audience. Does she intend the novel for the chronologically aged adolescent as depicted in the eighteen-year-old hero Hanno? Or are all humans adolescent, subjects in process? In *Divide and Rule* everything is caught in a temporal flux, and the quest for a unified self transcends physical time and place as well as the number of years one lives. The quest for subject identity fails if alterity is not embraced, and Mark implies that Hanno's (and civilization's) tragedy is the rejection of difference of either the self or the other. Again, in *Divide and Rule*, there are grave risks and terrible choices.

Hanno (a variant of Johann or John) is a significant name for the hero who lives at a time of breakdown in a religious institution; like John the Baptist, he is a precursor. Mark frames a segment of time—in this novel, a year in the life of a boy—and within that frame explores the past as a boundary, on the edge of knowing something more. Hanno has the practical insight to refuse to accept life as sacrificial victimhood, even though as the imagery suggests he is a sheep-like character, unwilling to accept his difference, wanting only to be led.

> Someone had once remarked unkindly that he looked like a sheep, and he did. A handsome sheep, but a sheep for all that; one of the long-faced marsh breed that walked through mire, impervious to foot rot. No one who had ever seen Hanno wading along the river margin, preceded by the questing prow of his nose, could fail to note the resemblance. (13-14)

In some ways, Hanno resembles a sub-human creature in an evolutionary process. As one who scorns the prevailing religion which each year chooses a youth of eighteen to be the ritual shepherd presiding over prayer-time in the temple, Hanno initially compromises his integrity by partaking in a religious ceremony in which he does not believe. This is his first choice and suggests he is "the fool that will not [take a stand] when he may" (vi). Only to please his family does Hanno partake in a ritual that he believes to be hollow and false. But even at the outset Hanno is interested in neither his integrity nor his internal life. He is completely captivated by the sheer physicality of the outside world of sensuous delight: earth, river, sky, women, and song. He must be converted, divided, literally split open, before he can be made whole—if he ever is made whole. (The novel's open, objective, unsentimental ending invites individual reader response.) But it is clear that by choosing to participate in a ritual that he scorns, Hanno embarks on an exploration of dark discovery. It is a totally lonely journey because, in Mark's view, any conversion requires a turning away, a separation from a lower plane of being. Surely, Peter Hunt missed the point when he wrote of *Divide and Rule* that "the only audience which could derive much pleasure from it would be a singularly masochistic group of manic depressives" ("Whatever Happened to Jan Mark?" *Signal* 31: [Jan. 1980] 11-19).[4] If Hunt were correct, the world would be exaggeratedly populated by manic depressives. On the contrary, *Divide and Rule* is concerned with the universal choice individuals must make when their dealings with any organized institution, particularly religion, conflict with their unique, individual insights.

Hanno's tragedy begins at the moment he decides to conceal the true nature of his disbelief. By undergoing what he believes to be a travesty in the ritual of choosing the shepherd, Hanno not only deceives himself but also denies his difference. His first deception imprisons him within a narrow, text-enclosed existence. Hanno, the lover of physical beauty, is trapped within a false symbolic structure, imaged by the shepherd's head-dress that physically limits his vision.

> The head-dress was of unyielding leather and it closed over Hanno's thick hair like a second scalp, covering his ears and cutting off the sound of the acolyte's prayer.... On either side a great curling horn came down and forward, blinkering his eyes, so that he could no longer see sideways without turning his head. (69)

Indeed, from the outset the reader recognizes that Hanno's vision has become impaired—a fact which he decides to hide from his family. His physical blindness echoes his inner, spiritual blindness. Ignored by the High Priest and treated contemptuously by his peers in the temple, the alienated and frightened Hanno lives alone. His sufferings, however, force him to live from the inside out, although he finds no joy or peace in inner communion.

Hanno's actualization of his place in time comes when he discovers the temple idiot has been murdered and resurrected as a god-like figure with miraculous powers. He must choose how to deal with the fraud and cover-up. Temple rites, supposed to have been unchanging and regulated by the Book since the dawn of civilization, are now being overturned for the crassest of reasons: money and its increase with an expanded church attendance generated by the "miracles" of the glorified idiot. In trying to expose the fraud and in refusing to go along with the official lie, Hanno betrays himself again by falsely admitting that he killed the idiot. The novel ends with Hanno, dismissed from the temple and ostracized by his family, wandering alone, incoherent and half blind. Yet, in stripping Hanno of all his illusions about the supernatural nature of religion, the sanctity of the priesthood, the stability of ritual and text, Mark plays on the title. Hanno has been divided, broken, split apart. He ends up where he began—by the river (symbol of continuity and of time), with a new dawn (a fresh start) and three travellers from a foreign land appearing in the distance. The process of maintaining subject identity begins anew. Hanno does not even know his name, but he is *not* the shepherd and he is no longer a sheep, led by others, as he was in the beginning of the book. Feeble and dark as is his discovery, terrible as has been the exploration, Hanno has found the beginnings of subjectivity. For Kristeva, the unitary subject is the result of an on-going process that is prior to meaning and mediates between drives and symbols. At the end of the novel, Hanno is an emptiness, lacking any bonding capacity. More precisely, the reader can only suspect he will attempt some form of bonding with the three strangers.

The total lack of bonding evident in *Divide and Rule*, which won for its author the Young Observer/Rank Organization Fiction Prize, becomes intensified in *Aquarius*. This novel has the same vagueness of setting and time, and the same unsentimental objectification of the young hero Viner, who has the power to find water with his divining rod. But Mark's manipulation of her readers' response to Viner, which evolves from initial sympathy to final detestation, is paralleled by her brilliant study of the destructive power of manipulation in the human psyche itself.

Kristeva notes that love probably always includes a love for power (*TL* 9). In *Aquarius*, Viner's drive for power proves to be stronger than that of love. Viner inevitably uses another, the Rain King (Morning Light), for his own gain. Despite Viner's devoted love for Morning Light (and Viner's sexual preference is dramatically clear), love is subordinated to power. Viner deliberately chooses to become the Saviour of the very people who betrayed him rather than be the lover/friend of the Rain King who cannot return his love.

Mark's delineation of Viner's character deserves meticulous scrutiny. Rescued from drowning in the flood-swollen river of a nameless town, rejected by his mother, and vilified by the villagers who blame him for the increasingly destructive rain, Viner becomes an outcast, separated from his family, fleeing into an unknown future. A traveller has told him of a kingdom where the people "take a man and make him dance, and when it rains they make him king, and he marries the queen" (13). Viner accepts his destiny and flees from ignominy to prosperity, from nothingness and emptiness to fulfillment—a subject in process. Captured by agents of the Rain King, Viner is brought to the drought-stricken land where his powers as a detector of underground water make him the Saviour. From the moment when Viner sees the Rain King's futile intercessory dance, in which he throws javelins into the air to bring down rain, Viner becomes devoted to the tragic king. But his devotion is tinged by a growing sophistication "in the ways of the world" (56). He is less concerned for inner fulfillment than for material gain.

The exploration of the double bind of one's need to belong to a group versus the need to be different resonates thematically in *Aquarius* as it does in all Mark's fiction. Viner decides to use his skill as a diviner "to assert his power and thus acquire power" (61). Already his subjective "good" is being vitiated in the struggle between his unselfish love of another and his self-aggrandizement. But Viner clearly knows his friend Morning Light better than the King's wife or any of his subjects does. He perceives the true potential of Morning Light when, on his first morning in the palace, he sees the king "absorbing the yellow light of the sun" (66): he is more of a Sun King than a Rain King. In his discovery of the alterity of another human being, Viner also discovers the magic of friendship. Subsequently, when the Rain King looks at the water which Viner's art has brought to the surface and kneels reverently to let it run over his arms and through his fingers, Viner feels "very tenderly toward him, a king brought to his knees by the handiwork of an orphaned and divided outcast" (93).

But even as Viner's love for the king deepens, his knowledge of the utility of friendship grows. He recognizes that "friendship here was a trade, like carpentry, or water-divining," but he does not realize that one day he too "would practice it as a trade" (74). "The agonizing moment of truth" comes when Viner realizes that Morning Light will not escape with him, will not barter his individual difference, and will not give himself over to be made in the image and likeness of Viner.

> Viner sat shaking with fury, remembering how kingship had been within his grasp and that on impulse he had turned his back on it to follow Morning Light. I gave up everything for you, he thought, and you won't do anything for me. I could have been king in your place. (176)

Viner expects reward for the loyalty of friendship, forgetting that love must accept alterity. If Viner cannot purchase the love of Morning Light, he will use violence to make the Rain King into a Sun King. He will force his friend to return to his old rain-soaked village and make him bring out the sun as Viner had been forced to bring forth rain.

The only source of hope in this powerful novel of lost chances rests in, as his name implies, Morning Light. Abandoned by his wife, used and abused by his friends, betrayed by the once-devoted Viner himself, the King never chooses power or status over love. He willingly relinquishes kingship so long as he can keep his beloved daughter Dark Cloud. Unlike Viner, who despairs at his entrapment when he knows "that his euphoria over the last two months had been a delusion, a deceiving sickness" (117), Morning Light accepts an even worse fate and survives—chooses to survive—all for love itself. For him devotion is never wasted, as Viner suspects (126), even though he gets nothing in return. "I should have been named Nothing," Morning Light tells Viner (208); but in recognizing his nothingness, his emptiness, he is in a better position than Viner to begin the process of subject identity.

Morning Light ultimately accepts the title "Sun King" and dances, as commanded by his tormentor, Viner, so he can keep his beloved daughter (223-4). We have our final glimpse of Morning Light, dispirited, dancing in despair "beneath the blue sky, the fleeing clouds, the inexorable sun." It is the only way he can save his daughter and insure that the unending cycle of life continues. For him, that is reason enough. Just as his mother, bearing "him at night, without a lamp" and seeing "nothing," still called him "Morning Light," so too Morning Light finds his reason for being in his daughter (209). Unwillingly, Morning Light has become Viner's Saviour. But Viner knows, as Mark would have her readers know, that humans cannot be kept prisoners forever. One day Morning Light will escape "Over the Top" with his loving daughter, and until that final escape comes, he will endure. The "water was tamed, the village secure, the people content" (224).

Mark interspersed these sombre works with an equally intelligent demonstration of her incomparable comic spirit, evident in younger people's books like *Hairs in the Palm of the Hand* (1981), *Handles* (for which she received her second Carnegie Medal in 1983), and *Trouble Half Way* (1985); also in works for older adolescents like *At the Sign of the Dog and Rocket* (1985). Works like these reveal the incredible versatility of this gifted English writer, who looks frankly at all those very real threats to a unified self—family breakdown, homophobia, sexism, racism, intolerance—and explores them with a seriousness tempered by a luminous wit.

The dynamism in Mark's works stems from her preoccupation with change. In commenting on her work in the short story, Mark wrote of her fascination with "the moment at which change occurs: the seminal moment—after which nothing will ever be the same again" (*The Horn Book* 64: 44). In both her short stories and her novels, she is adept at choosing the right moment and framing it. Her 1990 book of short stories, fittingly entitled *A Can of Worms*, describes the process Mark uses in demythologizing the concept of a unified self. To open a can of worms is to expose some fearfully twisted, convoluted creatures; to read a Jan Mark story is to isolate a wormy moment in time, note the quivering changes that moment brings, and laugh.

Consider the moment of change that a summer holiday brings to Erica Timperley, the tomboy heroine of the lead story in *Handles.* This short story reflects the Kristevan thesis that, because the psyche contains bisexual components, sexual stereotyping is pointless. In her essay "Oscillation between Power and Denial," Kristeva asserts:

> All speaking subjects have within themselves a certain bisexuality which is precisely the possibility to explore all the sources of signification, that which posits a meaning as well as that which multiplies, pulverizes, and finally revives it. (*New French Feminisms* 166)

Mark de-emphasizes sexual differences which are not fundamental to the psyche. Erica Timperley, in her love of motorcycles, is atypically masculine, but while liking the sense of power which her identification with motorcycles gives her, she also resents masculine domination. Uprooted from her city home to a remote English country village for her summer holidays, she must sort out the ambiguity of her sexual leanings. Erica is almost smothered by her aunt's patriarchically governed household: Rule Number One, Robert [her cousin] need do no work; Rule Number Two, Robert could do no wrong; Rule Number Three, no one was allowed to be rude to Robert; and Rule Number Four, Robert could be as rude as he liked (24). Erica oscillates between her desire for masculine power and her indignation at it.

From this male-dominated household Erica escapes to the Mercury Motor Cycle Shop where the proprietor, Elsie Wainwright, allows her to tinker and educates her in balancing the impossible dialectic between her desire for and hatred of male dominance. In her friendship with Elsie Wainwright, Erica learns the subtle dangers of stereotyping—of imposing "names" instead of creating "handles." How marvellous that a simple object like a bike should have such a glorious handle as the "cow with the crumpled horn" or the "iron cow," while she has "only a name" (79). As Erica discovers the evils of stereotyping, she learns, like her mentor Elsie Wainwright, to give people and events their proper "handles," which represent a synthesis of the semiotic and the symbolic. "Puddy Paws" or "Panda" is the cat; a Yamaha F.S.I.E. becomes "Fizzy"; Yerbert's brother is given the handle "Fang" because he has only two teeth that are his own; the "Gremlin" is the baby Gordon.

Elsie Wainwright's real name is Lynden C. (L.C.), but he is free enough to cross the straitened respectability which separates young from old, male from female, blue-collar from white-collar worker. Separated from his wife who wants him to go back to teaching, the "nice and respectable" career for which he was trained, Elsie chooses to be a bike mechanic, content to keep his feminine "handle" (155). At the same time, by never speaking down to Erica, he erases the dichotomy between youth and age. Wainwright, who "didn't seem to be any age at all," teaches Erica how to look at everything and "handle" it for herself (99).

In her problems with her Aunt Joan, Uncle Peter, and Cousin Robert, Erica learns to look on her relatives like the marrows they produce (147). In one of the funniest incidents in the book, Elsie helps Erica release her suppressed anger at male domination when he gives Erica the idea of carving liberating messages on the marrows while they are still courgettes. As the story unfolds, word and symbol mature together in the vegetables. The skin splits in the growing marrows and reveals hidden messages. The whimsicality of talking vegetables provides the humor: COME TO SUNNY CALSTEAD. ELSIE WAINWRIGHT RULES O.K. ROBERT IS A FAT TWIT. VOTE LABOUR (96-97, 143, 147). Objectifying her repressed anger in the vegetables, Erica escapes from the paternal, symbolic domination of her aunt's home.

At the end of her holiday, Erica has learned how to look at people and events independently, how to avoid stereotyping, and how to laugh—unlike her relatives whom she could not remember laughing except at a "proper joke" (147). She has transcended a stultifying propriety. For her growth, her mentor called her "woman," which she had never been called before (127), and gave her the handle Eroica (156). Though "boyish," she embraces her "girlness"; while still a "girl," she is also "woman"; in Kristevan terms the ordinary "Erica" is in process of becoming "Eroica." She no longer sees male and female as opposite but as different; what is more significant, she is comfortable with these differences.

Jan Mark, ever fascinated by change, delights in crossing boundaries—in the sexes, in class structures, in family relationships. Much of the humour in *Handles* comes from characters crossing boundaries and not realizing it because they have not yet cut loose from their misconceptions about themselves and others. Erica sees the incongruous double standard of her Uncle Peter and Ted gossiping "on either side of the hedge in the way housewives are supposed to do over the back fences" (56), but the humour arises from Uncle Peter's ignorance. What he would label "feminine gossip" in his wife or Erica becomes merely "neighbourly chatting" in his own case.

In a more serious boundary situation, Amy Calver must challenge her misconceptions about her new stepfather in *Trouble Half Way*. Amy's mother, remarried after the early death of her husband, is a compulsive housekeeper (she even irons baby Helen's diapers). In coming to a new awareness of Richard, her stepfather, Amy crosses another sex boundary in recognizing her new father as real mother. A debilitating shyness paralyzes Amy whenever she comes into her stepfather's presence. In one uncomfortable interview Richard asks: "Do you know what a pessimist is?"

> "No."
>
> "Look in the mirror then."
>
> "Me?"
>
> "Yes, *you*. Gripe, gripe, gripe. Anyone'd think you were going to cross the Alps on roller skates."
>
> "Mrs Varley [a neighbour] says I meet trouble half way...."
>
> "Half way? ... You don't meet trouble half way, you go to the door and yell through the letter box, 'Yoohoo, Trouble. Come on out. I've got a job for you!'" (47)

Amy laughs in seeing herself as object, and in doing so, for the first time, she loses a bit of her shyness in the presence of her truck-driving stepfather whom she later learns to love. In the hilarious events resulting from an enforced truck ride to Manchester with her step-father, Amy is nurtured in her understanding of the link between shyness and fear. She even learns to call Richard "father": "Richard as a wicked step-father was such a silly idea that she grinned, the first grin for days, it seemed" (124).

In the simple ordinariness of these lower-middle-class family situations, readers begin to appreciate the humour behind the search for identity in their own routine lives. Eleven-year-olds can identify with Amy, and sophisticated seventeen-year-olds can relate to the boundary situation faced by

Lilian Goodwin, a recent high-school graduate, in *At the Sign of the Dog and Rocket.* Lilian finds herself managing her parents' pub and hiring a former student-teacher whom she had (and detested) during the previous term. Beneath the comedy of collecting steak and kidney pies, getting rid of an obnoxious, underfoot dog, "bouncing" a disreputable drunkard (who should have been "respectable"), Lilian realizes that the quest for self-identity is not a quest for homogeneity but a constant breaking down of intermittent relationships and events. In overcoming her infantile antipathy to Tom Collins, she discovers the process of reassembling the diverse elements of the subject, which is always in a state of becoming.

Perhaps Mark is at her humorous best in two school stories which appear in *Hairs in the Palm of the Hand.* The story called "Time and the Hour" gives the book its title.

> "Watch his hands," says the schoolboy Hopkins. "The second sign of madness is hairs growing in the palm of the hand." But what's the first sign, then, asks his friend, Forbes. "Looking for them," said Hopkins. (30)

The unexpected characterizes Mark's humour. In her repertoire, no two stories are alike. She has an amazing versatility, as illustrated when Mark transforms an old joke into a clever story about school life in which a boys' class places bets on how much time can be wasted in week. In the companion piece in this volume, "Chutzpah," heroine Eileen Skeats invades a new school and, while hiding in a toilet cubicle, proceeds to frighten Lisa Donovan. Later, she assumes the subsequent aliases of Susan Tucker, Deborah Clarke, and Barbie—characters which aid her in her reign of terror in the school. Intruding for only one morning, Eileen initiates a women's liberation campaign by demanding that girls be allowed into woodworking. On one level, the story is another rollicking satire on sexual stereotyping; but on another level, it is a serious study of accepting the diverse elements in a given personality.

Another collection of short stories, *A Can of Worms* (1990), contains seven stories that illustrate Mark's ability to blend the comic and the tragic in the same story. She admits to preferring to write short stories (even though they are more difficult) than novels. "When I finish a novel, I feel tired. When I finish a short story, I feel clever" (*The Horn Book* 64: 43). That cleverness is shown in her skill at choosing a brief interval of time, an epiphanic moment, then emptying it, spilling its contents, and reassembling it in a story. "The Travelling Settee" concerns such a moment—a brief interview a student holds with a novelist. But even on her way to the meeting, after she had re-read the novels, the young journalist feels "really upset as if I had lost something." She even pinpoints the moment: "I knew then, as I passed the lamppost, that I was going to meet a dreadfully unhappy man" (8). But he isn't. The student comes to understand not only how the novelist had written all he was capable of, but also that he has come to terms with that desperate, unfulfilled search for the "garden" which obsesses the young. The interviewer recognizes, as the older novelist has already done, that the energetic search for happiness which young collegians put into their final days of university life is merely a recognition that the freedom from anxiety and worry that usually characterizes college life is over. "How happy they had been," the interviewer notes, "because they knew it couldn't last" (22).

Mark writes about the changes wrought by death in "Too Old to Rock and Roll." The surprise moment here is generated not by the father's loss of his wife, but by the son's expectations of the father. In "Front," a budding friendship is destroyed after one brief home visit; in "A Can of Worms," a visit to a bookstore changes a girl's perception of her mother's mother. In "Crocodile Time," the moment of change comes when a young man discovers his new girlfriend has no sense of humour. "Party Wall" catches the moment of change in a relationship. "Resurgam," perhaps the most ambiguous and richly textured of all the stories, focusses on one Easter celebration and the changes it brings—both to the characters and to the reader.

One cannot *not* read every word of a Jan Mark story. Fastidious in her respect for real life, she is often ambivalent about simple statements of fact in order to indicate the complexity of balancing social obligations and individual desires. Her framing of Dora in "A Can of Worms" is a good example. Instead of empirically stating that Dora's father had deserted the family, Mark notes that the father's capacity for "being happy had removed him from the scene six months after Dora's birth in search of fresh wife and children new" (80). Mark, albeit unconsciously, situates herself in the Kristevan dialectic, in that "constant alternation between time and its 'truth'" ("About Chinese Women" 38). The young girl in "Resurgam" hears the flower ladies' heels "gossip towards the door" (132), and the reader hears in the staccato sound of clacking heels the ever-recurrent hypocrisy to be found in Christianity; indeed in all humans. The gossiping "Christian" flower ladies in the church represent another form of dissimulation, paralleled by the miniaturized Garden of the Resurrection, which is an ironic dissimulation of the old church's real graveyard. In a lighter tone, Mark's creation and translation of Frodoxian (with its burlesque of Batman and Robin) in "Crocodile Time" must certainly be the funniest, freshest comic language in contemporary writing.

For all her comic art, however, Mark's is not a comic vision. Mark does not write from religious convictions. Ancient Greek Platonism—with its emphasis on endurance and the power of the heart to lead to the Good—is enough. She leaves no room for revealed religion or a personalized Saviour in the never-ending quest for the unified self. For her, recognizing the challenges of the fragmented self and having her young readers recognize them, are reward enough. Like Bellerephon on his Pegasus, she, with her gloriously versatile imagination, can defeat the delusive chimaera of the unified self. And she can laugh, because she can endure and will survive.

8

LAST WORDS

THIS BOOK had its beginning on a train ride from London to the south of England. Travels on three continents intervened before its ending in a tiny room whose one window offered a magnificent view of sweeping willows in the village of Gagny, France. During the eight year period of reading and research, I have travelled from Ayres Rock, sacred to the Australian Aborigines, to the Parisian apartment of Julia Kristeva,[1] and I have been nourished by the imaginative wisdom of the several writers whose works have been explored in this volume.

The train, with its pulsating rhythm, its stops, regressions, and active thrust forward, no matter what its destination, becomes a strange Kristevan hieroglyphic of language, of fiction, and even of time. Indeed, a train ride may be perceived as a metaphor for the creative act itself. Because of its rapid/slow, rhythmic/monotonous, space/time-defying pulsations, it may be viewed as a sign of contradictions: in language, because of the interactive elements of the semiotic and the symbolic; in fiction, because of the interpretive power of life on imagination, and of imagination on life; in our conception of time, because of the unending quest to objectify what Julia Kristeva has termed the "felt time of our subjective memories" (*Proust and the Sense of Time* 7). And indeed, Terry Eagleton succinctly captures Kristeva's own paradoxical teaching on the semiotic when he observes how

> the semiotic can still be discerned as a kind pulsional pressure within language itself, in tone, rhythm, the bodily and material qualities of language, but also in contradiction, meaninglessness, disruption,

silence and absence. The semiotic is the 'other' of language which is nonetheless intimately entwined with it. (*Literary Theory* 188)

That is why the impression of termination and of loss, initiated on that train ride, has long been dissipated by the forward-looking vision of the writers studied in this volume. After standing still or moving backward, the train always goes forward again. A young boy's belief in the power of evil may be acknowledged as simply an individual's recognition of evil as a form of Kristevan abjection—"immoral, sinister, scheming, and shady, a terror that dissembles, a hatred that smiles" (*PH* 4). But naming abjection may be simply a healthy acknowledgement of the chaos, turmoil and malice that lie deep within the heart and mind of humankind.

Whether one thinks this recognition of the power of abjection signals the age's loss of innocence or simply its coming of age—however one views it—the sense of confusion, waste and ruin evident in the last decade of the twentieth century cannot be denied. An adolescent's belief in the domination of evil has its counterpart in countless other images of grief and loss so powerfully depicted in the novels studied in this book. The only recourse we have in the face of meaninglessness, suffering, pain, and rejection is the art of living itself. This age is not so much interested in life after death as it is in the quality of life before death. And it is this art of living before death, of enduring, of hoping, that Julia Kristeva's psychoanalytic theory affirms. Her semanalysis is a search for balance between semiology and psychoanalysis, the semiotic and the symbolic, masculine and feminine, reason and emotion. The values of religion and art are wed in her psychoanalytic theory. Kristeva nourishes hope in the human psyche.

On that long-past train ride which, I admit, has dominated my imagination throughout the writing of this book, I claimed my own place in historical time. I realized that we, as parents and educators, cannot afford to miss society's opportunity to re-examine its consciousness, a consciousness often dulled by the bleatings of the media with its cult of imitation and conformity. I mused over several imponderable questions. How are we nurturing our young? Are the lives of children and adults too cramped, too stratified, too rushed? Are our children being cosseted, over-protected, over-regulated so that mental training, physical training, social training leave them no free time for silence, for strengthening individuality and developing interiority? Our generation will not find secure answers to these questions; the solutions to our problems are also in process.

Using Julia Kristeva's psychoanalytic theory, however, I have attempted to examine not so much those resolutions or answers given to the modern predicament by contemporary writers for the young, but rather the nature of our dilemma. If these studies have had one aim, it was to show how Kristevan theory offers a hope-filled dimension not only in our reading of contemporary literature but also, and more importantly, in our personal and social, never-ending quest for understanding and balance. Kristeva's conception of the chora and abjection, her probings of melancholia and sexual ambiguities, linear and monumental time, her hope-filled thesis on subject identity as being always in process—these insights provide an extraordinary penetration into the unconscious and its need for counterbalancing the semiotic and the symbolic polarities of the universal mind. Her alliance of psychoanalysis and literature helps both writer and reader explore and reorganize the psyche. Essentially her works defy soul-destroying despair. She gives back hope by teaching that humanity at the outset of the twenty-first century, like the individual adolescent, is capable of many resurrections in the on-going saga of identity formation.

Quoting Proust, Kristeva affirms that grief ends up killing us if we do not manage to extract an idea from it. "The sole recourse that we have in the face of this inevitable affliction is the art of living which is indeed dependent on a special form of intelligence." Intelligence becomes "special" when it is able to regard the person that hurts us as a "reflection," "fragment," "stage" of an Idea, a "divine form": in other words, a type of "divinity" (*PST* 79).

As far as I could research, not one of the writers considered in this book had ever studied the works of Julia Kristeva; yet every one of them shared with her a deep appreciation not only of the interpretive power of fiction on life but also of life on fiction. They likewise shared with her a profound conviction that literature can help us in our pain, and a preoccupation both in the ambivalent nature of adolescence and in the meaning of time. Although I concentrated on only one aspect of Kristevan theory in each writer—a facet of the semiotic/symbolic duality, the chora, abjection, the subject-in-process, melancholia in the human psyche, and monumental time—some consideration of these points appears in all the novels and underscores the importance of writing as a way of exploring the unconscious, of re-organizing the psyche, and of making us more accepting of the uncertainty of our place in time.

All six novelists are fascinated by time. Cormier, Mark, and Major dislocate the natural chronology of time. Wrightson seeks in the time past of the Australian Aborigines an antidote to modern materialism, while Paterson explores time past as memory and its effect on the imagination. For Chambers, the only way of understanding time is to record experience, tame it, frame it in the word. All the novelists considered in these studies offer life in time as both a spectacle and a spectacular challenge to seek salvation in recovering the lost kingdom of an interior life. These writers, as Kristeva expresses it, are "contrasting the disarray of the world and of the self with the unending search for that lost temple, that invisible temple which is *the felt time of our subjective memories*" (*PST* 7).

Patricia Wrightson discovered "felt time" in figures from Aboriginal folklore—the Bunyip, Nyol, and Nargun, for example— marvellous metaphors for the semiotic. The Aborigine's relationship to the land is like the child's relationship to the mother's body; Wrightson sees the Aborigines' association with the land as distinctly maternal and nurturing. Notwithstanding its positive force, Wrightson, like Kristeva, does not gloss over its negative aspects. The maternal function, according to Kristeva, provides both a means of identification and negation. The breast, to which the child relates most intimately and fully, also operates negatively when it is withheld at weaning time. The mother thus is a controlling figure ordering what goes into the body and what is withheld. Using authentic Aboriginal figures and creating stories based on a folklore not her own, Wrightson elucidates some of the most vexing problems of modern life. In the Australian Aborigine her imagination has found an allegory for a way to balance the semiotic and the symbolic within a maternal space, a space capable of healing the impending wounds of materialism, greed and racial divisions.

Space, too, does not lack a temporal component in Wrightson's work. In the cave scene of *The Dark Bright Water*, time and space are brought together to coalesce into a moment of intense sensuousness, a nodal point which will bulge, swell and explode in Ularra the beast. Ularra exerts a strange charm on Wirrun which the latter cannot fully understand until Ularra experiences his lustful longing for the Abuba girl. At this moment in time, Wirrun, once the bosom friend, becomes indifferent in Ularra's eyes and the dangerous Abuba becomes sweet and compellingly attractive. The analogy of Ularra as beast carries its own ontological truth for Wirrun. Flesh asserts its role in the nature of being. In their identification with and negation of the flesh, as well as by their identity with and by the land, Wrightson's characters must all come to grips with and re-enact the repressive/jubilatory state of the semiotic/symbolic cycle.

Kevin Major explores "felt time" through the word. He is fascinated both by the inability of the word to convey meaning fully and by the recognition that the only way of sustaining oneself is through the power of the word. His novels are all structured on some form of written communication: letters, reports, observations, different but deferential commentaries of the same phenomenon. For Major, the individual comes to grips with the hidden face of identity by encountering a space/time-defying chora experience which enables the stranger to lose its pathological aspect. The chora experience, intelligible but at the same time not totally comprehensible, offers nourishment and a new beginning because it provides the subject with a way to regress in order to progress. The chora, as the receptacle for the drives, allows the subject to enter into a pre-individual, pre-socialized state in order to recognize its separateness. The chora is usually associated with a moment of intense sensation—eating, drowning, snowballing. Kristeva, quoting Proust again, sees sensation as "a fragment of time in the pure state." It is "neither a reality nor mere solipsism," and "exists at the interface of the world and the self" (*PST* 53). In *Eating Between the Lines*, Jackson recollects through the metaphor of eating; recollecting and eating form the essence of Jackson's narration. Time past (memory) with time present (eating) merge into a future wherein equilibrium is restored because a young adult stabilizes loss by transferring it into meaning. In Kevin Major's novels, the adolescent, by undergoing a chora-like experience usually made comprehensible through the power of the word, finds a satisfying, if temporary, solution to the problem of separation from the parental dyad.

Katherine Paterson's novels explore abjection as a transitional, oft-repeated time of liberation. Abjection, according to Kristeva, is narcissism's counteractive force. In all Paterson's characters, abjection can be studied at the borders of subject identity. The phase of abjection within the maternal function marks the transition from dependence to independence. The borders, chronological and spatial, governing subject identity are hazy and ambiguous, fluctuating between the child and its mother, nature and culture, subject and other, but there is always a link in time, usually metaphorically captured. Thus, the postcard from Gilly's mother in *The Great Gilly Hopkins* forms a critical connection between Gilly and her mother. The arrival of the card is not a detached, sterile incident but a beginning which reaches toward a distant future when Gilly will face her own abjection. It becomes a metaphor for a metamorphosis. Gilly will cease to depend on a false, idealized figure of maternal love and recognize her individuality and independence. Abjection reveals a want, a lack, which must be recognized before identity is grasped. Gilly divests herself of her desire for the mother by debasing her, making her not an ennobling "womb" receptacle for new life but a useless flower child gone to wasted "seed." Identity is wrested from the experience of time; it is always in the process of forming, deforming, and reforming itself. Abjection and its acceptance are discarding and integrative processes, and all Paterson's fictional characters, like all humans, must wrestle with it in their allotted time.

No novelist is more aware of time's power on the unconscious than Aidan Chambers. The three novels discussed in this book all imply time's passage and its power. Time is explicit in the title *Breaktime*; in *Dance on My Grave*, the grave signals the end of time, a memorial to having been in time; in *Now I Know*, the emphasis is on the "now" of time. Chambers is acutely attentive to those clashes in perspective of time which separate child and parent, individual and society. He is equally observant of the constant time shifts from past to present and from present to future in human relationships. The stinging, bruising flavour of his protagonists' relationships are best seen in *Dance on My Grave*, where recollections of young Hal's homosexual relationship with Barry Gorman still slumber in the depths of memory which has an uncontrollable life of its own and thrusts itself into the present. The image of Barry's dead body surfaces again and again in the novel and endows the narration with the implosive power of the central incident—dancing on a friend's grave. Chambers' novel erupts inwardly with the tender as well as with the vicious aspects of Hal's erotic, homosexual secret, and with this eruption the heart of the universal adolescent is laid bare. In this novel, too, the silence of repression is violent. Hal and his analogical "can of beans," like Jack of the fairy tale who sold everything of value for a purse of worthless beans, is the allegory Chambers uses to explore the relationship between sexuality and language—a recurring theme in his three major novels. Examining the melancholia characterizing the sexual ambiguities in his characters' psyches, Chambers' novels become many-layered records of his protagonist telling stories about their lived experiences in time. The telling becomes a thinking, or processing of information, and it is this thinking with words that serves as an antidote to nihilism and despair. Chambers realizes that the act of writing may create the writer sometimes even more forcefully than the novelist creates his novel.

In all the novels studied, it is clearly evident that the novelists are primarily concerned with awareness and liberation of identity as on-going process. This topic is most closely analyzed, in Kristevan terms, in the writings of Jan Mark. She is courageous in depicting those youthful moments in time when meaning is pulverized, if not entirely destroyed. That memorable scene in *Thunder and Lightnings* when a young boy witnesses the destruction of an ideal of motherhood is a case in point. Andrew watches his friend's face being slapped by an angry mother simply because of a soiled sheet. In that moment time is encapsulated. All the unfairness of human life is wrapped up in that dirty sheet and stored forever in Andrew's memory. Mark shocks her readers into recognition and realization that a brief moment in childhood has absorbed the future destiny of Andrew as a subject-in-process, a subject who must constantly confront his illusions—in this case, the illusion of idealized maternal love.

Yet out of chaos and destruction, alienation and loss, there is always the possibility of change, of a resurrection, as long as the individual continues to search for the other as self and the self as other. The subject is always "in process," capable of being other than it is. So it is in her *Divide and Rule.* Hanno, the sheep-like character at the beginning of the novel, the slave of feeling, has become a thinker at the novel's close. This truth, on the individual dimension, carries through with that of society. Mark is unsentimental in her condemnation of the herd-like qualities of social groupings with their basis in imitation, an imitation inculcated by the media, religion, or political parties. Like Kristeva, Mark is interested in life as a series of splittings—at birth, at the mirror stage, at adolescence, at death—and her novels offer an apprenticeship in learning how to live in time with these necessary splittings, losses, and ensuing liberations.

Robert Cormier turns linear time into the monumental time of literature. In all his novels, the setting of the fictitious "Monument" in Massachusetts becomes not merely a name but a testament to time and timelessness. Often all that remains of a human being is a name and two dates. But the musing quality of the word's every syllable, its unobtrusive repetition in all his works, make Monument commemorative not only of his novels but also of their creator's place in time and in the literary history of his generation. The name releases in the reader's mind memories of all Cormier's subjects and their evanescence in time; it releases also memories of distinct sensations—from the screech of bicycle tires on a wet road to the smell of a burning school building—a plethora of impressions; jubilatory, yes, but also infinitely sad. Monument becomes metonymic for universal space and time, but space and time that is peopled with characters concerned with loss, abjection, subject formation, sexual ambiguities, and the semiotic. For Cormier, too, the maternal is the focus of the unconscious.

Just as the child's relationship to the breast operates both as a form of identification and negation, for him the mother's body provides a nexus for the ever-recurring pattern of escape from, and return to, the womb. Cormier, like Kristeva, sees the maternal figure of primary importance in leading the child from narcissism to time-and-space-transcending love. That is why time and love figure so prominently in all his novels, and why there can be no real love without the forgiveness that obliterates the mistakes of time and that offers extraordinary regenerative power to the psyche.

It is the symbolic that makes individual identities possible. But the symbolic function of reason has overdominated, repressed, and that is why a "revolution" in poetic language is in order. Radical social change would be impossible without a disruption in the authoritarian discourse articulated by religion, politics, and the family. Rebellion in some shape or form is endemic to adolescence. But just as clearly as Kristeva suggests that the semiotic is dominated by the symbolic, she is equally forceful in showing that what is rationally accepted must be continually tested by the irrational and the intuitive. Just as the subject is never entirely unified, neither are the semiotic and the symbolic. Reason is always challenged by pleasure. Humanity occupies a peculiar space across which physical and psychic impulses flow rhythmically. The flux is gradually regulated by the constraints of the symbolic which in turn are loosened by the demands of the semiotic. Thus, Julia Kristeva brings the body back into structuralism, into signification, into the very depths of language.

But she does infinitely more. Kristeva insists on the power of the imagination to offset the disappointment of present reality. Kristeva quotes Proust as remarking: "My work is not microscopic, it is telescopic" (*PST* 56). "Telescoping," she continues, "has its psychological point of departure in an original state of *disappointment*, which has been powerfully overcome by the *hallucinatory capacity* to reproduce the desired but lost impressions within the imagination (*PST* 56-57). For Kristeva, sensation can be recovered through imagination because memory, like time, "is but the servant of the imagination" (*PST* 90). Kristeva's own telescopic lens brings immense, deeply remote elements of the unconscious into closer view for ordinary inspection. The writers whose works were examined at length in these studies—Patricia Wrightson, Kevin Major, Katherine Paterson, Aidan Chambers, Jan Mark, and Robert Cormier—have also disdained the use of a microscopic lens which can merely produce a magnified image of a small fragment of reality. Bold in their novels' exploration of the most far-reaching reality of human existence—the mystery of suffering—these writers, by giving suffering meaning, have made us see despair as a splinter of the divine idea.

NOTES

Introduction

1 Zohar Shavit, *The Poetics of Children's Literature* (London and Athens: University of Georgia Press, 1986), ix.

2 There have been some very noteworthy critical studies of children's literature in the last twenty years. Certainly Jacqueline Rose's *The Case of Peter Pan* (London: Macmillan, 1984), which offers a Lacanian study of James M. Barrie's classic, is in a class by itself. Also significant and of help to me were Perry Nodelman's *The Pleasures of Children's Literature* (New York: Longman, 1992) and Roderick McGillis's "Another Kick at La/can," *Children's Literature Association Quarterly* 20.1 (1995): 42-46.

3 See Karin Lesnik-Oberstein's *Children's Literature: Criticism and the Fictional Child* (Oxford: Clarendon, 1994). Lesnik-Oberstein contends that "if children's literature criticism depends on, and is defined by, its claim to the existence of the 'real' child ... then it is indeed dead" (163).

1 Looking up the Devil's Nose

1 For a modern interest in the occult, see Jan L. Perkowski's *Vampires, Dwarves and Witches Among the Ontario Kashubs* (Ottawa: National Museum of Man, 1972).

2 See A.O. Lovejoy, *The Great Chain of Being* (Cambridge, Massachusetts: Harvard, 1936); also J. Hillis Miller's insightful introduction to his study *The Disappearance of God* (Cambridge, Massachusetts: Harvard, 1963), 1-16.

3 *Jouissance* is Kristeva's word to express the pleasures of infancy and sexuality, repressed by the Law of the Father. She uses it, for example, in *About Chinese Women* (London: Marion Boyars, 1977), 18-19. For feminists' connotations of the word, see *New French Feminisms: An Anthology*, Elaine Marks and Isabelle de Courtivron, eds. (Amherst: University of Massachusetts Press, 1980) 36, n. 8.

4 I am not arguing that there were no instances of parental failure in literature prior to the latter half of the twentieth century. Clearly the parents in *Clarissa*, for example, were dismal failures. Furthermore, when I claim that most fathers in fairy tales are guilty of benign neglect, I am not overlooking the tradition of the unnatural father who figures in many tales. "Cap o' Rushes" is an interesting illustration of these fathers.

5 See Donelson's and Nilsen's discussion on "nice" girls in their edition of *Literature for Today's Young Adults*, second edition (Glenview Ill, and London, England: Scott Forsman and Co., 1985), 13-18. Donelson and Nilsen look to 1967 as the pivotal year for "the new realism" (p. 104).

6 See, for example, S. Petzel and M. Riddle, "Adolescent Suicide: Psychosocial and Cognitive Aspects" in S.C. Feinstein et als. eds. *Adolescent Psychiatry: Developmental and Clinical Studies*, vol. 9 (Chicago: University of Chicago Press, 1981).

7 For futher background on the causes of suicide and depression see J.S. Wodarski, "Single Parents and Children: A Review for Social Workers," *Family Therapy* 9(3): 311-320; and F. Wenz, "Self-inquiry Behaviour, Economic Status and the Family Anomic Syndrome among Adolescents," *Adolescents* 14(54): 387-398.

8 See "Adolescent Suicide: A Review of Influences and the Means for Prevention," *Practice Applications* (St. Louis, Mo. Washington U. Center for adolescent Mental Health) 2:4 (Spring 1985): 1.

9 Between 1960 and 1980, the suicide rate in the United States rose from 5.2 to 12.3 per 100,000 for this age-group, representing a 136% increase. The 1986 statistics were no more encouraging and showed that despair grips even the 10–14-year-old age-group.

10 On the rise of suicide and parents' reluctance to report, the reader might consult A.L. Berman, "Testimony on Behalf of the American Psychological Association before the Committee on the Judiciary—Subcommittee on Juvenile Justice—United States Senate Hearing on Teenage Suicide," October 1984; B.L. Mishara, "The Extent of Adolescent Suicidality," *Psychiatric Opinion* 12 (6): 32-37; also A.D. Pokorny, "Self Destruction and the Automobile," *Self Destructive Behavior*, Albert R. Roberts, ed. (Springfield, Illinois: Charles C. Thomas, 1975).

11 In Canada between 1961 and 1981, the suicide rate more than quadrupled among males aged 15–19 and almost tripled among the males in the 20–24 age-group. Over the same period the rate for females in the 15–19 group jumped from 0.8 to 3.8 per 100,000 population. The overall rate for the country was 15.1 per 100,000 people. In 1986 suicide represented 22% of deaths among males aged 15-24 and 13% of deaths among females of the same age-group (*Statistics Canada*), 1989). The comparative figures among the four major English-speaking countries produce some anomalies. For the male population 15–24 years of age, the statistics per 100,000 are as follows: Australia (1988) 27.8; Canada (1990), 25.2; UK, 2; US, 4.2 (*Statistical Abstract of the US* 1993, Table 1382). While males in general have a higher rate of suicide than females, the latter make more attempts.

12 Annie Gottlieb accused Cormier of robbing youth of hope in her review of *The Chocolate War*, "A New Cycle in 'YA' Books," *New York Times Book Review* (June 17, 1984): 24-25.

13 Jacqueline Rose argues that "childhood is seen as the place where an older form of culture is preserved" (50) and "what seems to have happened in recent discussions of children's books is that, in response to the realist aesthetic in the modern adult novel, writers have been arguing with increasing vehemence for its preservation in writing intended for children" (60).

14 For an account of Cormier's contribution to young adult fiction see Patricia Head's insightful article "Robert Cormier and the Postmodernist Possibilities of Young adult Fiction," *Children's Literature Association Quarterly* 21:1 (Spring 1996): 28-33.

15 Plumb's essay reechoes the main ideas of Philip Aries' seminal work *Centuries of Childhood*, trans. Robert Baldwick (London: Jonathan Cape, 1962).

16 The "Honor Sampling" comprises a list of books culled by Alleen Pace Nilsen and Kenneth L. Donelson in which the "best books" recommended by the Young Adult Services of the American Library Association, the *School Library Journal*, the *New York Times Book Review, The English Journal*, the books for Young Adults Program founded by G. Robert Carlsen at the University of Iowa, and a survey of books assigned by approximately 100 college instructors of young-adult literature.

17 Foremost among Parisian intellectuals, Julia Kristeva was born in Bulgaria in 1941 and emigrated to Paris in 1965 in order to study linguistics. Kristeva quickly became one of the guiding theorists of the avant-garde journal *Tel Quel*. In the 1970s and 1980s, she published a series of very erudite, sometimes controversial, books on semiotics, narrative theory, and psychological analyses of literature. English translations of *Desire in Language, Powers of Horror, Revolution in Poetic*

Language, Tales of Love, In the Beginning Was Love, Language, the Unknown, Black Sun, and *Strangers to Ourselves* have all been published by Columbia University Press.

18 Kristeva's "The Adolescent Novel" is the lead essay in *Abjection, Melancholia and Love,* John Fletcher and Andrew Benjamin, eds. (London and New York: Routledge, 1990), 1-23.

2 The Semiotic/Symbolic Dyad

1 In his introduction to Kristeva's *Revolution in Poetic Language,* Leon S. Roudiez uses the term "writing subject" rather than "author" to counter the illusion that the author has "author-ity" over the meaning of his work (7).

2 Kristeva privileges the maternal body and emphasizes the period before Lacan's mirror stage—the space before the entry into the use of the symbolic sign in language. She does not limit the semiotic to that period, however. The semiotic for Kristeva, as Roudiez explains in his edition of *Desire in Language,* "is seen as one of the two components of the signifying process—the other being the symbolic. The semiotic refers to the actual organization, or disposition, within the body, of instinctual drives as they affect language and its practice, in dialectical conflict with the symbolic" (*DL* 4).

3 According to Kristeva, maternal regulation prefigures paternal prohibition, and bodily drive force is never completely repressed within signification (Oliver 19). Expanding on Freud's view of the unconscious and on Lacan's mirror stage, Kristeva emphasizes the fluidity of the semiotic which disrupts the symbolic order and underscores the subject's capacity to transgress and transcend the existing linguistic and social institutions in which it is encoded. Her semiotic, so closely associated with the maternal, is seemingly opposed to all fixed ideologies of a male-dominated society with its symbolic reliance on established signs like God, father, state, and property. In modern history, Kristeva maintains, poetic language "has deserted beauty and become a laboratory where, facing philosophy, knowledge, and the transcendental ego of all signification, the impossibility of a signified of signifying identity is being sustained" (*DL* 145).

4 I have found M.J.E. King-Boys' study *Patterns of Aboriginal Culture: Then and Now* (Sydney; McGraw-Hill, 1977) extremely helpful in my study of the Australian Aborigines; also helpful was Kenneth Maddock's *The Australian Aborigines: A Portrait of Their Society* (London: Penquin, 1972). Readers wishing to pursue further readings of the Australian Aborigines should consult John Greenway's *Bibliography of the Australian Aborigines and The Native Peoples*

(Angus & Robertson, 1963); also the regional and periodic bibliographies published by the Australian Institute of Aboriginal Studies (Box 553, Canberra City, A.C.T., 2601). To keep up to date on the progress of Aboriginal studies it is necessary to read learned journals, of which the most important are *Oceania*, *Mankind*, and *Anthropological Forum*, the first two issued from the University of Sydney and the third from the University of Western Australia.

5 For insights into Aboriginal identity, I am grateful to Ernest M. Hunter's essay, "On Gordian Knots and Nooses: Aboriginal Suicide in the Kimberley," *Australian and New Zealand Journal of Psychiatry* 23:2 (June 1989): 264-71. For a more detailed analysis of this kinship among the Aborigines of Yirrkala and Pintupi, for example, see J. Reid, *Sorcerers and Healing Spirits: Continuity and Change in an Aboriginal Medical System* (Canberra: Australian Institute of Criminology, 1986); also see F.R. Myers, *Pintupi Country, Pintupi Self: Sentiment, Place and Politics among Western Desert Aboriginals* (Canberra: Australian Institute of Aboriginal Studies, 1986). For Aboriginal religious belief consult Tony Swain, *Interpreting Aboriginal Religion: An Historical Account*, Special Studies in Religion No. 5 (Bedford Park, S.A. Flinders University, 1985), 123-30; M.J.E. King-Boys, *Patterns of Aboriginal Culture: Then and Now* (Sydney; McGraw-Hill, 1977), 1-2; and Kenneth Maddock *The Australian Aborigines: A Portrait of Their Society*. London: Penguin, 1972.

6 Author interview with Patricia Wrightson, Maclean, N.S.W., March 4, 1991.

7 For biographical information on Patricia Wrightson consult *The Oxford Companion to Australian Literature,* William H. Wilde, Jay Horton, Barry Andrews, eds. (Melbourne: Oxford University Press, 1985), 757.

8 See Eggan's discussion of land in *The American Indian.* (London: Weidendeld & Nicolson, 1966), 18-19.

9 This article in *Reading Time* is an excerpt from Wrightson's acceptance speech, written when she was presented with *The Boston Globe/Horn Book* Award in 1984. The speech was read for Wrightson by Margaret McElderry.

10 Following the tradition of Tolkien, Wrightson's fantasy may be termed "high" since she is concerned with such serious topics as the psychological quest for self-identity, the never-ending search for unity, the unending conflict between good and evil, ecological conservation, and, above all, the importance of love; but her characters are far more realistic both in their human and racial generation.

11 Letter of 19 June 1979, quoted in "Australian Fantasy and Folklore, Part Two," *Orana* 17:3 (August 1981): 112-33.

12 In a letter written to the author, dated 24 May 1994, Wrightson insists: "If I haven't made it clear that they [Bunyip, Nyols, Nargun] all come out of the folklore, I should have done so.... So much, including Ularra's transformation into a beast, the process for restoring him, Wulgaru, the man-made death and so on, come direct from the folklore, and authenticity was a prime objective.... To use the authentic figures in invented stories, and to achieve an authenticity in a folklore that wasn't my own, was the hard thing. It involved fitting them truly to the land that gave rise to them...."

13 Wrightson maintains that *The Book of Wirrun* "has never seemed like a trilogy to me.... To me it's a single, continuous story of the growth of a man into herohood, and only for convenience of size is it in three parts" (Patricia Wrightson to Martha Westwater, May 24, 1994).

14 Patricia Wrightson, "Some Comments on the Books of Wirrun," *Reading Time* 84 (July 1982) 13.

15 Murra "is taken, badly against her will, but just as she knew all along she must be.... Murra is one of the fairy-wives men dream of but can never hold; the sealies and swan maidens and mermaids of Europe and the water-girls of Australia. Happy, faithful and loving wives, lost through some failing of their husbands. In this case Murra, happily discovering love, warned Wirrun early and told him he should keep her away from water. ...Wirrun failed her" (Patricia Wrightson to Martha Westwater, May 24, 1994).

3 Kevin Major and the Chora Experience

1 For biographical information on Kevin Major see Diane Turbide's article "Boyhood on the Rock" in *Maclean's* (April 17, 1989).

2 Kristeva's authoritative account of the generation of otherness that arises out of the I/me split is based on Jacques Lacan's theory as presented in his "Signification du Phallus," *Ecrits*, vol. 2 (Paris: Editions du Seuil). Here Lacan remarks that the "mirror stage" in the child's development occurs when, at the age of approximately eighteen months, the child looking in a mirror recognizes himself as other and begins a separation of the self from the mother.

3 In citing the pervasive and distinctive Newfoundland ambience of *Hold Fast*, Silver Donald Cameron noted that the world in which Major's young characters live is recognizably the rock-island on Canada's east coast, a world in which traditions like jigging squid, cutting firewood, and snaring rabbits give the universal experience of adolescence through Newfoundland particularities (Cameron 64). Gray also attests to Major's love of Newfoundland when he

quotes the novelist as saying, "I want our boys [his two sons] to have a sense of belonging, to understand the importance of family, to care about their neighbors as Newfoundlanders always have" (42). But Muriel Roberts (discussing *Hold Fast*) maintains that Major's hero is more a Canadian than a Newfoundlander. I disagree. I suggest that the Newfoundlander character is more complex, perhaps more universal than the stereotypical quiet Canadian. See Roberts' article "Canadian Books for Canadian Children" in *Book News.*

4 Kevin Major's first novel *Hold Fast* won three major Canadian awards including the Canada Council Children's Literature Prize. It was placed on the Hans Christian Andersen Honors List during the International Year of the Child in 1979. It has been translated into French, German, Spanish, Hebrew, and Danish, and was dramatized for the stage by St John's Rising Tide Theatre in 1990. See C.M. Sullivan's account of a Newfoundland writer with five adolescent novels to his credit. See also Helen Porter's essay in which she notes that *Hold Fast* "made the short list for the third annual Books in Canada Award ... unusual for a juvenile novel."

5 The masturbation scene in this and in his other novels has not been without its critics. See Margaret Montgomery and Ken Adachi.

6 The subject is split into the "I" that sees and the "me" that is seen. The "me" as other exists only in the mirror; it is therefore a creation of the imaginary. Following Lacan, Kristeva expands the effects of the mirror stage on language acquisition, by explaining how, at the same time that the child is recognizing self and other, he is undergoing other concrete operations which precede the acquisition of language and which organize pre-verbal semiotic space according to logical categories (Moi 94-95). These concrete operations help define a child's body and include physical activities like eating and excreting. Such operations lead to the development of urgent tendencies, desires, or drives in the child's mental landscape. Drives, always ambiguous, simultaneously assimilative and destructive, tend to generate a dominant destructive wave. As Roudiez explains, Kristeva's "speaking subject" is always split—"divided between unconscious and conscious motivations, that is, between physiological processes and social constraints" (*DL* 6).

7 For the meaning of this word and others, see the *Dictionary of Newfoundland English*, edited by G.M. Story, W.J. Kirwin, and J.D.A. Widdowson (Toronto: University of Toronto Press, 1982).

8 Major does not like to repeat narrative techniques. Jenkinson quotes Major as saying, "One thing I'm interested in doing is telling a story in different ways" (67) (*Far from Shore* uses five narrators.) "I'd seen the multi-narrative technique work quite well in one of Faulkner's books, *The Sound and the Fury.* I don't know if the idea of doing the multi-narration came from that, and I don't know why I chose it. Perhaps I wanted to try something a little bit different" (66).

9 Major has claimed that Lorne in *Thirty-Six Exposures* is closest in temperament to the adolescent he was, "at times—unsure of himself and confused about his place in life" (Duffy 255).

4 Abjection in the Novels of Katherine Paterson

1 I am grateful to James P. Carsels, *Finite and Infinite Games* (New York: Ballantine, 1986), 32. Carse emphasizes the joy in the game; Kristeva, its necessity; Paterson, its reality.

2 Kristeva defines this trinity of psychic life in *Tales of Love* when she writes, "The experience of love indissolubly ties together the *symbolic* (what is forbidden, distinguishable, thinkable), the *imaginary* (what the Self imagines in order to sustain and expand itself), and the *real* (that impossible domain where affects aspire to everything and where there is no one to take into account the fact that *I* am only a part)" (7).

3 "*Park's Quest* is patterned after Wolfram's 13th century romance, *Parcival.*" Letter from Katherine Paterson to Martha Westwater, June 24, 1994.

5 The Dilemma of Melancholia

1 Quoted from the author's interview with Aidan Chambers (Stroud, UK, April 19, 1991). Chambers has earned other awards in addition to the Farjeon. Three times he has won a Dutch Silver Pencil Award for his novels *Seal Secret* (1980), *The Present Takers* (1983), and *The Toll Bridge* (1992). Of the latter, a good example of Chambers' innovation, he wrote "it was a book in which I consciously and directly explored the Recognition narrative set in the modern(ist) context of an indeterminate ending, the ending that isn't an ending, and where closure isn't possible." Letter from Aidan Chambers to Martha Westwater, August 21, 1994.

2 Kristeva herself has admitted to feeling an exile, and her interest in psychoanalysis resulted at least in part from her being an exile from her native Bulgaria (Kurzeil 216).

3 Besides his fiction, Aidan Chambers edits, with his wife Nancy Chambers, *Signal*, a journal for children's literature. They also began Thimble Press, dedicated to the cultural health of children's literature in the United Kingdom and in the English-speaking world. He has also been a frequent contributor to *The Horn Book*.

4 Chambers expands Kathleen Tillotson's use of the "second self" in "The Reader in the Book," *Booktalk: Occasional Writing on Literature and Children* (London: The Bodley Head, 1985), 35. Here Chambers developed for critics of children's literature F.H. Langham's thesis that the literary critic must recognize the idea of the reader implied by the work. Not only correct understanding but also evaluation often depends principally upon correct recognition of the implied reader. This essay, "The Reader in the Book," was based on a talk titled "A Children's Book Is for Children," given in February 1977 at the University of Bristol School of Education. It was first published in *Signal* 23 (May 1977) and it received the first award for excellence in literary criticism given annually by the Children's Literature Association in the US (1978).

5 See James DiCenso's article "New Approaches to Psychoanalysis and Religion: Julia Kristeva's *Black Sun*" in *Studies in Religion* 24:3 (1995): 279-95. Here DiCenso explicates that ways that Kristeva links melancholia with a developing sense of self (280).

6 Chambers admitted that, born into a working-class background and educated out of it, he had experienced a broken relationship with his own father (Martha Westwater interview with Aidan Chambers, April 19, 1991.)

7 Anton Chekhov, *The Seagull*, Act 4, quoted in David Magarshack's *Chekhov The Dramatist* (London: Methuen), 191.

8 Nik's name read backwards is "kin," and an anagram of it is "ink;" the name is often associated with the Christian Saint Nicholas, patron of Christmas, and also with the "old Nick," the devil. See Peter Forrestal's "An Interview with Aidan Chambers," *Magpies* 4 (September 1987), 16-18.

9 In Peter Forrestal's interview with Aidan Chambers, already cited, Chambers elaborated on the significance of setting as well as of time: The setting is "Stroud mythologized. All the characters in the book have names which are place names in Stroud. The boy is called Nicholas Frome and the Froom is the river that flows through Stroud.... You will find that the characters make a cruciform shape on the map. They actually make a rough cross with the middle of the cross running through where ... there is a crucifixion in the book and the place where it happens is where the crosses cross" (18).

10 Chambers admits that the ideas appearing in Nik's book for Julie owe their inspiration to the work of Tom Phillips, especially his book *A Humument* which Nik uses in his "book scrap" (235-37).

11 John Bunyan, *The Pilgrim's Progress* (London: Cassell and Co., 1908), 107.

6 Robert Cormier and Monumental Time

1 In an interview (August 1991), Cormier admitted that he intended *The Chocolate War* for the adult market. It was a percipient editor who felt it would be more suitable to an adolescent readership.

2 Kristeva provides a complete examination of the mother's relation to time and space in her discussion of childbood language. See "Place Names," *Desire in Languages*, 271-94.

3 See Kristeva's essay "Women's Time," wherein Kristeva maintains her belief that space, specifically maternal space, is more important than time in generating and forming the human species. *The Kristeva Reader*, 188-213.

4 The question, "Do I dare disturb the universe?" comes from T.S. Eliot's poem "The Love Song of J. Alfred Prufrock."

5 Kristeva maintains that "All enunciation, whether of a word or of a sentence, is thetic. It requires an identification; in other words, the subject must separate from and through his image, from and through his objects" (*Revolution in Poetic Language* 43.). Lechte further clarifies the term: "The 'thetic,' then, is precisely the positionality deriving from the distinction between subject and object" (*Julia Kristeva* 134).

6 What distinguishes common usage of *jouissance* from that of Jacques Lacan and Julia Kristeva is that in the earlier meaning of the word, the different connotations are kept separate. Kristeva in particular emphasizes their simultaneity. "'Jouissance' is sexual, spiritual, physical, conceptual at one and the same time." Furthermore, the "jouissance" of the other, which in Lacanian-Kristevan terms is the "place in which is constituted the I who speaks with him who hears," can be fostered only through infinitude (Roudiez, *Desire in Language*, 16).

7 For a postmodernist study of *Fade* see Patricia Head's essay "Robert Cormier and the Postmodernist Possibilities of Young Adult fiction" *Children's Literature Association Quarterly*, 21:1 (Spring 1996) 28-34.

7 Chuckling with the Chimaera

1 In the course of writing this book, I have had several meetings with Jan Mark; the first of these meetings, in which I tested the thesis of this chapter, took place on April 14, 1991.

2 Kristeva's clearest exposition of the stranger within the self is found in her book *Strangers to Ourselves*, Leon S. Roudiez, tranlator (New York: Columbia University Press, 1991).

3 C.S. Lewis expresses this idea in his *Voyage to Venus*: "It is words that are vague. The reason why the thing can't be expressed is that it's too definite for language." Quoted in Paul Hawken, *The Magic of Findhorn* (New York: Harper and Row, 1975), 231.

4 Hunt is uncharacteristically harsh in some of his comments; for example, he claims that Jan Mark's talent had been "lost through egoism and ill advice to the proper pursuit of producing superlative, *relevant* books for children" (13). I disagree.

8 Last Words

1 I met the gracious, generous Julia Kristeva in Paris on July 6, 1994. In person she is not nearly so mystifying as she is in prose.

WORKS CITED

Adachi, Ken. "Novelist Expects More Censorship." *Toronto Star* 26 November 1984: C3.

"Adolescent Suicide: A Review of Influences and the Means for Prevention." *Practice Applications.* St. Louis: Washington University Center for Adolescent Mental Health 2:4 (Spring 1985).

Anonymous. *Go Ask Alice.* Englewood Cliffs, New Jersey: Prentice Hall, 1971.

Aries, Philip. *Centuries of Childhood.* Robert Baldwick, trans. London: Jonathan Cape, 1962.

Atkinson, Maxwell. "Some Cultural Aspects of Suicide in Britain." *Suicides in Different Cultures.* Norman L. Farberow, ed. Baltimore, London, Tokyo: University Park Press, 1975.

Bann, Stephen. "Introduction." In Julia Kristeva, *Proust and the Sense of Time.* London: Faber and Faber, 1993.

Benjamin, Andrew and John Fletcher, eds. *Abjection, Melancholia and Love.* London and New York: Routledge, 1990.

Berman, A.L. "Testimony on Behalf of the American Psychological Association before the Committee on the Judiciary-Subcommittee on Juvenile Justice—United States Senate Hearing on Teenage Suicide." October 1984.

Bixler, Phyllis. "*I Am the Cheese* and Reader Response." *Children's Literature Association Quarterly* 10:1 (1985): 13-16.

Blakeslee, Sandra and Judith Wallerstein. *Second Chances: Men, Women and Children a Decade after Divorce.* New York: Ticknor and Fields, 1989.

Bunyan, John. *The Pilgrim's Progress.* London: Cassell, 1908.

Cameron, Silver Donald. "A Major Author for Minors." *Atlantic Insight* (March 1981): 64.

Chambers, Aidan. *Breaktime.* London: Bodley Head, 1978.

———. *Dance on My Grave.* London: Bodley Head, 1982.
———. *Now I Know.* London: Bodley Head, 1987.
———. *The Toll Bridge.* London: Bodley Head, 1993.
Cormier, Robert. *Beyond the Chocolate War.* New York: Pantheon, 1985.
———. *The Bumblebee Flies Anyway.* New York: Pantheon, 1983.
———. *The Chocolate War.* New York: Pantheon, 1974.
———. *Fade.* New York: Delacorte, 1988.
———. *I Am the Cheese.* New York: Pantheon, 1977.
Cuskey, W.R., I.F. Litt, and S. Rudd. "Emergency Room Evaluation of the Adolescent Who Attempts Suicide: Compliance with Follow-up." *Journal of Adolescent Health Care* 4 (1983): 106-08.
DiCenso, James. "New Approaches to Psychoanalysis and Religion: Julia Kristeva's *Black Sun.*" *Studies in Religion* 24:3 (1995): 279-95.
Donelson, Kenneth L. and Alleen Pace Nilsen. *Literature for Today's Young Adults.* Second ed. Glenview, Illinois and London, UK: Scott Forsman, 1985.
Donovan, John. *Wild in the World.* New York: Harper, 1971.
Duffy, Mary. "A Sense of Truth: A Profile of Kevin Major." *Canadian Materials* 17:6 (1989): 255-56.
Eagleton, Terry. *Literary Theory: An Introduction.* Minneapolis: University of Minnesota Press, 1983.
Eggan, F. *The American Indian.* London: Weidenfeld & Nicolson, 1966.
Eliot, T.S. "The Love Song of J. Alfred Prufrock." *Collected Poems* 1909-1935. London: Faber & Faber, 1937.
Feinstein, S.C. et al., eds. *Adolescent Psychiatry: Developmental and Clinical Studies* 9. Chicago: University of Chicago Press, 1981.
Fraser, Matthew. "Writer Probes Youthful Worries with Rare Insight." *The Globe and Mail* 26 March 1988: C3.
Gottlieb, Annie. "A New Cycle in 'YA' Books." *New York Times Book Review* 17 (June 17 1984): 24-25.
Gray, Charlotte. "What Kind of Canada Do You Want for Your Kids? Part 4." *Chatelaine* (June 1991): 41-46.
Greenway, John. *Bibliography of the Australian Aborigines and the Native Peoples.* London: Angus & Robertson, 1963.
Hatton, Peter. "Patricia Wrightson." *Aspects of Children's Literature.* Ed. Ken Watson. 23-30.
Head, Patricia. "Robert Cormier and the Postmodernist Possibilities of Young Adult Fiction." *Children's Literature Association Quarterly* 21:1 (Spring 1996): 28-34.

Heins, Ethel L. "Review of *Under the Autumn Garden*." *Horn Book Magazine* 55 (1979): 415-17.
Hendin, H. "Growing up Dead: Student Suicide." *American Journal of Psychotherapy* 29 (1975): 327-28.
Hillis Miller, J. *The Disappearance of God.* Cambridge, Massachusetts: Harvard University Press, 1963.
Holland, Isabelle. *The Man Without a Face.* New York: Lippincott, 1972.
———. *Perdita.* Boston: Little Brown, 1983.
Homze, Alma. "Interpersonal Relationships in Children's Literature 1920–60." *Elementary English* 43 (1966): 26-28.
Hunt, Peter. "Whatever Happened to Jan Mark?" *Signal* 31 (1980): 11-19.
Hunter, Ernest. "On Gordian Knots and Nooses: Aboriginal Suicide in the Kimberley." *Australian and New Zealand Journal of Psychiatry* 23:2 (1989): 264-71.
Iskander, Sylvia Patterson. "Readers, Realism and Robert Cormier, *Children's Literature.* 15. New Haven and London: Yale University Press, 1987, 7-18.
Jacobs, J. and J.D. Teichor. "Broken Homes and Social Isolation in Attempted Suicides of Adolescents." *The International Journal of Social Psychiatry* 13 (1967): 139-49.
Jardine, Alice. "Introduction to Julia Kristeva's 'Women's Time'." *Signs* 7:1 (1981): 5-12.
Jenkinson, David. "Portraits: Kevin Major." *Emergency Librarian* 19:3 (1992): 66-67.
Johnston, William, ed. *The Cloud of Unknowing.* New York: Image, 1973.
Katz, Welwyn Wilton. *Whalesinger.* Toronto: Douglas & McIntyre, 1990.
King-Boys, M.J.E. *Patterns of Aboriginal Culture: Then and Now.* Sydney: McGraw-Hill, 1977.
Kristeva, Julia. *About Chinese Women.* Trans. by Anita Barrows. London: Marion Boyars, 1977.
———. "The Adolescent Novel." *Abjection, Melancholia and Love.* Eds. John Fletcher and Andrew Benjamin. London and New York: Routledge, 1990.
———. *Black Sun: Depression and Melancholia.* Trans. Leon S. Roudiez. New York: Columbia University Press, 1989.
———. *Desire in Language.* Ed. Leon S. Roudiez. Trans. Thomas Gora, Alice Jardine, and Leon S.Roudiez. New York: Columbia University Press, 1980.
———. "Evenement et revelation." *L'Infini* 5 (1984): 3-11.
———. *In the Beginning Was Love.* Trans. Arthur Goldhammer, M.D. Introduction by Otto F. Kernberg, M.D. New York: Columbia University Press, 1987.

———. *The Kristeva Reader*. Ed. Toril Moi. New York: Columbia University Press, 1986.
———. *Powers of Horror: An Essay on Abjection*. Trans. Leon S. Roudiez. New York: Columbia University Press, 1982.
———. *Proust and the Sense of Time*. Trans. Stephen Bann. London: Faber & Faber, 1993.
———. *Revolution in Poetic Language*. Trans. Margaret Waller. New York: Columbia University Press, 1984.
———. *Strangers to Ourselves*. Trans. Leon S. Roudiez. New York: Columbia University Press, 1991.
———. *Tales of Love*. Trans. Leon S. Roudiez. New York: Columbia University Press, 1987.
Kurth, Anita. "Biting the Hand That Feeds You: Parents in Adolescent Novels of the 70's." *School Library Journal* (April 1982): 26-28.
Kurzeil, Edith. "An Interview with Julia Kristeva." *Partisan Review* 53:2 (1986): 216-229.
Lechte, John. *Julia Kristeva*. London and New York: Routledge, 1990.
———. "Art, Love, and Melancholy, in *Abjection, Melancholia and Love*. Eds. John Fletcher and Andrew Benjamin. London and New York: Routledge, 1990.
Lesnik-Oberstein, Karin. *Children's Literature: Criticism and the Fictional Child*. Oxford: Clarendon, 1994.
Lovejoy, A.O. *The Great Chain of Being*. Cambridge: Harvard University Press, 1936.
Lukenbill, Bernard. "Family Systems in Contemporary American Novels: Implications for Behaviour Information Modelling," *Family Relations* 30 (1981): 219-27.
Maddock, Kenneth. *The Australian Aborigines: A Portrait of Their Society*. London: Penguin, 1972.
Major, Kevin. *Blood Red Ochre*. New York: Dell, 1989.
———. *Dear Bruce Springsteen*. New York: Dell, 1987.
———. *Eating Between the Lines*. Toronto: Doubleday, 1991.
———. *Far From Shore*. Toronto: Stoddart, 1991. (First published by Clarke Irwin in 1980.)
———. *Hold Fast*. Toronto: Clarke Irwin, 1978.
———. *Thirty-Six Exposures*. New York: Dell, 1984.
Manyweathers, Jeannette. "Why Patricia Wrightson?" *Scan* 5:4 (1986): 76-78.
Mark, Jan. *A Can of Worms*. London: The Bodley Head, 1990.
———. *Aquarius*. Harmondsworth: Kestrel, 1982.
———. *At the Sign of the Dog and Rocket*. Harmondsworth: Kestrel, 1985.
———. *Divide and Rule*. Harmondsworth: Kestrel, 1979.

———. *The Ennead.* Hammondsworth: Kestrel, 1978.
———. *Hairs in the Palm of the Hand.* Harmondsworth: Kestrel, 1981.
———. *Handles.* Harmondsworth: Kestral, 1983.
———. "The Short Story." *Horn Book Magazine.* Jan.-Feb. 1989: 42-45.
———. *Thunder and Lightnings.* Harmondsmith: Kestrel, 1976.
———. *Trouble Half Way.* Harmondsworth: Kestrel, 1985.
———. *Under the Autumn Garden.* Harmondsworth: Kestrel, 1977.
Marks, Elaine and Isabelle de Courtivron. *New French Feminisms: An Anthology.* Amherst: University of Massachusetts Press, 1980.
McGillis, Roderick. "Another Kick at La/can," *Children's Literature Association Quarterly* 20:1 (Spring, 1995): 42-46.
Meisel, Perry. "Interview with Kristeva," *Partisan Review* 51:1 (1984): 128-32.
Minow-Pinkney, Makiko. "Virginia Woolf: 'Seen from a Foreign Land'." *Abjection, Melancholia, and Love.* Eds. John Fletcher and Andrew Benjamin. London and New York: Routledge, 1990.
Mishara, B.L. "The Extent of Adolescent Suicidality," *Psychatric Opinon* 12, 6 (1975): 32-37.
Moi, Toril, ed. "Introduction," *The Kristeva Reader.* New York: Columbia University Press, 1986.
Montgomery, Margaret, "Letters to the Editor," *Canadian Materials* 5 (1980): 6.
Myers, F.R. *Pintupi Country, Pintupi Self: Sentiment, Place and Politics among Western Desert Aboriginals.* Canberra: Australian Institute of Aboriginal Studies, 1986.
Nodelman, Perry. *The Pleasures of Children's Literature.* New York: Longman, 1992.
Oliver, Kelly. *Reading Kristeva: Unravelling the Double Bind.* Bloomington and Indiannapolis: Indianna University Press, 1993.
Paterson, Katherine. *Bridge to Terabithia.* New York: Crowell, 1977.
———. *Come Sing, Jimmy Jo.* New York: Dutton, 1985.
———. *The Great Gilly Hopkins.* New York: Crowell, 1978.
———. *Jacob Have I Loved.* New York: Crowell, 1980.
———. *Lyddie.* New York: Crowell, 1991.
———. *The Master Puppeteer.* New York: Harper, 1975.
———. *Of Nightingales That Weep.* New York: Harper, 1974.
———. *Park's Quest.* New York: Puffin, 1989.
———. *Rebels of the Heavenly Kingdom.* New York: Dutton, 1983.
———. *The Sign of the Chrysanthemum.* New York: Thomas Crowell, 1973.
Perkowski, Jan L. *Vampires, Dwarves and Witches Among the Ontario Kashubs.* Ottawa: National Museum of Man, 1972.

Petzel, S. and Riddle, M. "Adolescent Suicide: Psychosocial and Cognitive Aspects" in S.C. Feinstein et al. eds. *Adolescent Psychiatry: Developmental and Clinical Studies* 9. Chicago: University of Chicago Press, 1981.

Plumb, J.H. "The Great Change in Children," *Horizon* (Winter 1971): 5-12.

Pokorny, A.D. "Self Destruction and the Automobile." *Self Destructive Behavior.* Ed. Albert R. Roberts. Springfield, Illinois: Charles C. Thomas, 1975.

Porter, Helen. "Children's Literature Prizewinner," *Apla Bulletin* (Nov. 1979).

Rae, Arlene Perley. "A Major Newfoundland Talent," *Toronto Star* (21 Sept. 1991): K16.

Rees, David. "Jan Mark: There's No Such Thing As Fairness, *Painted Desert, Green Shade.* Boston: Horn Book, 1984.

Reid, J. *Sorcerers and Healing Spirits: Continuity and Change in an Aboriginal Medical System.* Canberra: Australian Institute of Criminology, 1986.

Roberts, A.R. *Self-Destructive Behaviour.* Springfield, Ill: Charles C. Thomas, 1975.

Roberts, Muriel. "Canadian Books for Canadian Children," *Booknews*, Burnaby Public Library 9:3 (1979).

Robinson, T.M. *Plato's Psychology.* Toronto: University of Toronto Press, 1970.

Roudiez, Leon S., ed. *Desire in Language.* New York: Columbia University Press, 1986.

Rose, Jacqueline. *The Case of Peter Pan.* London: Macmillan, 1984.

Shakespeare, William. *The Complete Works.* Baltimore: Penguin, 1970.

Shavit, Zohar. *Poetics of Children's Literature.* Athens and London: Georgia University Press, 1986.

Siege, Selma R. "Heroines in Recent Children's Fiction: An Analysis." *Elementary English* 50 (1973): 1039-43.

Story, G.M., W.J. Kirwin, and J.D.A. Widdowson, eds. *Dictionary of Newfoundland English.* Toronto: University of Toronto Press, 1982.

Sullivan, J.M. "Newfoundland Writer Steps to Centre Stage." *Globe and Mail* 3 February 1990: C3.

Swain, Tony. *Interpreting Aboriginal Religion: An Historical Account.* Special Studies in Religion No. 5. Bedford Park, SA: Flinders University, 1985, 123-30.

Tennyson, Lord Alfred. *The Poems of Tennyson.* Second ed. 3 vols. Christopher Ricks, ed. London and New York: Longmans, 1987.

Turbide, Diane. "Boyhood on the Rock." *Maclean's* 17 April 1989: 61.

US Bureau of the Census. *Statistical Abstract of the United States*: 1993 (113th ed.). Washington, DC: 1993.

Veglahn, Nancy. "The Bland Face of Evil in the Novels of Robert Cormier." *The Lion and the Unicorn*: 12:2 (1988): 12-18.

Voight, Cynthia. *The Homecoming*. New York: Atheneum, 1981.

Walch, S.M. "Adolescent Attempted Suicide: Analysis of the Differences in Male and Female Suicidal Behavior." *Dissertations Abstracts International* 38 (B: 1977): 2892-93.

Wenz, F. "Self-inquiry Behaviour, Economic Status and the Family Anomic Syndrome among Adolescents." *Adolescents* (1979): 387-98.

Wodarski, J.S. "Single Parents and Children: A Review for Social Workers." *Family Therapy* (1982): 311-20.

Wrightson, Patricia. *A Little Fear*. Victoria: Hutchinson, 1983.

———. "A Little Fear." *Reading Time* 92 (1984): 14.

———. *An Older Kind of Magic*. London and Melbourne: Hutchinson, 1972.

———. "Australian Fantasy and Folklore, Part Two." *Orana*. 17:3 (1981): 112-33.

———. *Behind the Wind*. London and Melbourne: Hutchinson, 1981.

———. *The Bunyip Hole*. London and Melbourne: Hutchinson, 1957.

———. *The Crooked Snake*. London and Melbourne: Hutchinson, 1955.

———. *The Dark Bright Water*. London and Melbourne: Hutchinson, 1978.

———. *Down to Earth*. Illus. Margaret Horder. London and Melbourne: Hutchinson, 1965.

———. *The Feather Star*. London and Melbourne: Hutchinson, 1962.

———. *The Ice Is Coming*. London and Melbourne, Hutchinson, 1977.

———. *I Own the Racehorse*. Illus. Margaret Horder. London and Melbourne: Hutchinson, 1968.

———. *The Nargun and the Stars*. London and Melbourne: Hutchinson, 1973.

———. *The Rocks of Honey*. London and Melbourne: Hutchinson, 1960.

———. "Some Comments on the Books of Wirrun." *Reading Time* 84 (July 1982).

"Wrightson, Patricia". *The Oxford Companion to Australian Literature*. William H. Wilde, Jay Horton, and Barry Andrews, eds. Melbourne: Oxford University Press, 1985.

INDEX